"In this age of picture-perfect models, airbrushed photography, and a weakened family, eating disorders among young women have become a real deal. Sharon Hersh has written not only a timely book but one that will equip mothers and fathers as they raise their daughters. This is the help and hope that parents need today!"

—DENNIS RAINEY, executive director of FamilyLife

"Finally, a book that says out loud what most moms worry about in secret! This book is not only full of advice on eating disorders, but it also has great questions to spark deeper conversations between any mother and daughter."

—SUSAN ALEXANDER YATES, best-selling author of several
books, including *And Then I Had Teenagers: Encouragement for Parents of Teens and Preteens*

"This book provides excellent information for the prevention of eating disorders and offers hope and wisdom for mothers whose daughters are struggling."

—WARD KELLER, president of the Remuda Ranch Center
for Anorexia and Bulimia, Inc.

"Mom, I feel fat!" is timely, culturally informed, realistic, and biblically based. This book will open the lines of mother-daughter communication on issues that our daughters are literally dying to talk about."

—WALT MUELLER, founder and president of the Center
for Parent/Youth Understanding

"This well-written book is not a formula for an easy fix to the complex struggles of disordered eating but an honest, refreshing, and practical resource for families struggling to overcome a serious challenge to the health of young women. Anyone who cares about the plight of young women today will benefit from reading *"Mom, I feel fat!"* I highly recommend it to parents, adolescent girls, youth workers, and teachers—in short, to anyone in a place of influence."

—BRETT ANDREWS, national training director of Youth for
Christ Canada

"Sharon Hersh has written a sensitive, thoughtful, and extremely valuable resource for mothers of girls. Her encouragement to love our daughters as God loves us, have faith in our mother heart, and be real with our daughters is very wise. This book will help us raise young women with healthy body images and self-esteem and create a lifetime mother-daughter bond."

—SANDY RICHARDSON, executive director of the Remuda
Foundation and the author of *Soul Hunger*

a hand-in-hand book

"Mom, *I feel fat!*"

Becoming your daughter's ally
in developing a healthy body image

sharon a. hersh

SHAW BOOKS

an imprint of WATERBROOK PRESS

"Mom, I feel fat!"
A SHAW BOOK
PUBLISHED BY WATERBROOK PRESS
2375 Telstar Drive, Suite 160
Colorado Springs, Colorado 80920
A division of Random House, Inc.

ISBN 0-87788-538-9

Library of Congress Cataloging-in-Publication Data
Hersh, Sharon A.
    "Mom, I feel fat!" : becoming your daughter's ally in developing a healthy body image / Sharon A. Hersh.
        p.   cm.
    Includes bibliographical references.
    ISBN 0-87788-538-9
    1. Body image in children. 2. Body image in adolescence. 3. Teenage girls—Mental health. 4. Eating disorders in children.   I. Title.

RA777.25 .H47 2001
612'.04243—dc21

2001026828

Printed in the United States of America
2001—First Edition

10 9 8 7 6 5 4 3 2 1

To my mother,
who taught me that even failure leads to love

CONTENTS

FOREWORD

I am sure that my own mother would have loved to have gotten her hands on this book. She watched me travel down a road of personal destruction during my teenage years. She longed to travel alongside me, point me to an exit, or take over the wheel. But it was my journey. I had found control and independence in one part of my world that was entirely my own—what I put into my mouth.

As I steadily lost weight, reaching a low of seventy-eight pounds my senior year of high school, my addiction to losing weight steadily grew. I was constantly fatigued, emotionally withdrawn, and spiritually confused. My periods stopped, my hair thinned, and I was constantly cold. My family and friends were understandably alarmed, but my mother was devastated. She, who brought me into the world and was a world-class caring mom, wanted to help. And she wanted to know *why.*

It was a frustrating time for girls with eating disorders. Unlike today, there were no books or articles with research and advice. Body image was not addressed, and anorexia was simply the clinical term for lack of appetite. I certainly seemed to have anorexia (although I was often ravenous but learned to ignore—even enjoy—the hunger), but numerous medical exams provided no clues. I would be sent on my way with a weight-gaining diet: three eggs, bacon, and toast every morning, milk shakes, beef, and potatoes. In the true "face the world with a smile" fashion that I had learned, I would simply grin, accept the diet, and discreetly throw the food away.

Many years later, after a long healing process (which still continues!) according to God's timetable, I look back and ask my mother's question: *Why?* Why would a girl who was not overweight join her best friend on a crash diet—and then stay on it for more than seven years? Why would someone rooted in the church, raised in a Christian home, and serious about her Christian faith virtually starve herself while at the same time never missing a church function? Why would she feel, at a skeletal weight, *fat?*

To this day I don't know all the answers to my questions. Sharon Hersh, however, has powerful insights into why girls fall prey to the lie of the importance of an ideal body. *"Mom, I feel fat!"* not only helps me understand myself but also gives me tools to relate to my own three daughters. Certain ungodly pressures, cultural demands, and Enemy tactics uniquely target girls. A parent's best defense is to outsmart the Enemy—by being informed and putting Hersh's principles into practice.

For those of you loving a daughter who is caught in the snare of an eating disorder, take heart. As this book will assure you, her Creator—who is her perfect parent and the lover of her soul—cares for her more than you do! Your prayers, your love, and your wisdom are the keys to her health. The "end of my story" should encourage anyone facing the eating disorder battle: By God's grace, I am married to a wonderful man and am the busy mother of five amazing children. God's faithfulness, not my own, brought me through the darkest hours of my soul. He answered the prayers of a mother's heart—*my* mother's prayers. And I pray that *"Mom, I feel fat!"* will equip you in the defense of your daughter, knowing that with God, all things are possible.

—DEBBIE SMITH, songwriter, wife of Michael W. Smith,
and mother of Ryan, Whitney, Tyler, Anna, and Emily

ACKNOWLEDGMENTS

My deepest love—

To my husband, Dave. You are my anchor and my ally.

To my son, Graham, who wonders if I'll ever write a book about boys. Probably not. You are the best.

To my *braveheart* daughter, Kristin. Thank you for letting me share our stories. This book is as much yours as it is mine.

My utmost respect—

To the mothers and daughters who have allowed me to be a part of your lives and to share your struggles, stories, successes, and failures.

To my friends Shari Meserve, Joan Shearer, and Cathy McWilliams for your insights and support during the writing of this book.

My heartfelt thanks—

To Don Pape and Shaw Books for believing in this book and for having a passion to encourage mothers to make the most of their mothering.

To my editor, Traci Mullins of Eclipse Editorial Services. Our alliance not only produces fresh ideas and good writing, it provokes me to growth and delights me with the joy of a rich relationship!

"Fat" Is Not a Feeling

Mothering is a mysterious task.
First you create an intimate, all consuming attachment
with your daughter,
then you spend the rest of your life
learning to let her go.[1]

JUDY FORD AND AMANDA FORD, *Between Mother and Daughter*

Mysterious. Miraculous. Maddening. All three words are apt synonyms for mothering.

Mysterious. Perhaps the mystery began for you, as it did for me, when you discovered that you were going to have a baby—to be a mother.

Miraculous. Can you remember the moment when the doctor or the adoption agency announced, "It's a girl!"? I don't know about you, but I could hardly contain the joy of that moment.

Maddening. And we've all known our moments of mothering madness—when our child bites the baby-sitter or she draws with a magic marker on her bedroom walls.

Let me share with you one of my maddening moments, which occurred not long ago and planted one of the seeds for this book.

"Mom, I am so fat! I look awful. I can't go to school today," my daughter, Kristin, pleaded.

"You are not fat. You look fine." I tried to answer calmly and confidently. We'd had this conversation before.

"I am fat. Look at my legs. I'd be fine if I could just cut my body off from the waist down."

I turned my attention to clearing the breakfast table and loading the dishwasher, hoping that if I just ignored my daughter's remarks she would happily be on her way to school.

"I feel awful," Kristin groaned. "Nothing I wear looks right. Isn't there a pill or something I can take to lose weight? I mean it. I can't go to school!"

Fear gripped my heart and stopped me in my tracks. I didn't know what to say. As a therapist, I was all too aware of the potential for eating disorders like anorexia and bulimia, as well as the epidemic of dieting among adolescent girls.

"You are not fat," I answered firmly.

"You just don't get it, Mom! You don't understand!" Kristin headed for her room, tears beginning to stream down her face.

"Maybe we can take an aerobics class together after school," I called after her, grasping at anything to turn the conversation in a more positive direction.

"I knew it!" Kristin cried harder. "You think I'm fat too!"

Whenever I tell other mothers about this conversation with my daughter, they laugh and groan, understanding immediately this familiar minefield that we moms attempt to navigate repeatedly. Maybe a conversation like this one with your own daughter is why you picked up this book.

Or perhaps you were drawn to this book because you know the statistics about eating disorders and fear that your daughter might become entangled in these life-threatening behaviors. Your fears are well founded. The most recent statistics from Eating Disorders Awareness and Prevention report that "*at least* 40 percent of all adolescent girls suffer from some form of disordered eating."[2] And studies suggest that girls become concerned about body image at young ages. More than fourteen years ago, one study of nine- and ten-year-old girls discovered that 50 percent of nine-year-old girls thought they were fat and that 80 percent of ten-year-olds felt fat![3] It's frightening to consider how girls in the new millennium feel about themselves.

Now, don't panic! Put down the yellow pages, and stop looking for a body-image consultant to help your daughter. *No one is better equipped to walk her through this confusing terrain than you are.* Since my maddening moment with my daughter, I have learned a lot about my daughter and me, and I have discovered that her inevitable concerns about weight loss and body image can be wonderful gifts to our relationship. Yes, *gifts.*

This book is full of good news! You can enter your daughter's world, connect with her, and engage with her about the tricky topics of body image and eating behavior in the midst of a developing and delightful relationship. You can help her identify and deal with the myriad emotions she feels as a growing girl, helping her to understand that "fat" is not a feeling. And in a culture where your daughter is bombarded with skinny, glossy, and superficial images, you can be a mirror that she can look into without fear as you reflect understanding, reassurance, wisdom, and love.

This book is about becoming your daughter's ally in developing a healthy body image and preventing eating disorders. But it also examines how a mom with a daughter who is dabbling in or is already ensnared by an eating disorder can be an ally to her daughter in overcoming this dangerous behavior.

Becoming allies. It sounds good, doesn't it? It is invigorating to discover that amid the challenges of raising a daughter, you can become not just mother and daughter and not just friends, but you can become allies. An ally is one who knows the enemy, understands the battle, and is always ready to lend a hand. This book will help you be the most effective and powerful ally possible to your daughter. And as you cement this bond with her, you will have opportunities to experience the reality of God's promise: "Two are better than one, because they have a good return for their work" (Ecclesiastes 4:9).

In the chapters ahead I want to help you build the framework for becoming your daughter's ally in three ways—first, by understanding your daughter's world, as well as understanding your own. You'll look in depth at your own ideas and experiences with regard to body image and weight management. You'll also explore ways to understand your daughter's world and her emotional life with wisdom and compassion. Second, I'll help you uncover as many means as possible to bridge your two worlds. Surprisingly, the questions and struggles your daughter has with regard to body image, dieting, and other ideas about eating and self-care can become the most powerful means to connect the two of you. Finally, you'll take a look at some of the serious roadblocks that can keep you from becoming your daughter's ally and even derail you from relationship completely.

Throughout this book you will see sections entitled "Just for You" and "Just for the Two of You." The questions and practical exercises in these sections are designed to help you address your own attitudes about mothering, the culture, eating, weight loss, body image, and so forth, and then to inspire you to translate your own experience and understanding into walking hand in hand with your daughter through this territory. Don't feel pressured to answer all the questions or do all the exercises right away. You will want to pick and choose based on your daughter's age and her current questions and struggles. These sections can be an ongoing resource to help you discover as many ways as you can of responding to your daughter out of a heart set free to love purposefully and passionately.

As your daughter approaches and enters adolescence, you can be sure there will be a few more moments of mothering madness! But as you walk hand in hand with your daughter, you can also be sure of the mystery and miracles that await you both.

Part I

Understanding Your Worlds

Knowing our children—knowing anyone, in fact—is a two-way street. We get to know someone based on how they respond to who we are. But, conditioned by best-selling pediatricians, child developmentalists, and therapeutic experts, we listen exclusively to our children, and fail to give back ourselves. In this we forfeit our part of the equation.... Delight in [the relationship] can only wither away. To create a [relationship] that lasts past the feeding-by-spoon stage, the can-I-borrow-the-car stage, means giving your personality, your identity, your presence, to your children so that they have something to come back to, namely you. That's a [relationship] that lasts.[1]

GINA BRIA, *The Art of Family*

Chapter 1

Being a Mom

Oh, what a power is motherhood,
possessing a potent spell.
All mothers alike fight fiercely for their child.

EURIPIDES

I'm not sure exactly what Euripides meant when he wrote about the potent spell of motherhood, but I am certain I was under this spell on my daughter's first day of high school.

Kristin set her alarm so she could get up three hours before we needed to leave for school. Although she'd already carefully laid out her chosen outfit the night before, she still tried on at least eight other outfits before returning to her first choice. She ran into my bedroom, modeled her outfit, and asked, "Mom, does this make me look fat?" I reassured her that she looked great and found some satisfaction in her question. She still needed me. I could not help but think back to nine years earlier—her first day of kindergarten. With anticipation and a little sadness, I'd laid out her clothes the night before. I'd helped her get dressed, reminded her to brush her teeth, and braided her hair. How things had changed!

Kristin and I were quiet on the drive to Heritage High School. She was reviewing her class schedule, locker combination, and lunch plans. My heart was in my throat while I was reviewing fourteen years of parenting and at the same time worrying about what might meet Kristin in the hallways of high school. I could tell we were nearing the school as other cars began to zip around me. I slowed down, and those cars (with drivers who looked all of thirteen) sped up. I slowed down even more when the drivers began to honk their horns at one another and passengers stuck their heads and arms out of the moving cars to wave to one another. Kristin quietly interrupted my panic. "Mom, the speed limit *is* twenty-five miles per hour."

I pulled up to the drop-off spot and stopped. Kristin opened her door and turned to say good-bye. I swallowed all my warnings and motherly admonitions when I saw the look of joy-filled anticipation on her face. "Mom," she said, "I'm ready. I can't wait!" And she took off.

My mind immediately returned to that first day of kindergarten when, holding her hand tightly, I walked Kristin into her classroom. She didn't want to let go of my hand, and I thought I might just stay with her for her first day of school. Her teacher assured me that she'd be okay and that it was probably better for me to leave. Reluctantly and tearfully, my little girl let go of my hand.

I watched for a few minutes as teenagers filed into the high school. I noticed the girls who must have decided to make a first impression by showing off their bodies with midriff-baring shirts, tight-fitting tank tops, and short shorts. I saw girls who looked comfortable in their clothes and their bodies. I wondered about the girls with heavy black shirts, big black boots, stiff black hair, and multiple studs and rings piercing various parts of their bodies. I winced when I saw girls who looked scared, uncomfortable, and lonely. I watched one young woman with the most gorgeous hair as she hung back from the steady stream of students. Her larger, more developed body stood out from the ranks of her peers. She bent her head to one side, bit her lip, and looked at her shoes. I wanted to know what she was thinking. But most of all, I wanted to run into that school, find Kristin, grab her by the hand, and say, "Let's go home and try again next year!"

Reluctantly and tearfully I drove home.

MOTHERING MANUALS

From the time I learned I was pregnant with Kristin, I've read books about mothering. I've read *What to Expect When You're Expecting, The First Three Months, Raising a Toddler, Parenting with Love and Logic, A Totally Alien Life-Form—Teenagers, The Strong-Willed Child,* and *Raising Kids Who Turn Out Right,* just to name a few. I imagine you've read your share of books as well and, like me, have your favorites—the well-worn editions that you consult regularly.

When Kristin was in the fifth grade, she came home with a question that sent me scrambling to my library of parenting books. She plopped down on a stool in the kitchen and asked a question that threw me for a loop: "Mom, am I fat?" I quickly replied, "No." She ignored my answer and barely skipped a beat during the next five minutes as she gave me a glimpse into a part of her ten-year-old world that I didn't know existed.

"Well, Kelly thinks she's fat," Kristin said, "and she's on a diet. She can't eat anything with fat in it. Do we have fat-free potato chips? And Ashley hates her legs and wants a flatter stomach. She's started doing sit-ups in her bedroom every night. And Katie says that her mom drinks a diet drink that helps her lose weight. She says it tastes gross but that she's going to start drinking it for breakfast. Do we have any diet drinks? Have you ever been on a diet, Mom? How tall do you think I'm going to be? I want to be really tall and maybe even be a model."

Today, six- and seven-year-old girls are concerned about their weight.
Standing on the cusp of puberty, nine-year-old girls talk about feeling fat
before their bodies have even begun to change.
At ten and eleven, feeling fat has been incorporated
into their everyday language.
It influences how they see themselves
and the way they interact in the world.[1]

SANDRA SUSAN FRIEDMAN, *When Girls Feel Fat*

I know my eyes glazed over during Kristin's questions and reflections on appearance and body image. My heart started to beat faster, and my palms got sweaty. I didn't know what to say. Of course I've dieted and worried about my weight. I've not only experimented with destructive eating behaviors, but this experimentation also led me into a struggle with the eating disorder bulimia. And I know that eating disorders are rampant among girls today. I was afraid I'd say the wrong thing to my daughter. I mumbled some response to Kristin and determined to find an expert to give me the right words to say.

I began to read everything I could find on appearance, body image, and eating disorders. Much of what I read was too political for my taste (thoughtful feminists attaching these struggles to a male-dominated culture) or too clinical (addressing only crisis behaviors). I discovered that much has been written to girls—workbooks, magazines, and beauty books—on the challenges facing them with regard to body image, but little has been written on how to *mother* girls struggling with these inevitable issues. I longed to read a book that not only addressed eating and body-image problems, but also focused on preparing for the future—responding before full-blown adolescence and its often full-blown crises related to self-esteem and eating disorders.

My own longings, conversations with many other moms and daughters, and subsequent discussions with my daughter gave birth to this book. From the conception of the idea for "*Mom, I feel fat!*" I knew that I had a lot to learn and would once again have to confront my questions about body image, recall my history, and disclose my fears and limitations. When I've felt overwhelmed or ill equipped for the task, I look at a picture of my daughter that sits on the corner of my desk. Kristin's courage, beauty, sense of humor, and sheer passion for life are my inspiration. When my mother heart swells with love and longing for my daughter, I dare to believe I am up to the job. Which is precisely the point of this book. Although we will examine the advice of "experts" and I'll suggest practical exercises and ask thought-provoking questions, the premise of this book is that the best mothering does not come out of formulas, scientific evidence, or ideological agendas, but rather it comes from consulting our love for our daughters.

When God wants an important thing done in the world or a wrong righted,
He goes about it in a very singular way....God simply has a tiny baby born....
And God puts the idea or purpose into the mother's heart.
And she puts it in the baby's heart, and then...God waits.
The great events of this world are...babies, for each child comes
with the message that God is not yet discouraged with humanity,
but is still expecting goodwill to become incarnate in each human life.[2]

MCEDMOND DONALD, *Presbyterian Outlook*

Consider this: God has entrusted you with both a daughter and a mother's heart for your daughter. Don't be afraid to trust yourself as God has trusted you! If you don't trust yourself, perhaps it's because you don't really know yourself—your strengths, weaknesses, and unique abilities to mother. Before you can enter your daughter's world in a truly loving and effective way, you need to understand your own.

FEAR SHOUTS LOUDER THAN LOVE

Marilyn brought her daughter to see me for counseling because she was concerned about Britney's eating behaviors. Fear was written all over Marilyn's face as she practically pushed Britney into my office. "I'm scared to death," Marilyn confessed.

Britney plopped down on my couch, crossed her legs, and started shaking her foot furiously. "Oh, Mom," she moaned, "you're being overly dramatic." I smiled. I suspected that Britney could be a bit dramatic herself, and I knew that nothing draws us mothers into drama like our daughters' stories.

Britney's story was unique. She had decided, in an effort to control her caloric intake, that for dinner she would eat only lettuce leaves adorned with mustard. Her mother had tried forcing her to sit at the table until she ate something else, putting her on restriction, preparing her favorite meals, and ignoring her. Understandably, Marilyn feared that Britney was not getting a balanced diet, might be developing an eating disorder, and was setting a bad example for her younger siblings. Britney's mother was ready to hand her off to an "expert."

Mothers everywhere understand and empathize with Marilyn's fears. We're afraid for our daughters in this culture that worships thinness and exalts appearance above all else. We're afraid peer pressure is stronger than our influence. We're afraid we'll say the wrong things and make matters worse. We're afraid to share our experiences, because it might encourage our daughters to make the same mistakes we did. We're afraid of being bad mothers. We know that the literature of psychology from Freud to present-day thinking is saturated with suggestions that mothers are the cause of everything that goes wrong in our daughters, from bedwetting to making bad marriage choices!

We've read the literature that attaches some pretty intimidating words to bad mothering—smothering, controlling, overbearing, clinging, abandoning.

If our daughters talk about being fat, want to go on diets, or begin to eat only lettuce for dinner, it must be our fault! It's understandable when we, like Marilyn, mother out of fear. We don't like what fear does to us, turning us into shrill, frantic, ineffective, or even paralyzed mothers. But how can we keep from being afraid in the midst of such a daunting task, fraught with so many dangers and difficulties?

When we are afraid of our daughters, of their problems, and even of ourselves, we can't use the natural longing, love, and leading that God has planted in our mother hearts. No matter what stage of mothering you find yourself in as you read this book, I suspect something just leaped in your heart as you read the previous sentence. You know it's true. There is a connection with your daughter that words can't adequately articulate. Perhaps you first felt it when you discovered you were pregnant, or when you held your daughter for the first time, watched her tie her shoes, listened to her read from her own book, or watched her walk in the front door of kindergarten! You've awakened in the middle of the night and thought of something you need to talk about with your daughter; you've sensed that she was in danger or trouble when she wasn't even in your presence; you've known when she needed you even before she asked. We know that no one loves our daughters as we do, and we want to believe that counts for something. *It does.*

A mother understands what a child does not say.

JEWISH PROVERB

Many fathers take an active role in parenting their daughters, and the premise of this book is not that fathers don't matter or can't help their daughters when it comes to body image or eating struggles. Fathers can have a significant impact on their daughters, and supportive fathers generally have daughters with good self-esteem and self-confidence. I encourage fathers to read this book to gain more understanding about their daughter's concerns regarding body image and weight control.

But not all fathers are supportive and involved in parenting their daughters, and some fathers may actually contribute to their daughter's risk of developing a distorted body image, and even an eating disorder. According to psychologist Margo Maine, author of *Father Hunger,* many girls experience a hunger for emotional connection with their fathers, and when that is not available, girls may seek emotional satisfaction in harmful behaviors.[3] For mothers whose spouses are absent or abusive, this book will encourage you that you are not alone, and that your love for your daughter can feed her hungry heart.

HAND-IN-HAND MOTHERING

I hope this book encourages you to relax so that you are no longer ruled by anxiety but by love. My prayer is that as we embark on walking hand in hand with our daughters through the complex and difficult issues with regard to eating and body image, we will echo the words of the apostle John: "There is no room in love for fear. Well-formed love banishes fear" (1 John 4:18, MSG).

Throughout the rest of this book we will examine in depth what it means to understand, respect, and listen to our mother hearts, as well as live out of "well-formed love" for our daughters. But for now, the good news is that the mothering we're going to discuss is not about doing everything right, being all-nurturing, all-loving, selfless, and perfect in every response. *Hand-in-hand mothering is simply a willingness to learn as many ways as you can of responding to your daughter out of a heart filled with limitless love for her.*

This type of mothering is filled with hope, because you believe that every struggle, question, failure, and victory is an opportunity for transformation—for both you and your daughter. Hand-in-hand mothering becomes possible as you become convinced in the very depths of your being that there is One who walks beside you, takes *your* hand, and is committed to helping you find your way. We long for nothing less for our daughters. And we are the ones, who, by our love in the very midst of our daughters' struggles, will invite them to know God deeply and assist them in seeing the path of life clearly.

I hope this book will help you understand your daughter and the questions and struggles she will most certainly encounter with regard to her body image—the way she perceives her size, shape, and proportions, and how she feels about her body. We will delve into the culture and its influence and look at how we can surpass its appeal to, authority over, and influence on our daughters. We will examine the continuum of eating disorders and what we can do to prevent them or assist our daughters in overcoming them. But throughout this book you will be encouraged first to reclaim the mother-daughter relationship as one of the most powerful relationships there is for closeness, support, friendship, and modeling. Once you deeply acknowledge this God-designed connection between you and your daughter, your way of relating to her will begin to change.

A HOLY LONGING

"I don't think I'm the one to help Britney," Marilyn told me in our first session. "My own mother and I don't have a close relationship, and it looks like Britney and I won't either."

Marilyn's shoulders slumped, and tears began to stream down her face. After meeting with Britney and making an assessment that she was just beginning to experiment with eating behaviors and that her health was not at imminent risk, I asked if I could spend a few sessions with Marilyn alone. Marilyn suspected that I thought *she* was the problem and therefore needed counseling first. She was about to learn that I knew she was the *answer*, but we needed to figure out what was keeping her from being the powerful, awesome mother she wanted to be and her daughter needed her to be.

I asked Marilyn about her tears, and she was surprised by her own answer. Choking back sobs Marilyn cried, "I guess I still want *my* mother." We never stop wanting a mother—someone whose love is limitless, who never forgets who we are, who keeps believing in who we can be, who holds our hand when we're afraid, uncertain, or filled with anticipation. Even if our childhood experiences did not fulfill our longings for a mother, we still want this kind of mothering. Novelist Janet Fitch poignantly describes her observation of this longing in a hospital maternity ward:

> All down the ward, they called for their mothers. *Mommy, ma, mom, mama.* Even with husbands at their sides, they called for mama.... A grown woman sobbing like a child. *Mommy...*But then I realized, they

did not [necessarily] mean their own mothers. They wanted the real
mother…mother of a fierce compassion, a woman large enough to
hold all the pain, to carry it away…mothers who would breathe for us
when we could not breathe anymore, who would fight for us, who
would kill for us, die for us.[4]

Where does this longing come from? My first book, *Bravehearts: Unlocking the Courage to Love with Abandon,* explores in depth God's design of
women with a longing for relationships as the very core of our being. I believe
that God created women uniquely to "birth" relationships and implanted
within us a longing for relationships to motivate us to pursue them passionately. Scientific and psychological studies also conclude that there's something
unique about the female's longing for relationships, and it begins with her
longing for her mother.

Researcher of feminine development Janet Surrey explains in her essay
"The Self-in-Relationship: A Theory of Women's Development" that from
birth girls develop a "self-in-relation" to their mothers, whereas boys develop
a "self-in-separation." Girls, Surrey says, develop their identities in the context
of the mother-daughter relationship beginning at infancy and continuing as
the relationship becomes more complex.[5]

The first primary relationship we experience powerfully impacts what we
believe about ourselves and relationships. But whether we are cared for or
neglected, nourished or left hungry, nurtured or abandoned by our mothers,
the seeds of our divinely-implanted longing for relationships remain within
us. God's intention is that mothering provide the nourishment for these
seeds.

In God's stories about mothers, he fleshes out his purposes beginning
with Eve, "the mother of all the living" (Genesis 3:20). The stories in the Bible
about mothers are as diverse as our own, and they are filled with mothers who
made mistakes and certainly didn't do it all perfectly. But each story clearly
reveals the power of a mother's love.

Consider Sarah's fierce protection of her son (Genesis 21); Rachel's joy in
having two sons even though the birth of her second son resulted in her death
(Genesis 35:16-18); Jochabed's creativity and courage in caring for Moses

(Exodus 2); Deborah's rescue of a nation out of her mother heart (Judges 5:7); Hannah's selfless surrender of her son (1 Samuel 1–2:10); and of course Mary—Jesus' mother—pondering in her heart the coming of a baby and then weeping at his feet over the terrible loss of her dear son (Luke 2:19 and John 19:25-27).

Twice in the Scriptures God uses the metaphor of a mother as the best representation of his own fierce love:

> Jerusalem! Jerusalem!... How often I've ached to embrace your children, the way a hen gathers her chicks under her wings, and you wouldn't let me. (Matthew 23:37, MSG)

> For this is what the LORD says:... "As a mother comforts her child, so will I comfort you." (Isaiah 66:12-13)

Marilyn's longing for a mother during a crisis in her own mothering makes sense. We innately seek what God created us to experience: comfort, protection, direction, and unconditional acceptance. Regardless of our childhood experiences, our hearts always long for these qualities in a mother. The poet Adrienne Rich penned her conclusion about the disappointment that often occurs in our relationships with our mothers: "The loss of the daughter to the mother, the mother to the daughter, is the essential female tragedy."[6] She may be right, especially since the mother-daughter relationship is such a powerful and influential bond. But it is a tragedy that can be rewritten for future generations. If your relationship with your mother has been rich and rewarding, that, too, can continue in future generations, even with the distinct and demanding struggles of girls in this generation.

A HOLY CALLING

Marilyn and I talked about her disappointments in her relationship with her own mother. Her mother often placed herself at a distance from Marilyn, and hope began to grow in Marilyn's heart once she acknowledged that when she is frustrated or afraid in her own mothering, she, too, often ends up distancing herself from her daughter. Marilyn confessed that seeking counseling for

Britney stemmed, in part, from a decision to push Britney away into the hands of someone else.

Hope arrives when we recognize our responsibility and determine to move in a new direction. Marilyn's mother heart awakened when she realized that *she* could be the mother she always dreamed of. Her heartbeat changed from "what I lack" to "who can I be?" She began to believe that her holy longing for a close relationship with her own mother could be transformed into a holy calling to be the mother her daughter needed. Britney's strange eating behaviors became a wake-up call to her mother that a change must come—not just in Britney's dinner choices, but more importantly in Marilyn's mothering choices. Mustard on lettuce for dinner became a messenger of transformation.

What about you? Do you see mothering your daughter as a holy calling? Do you believe that your relationship with her will model for her how she's supposed to live passionately and joyfully with her God-instilled heart for relationships? Do you believe that no one is more qualified to help your daughter than you are?

While mothering your daughter through the questions, conflicts, and struggles of growing up may require that you consult an "expert" or seek advice from a counselor, it must begin with faith in your mother heart.

JUST FOR YOU

1. What did your relationship with your mother teach you about yourself and relationships?
2. What do you think are your talents and authentic gifts? How are you using them in mothering?
3. Do you believe others' opinions over your own about parenting your daughter? Why or why not?
4. Make a list of the positive things you have to give your daughter.
5. Write down qualities and characteristics that you value about yourself. How can you model these for your daughter?

Although you will glean all the wisdom from others that you can, you are the one who will take your daughter's hand and lead her in the way of life. A study conducted in 1998 by Teenage Research Unlimited found that 70 percent of teenagers name their mom or dad as the person they most admire. You are a perfect match for your daughter!

A HOPE-FILLED HEART

Marilyn came to a later counseling session with a sparkle of hope in her eyes. She sat across from me and began unfolding a picture, obviously drawn by a child. She explained that she had been cleaning Britney's room and had come across a drawing that had fallen behind a bedroom dresser. Marilyn remembered when Britney drew the picture. She was eight years old and trying to help her mom make dinner. Britney kept spilling ingredients and interrupting the process with questions and stories until Marilyn's patience ran out. She snapped at her daughter, "Can you just find something else to do?"

Several minutes later Britney came back into the kitchen and handed her mother a picture she'd just drawn. In the picture mother and daughter were standing in the kitchen holding hands. Britney had drawn a big smile on both of their faces, and over her mother's head she'd colored a shiny gold halo.

"I can do it," Marilyn said, pointing to the picture. "I can be the mother Britney saw me as back then, even when I wasn't doing a real great job. And I can be the mother she needs me to be right now." I could almost see the glow of hope and joy coming from Marilyn's "halo" in that moment!

Hand-in-hand mothering begins with a fervent belief that you are the right mother for your daughter, that God has implanted in you the seeds of longing for relationship that can bloom into an empowering alliance between you and your child.

Are you ready to learn how to relax, listen to your mother heart, and allow love to light your path? The next chapter will help you identify your predominant style of mothering and encourage you to be the mom you always dreamed of.

JUST FOR THE TWO OF YOU

1. Tell stories to your daughter about learning of her conception, discovering she was a girl, welcoming her into your family, etc. Let your mother heart for your daughter shine brightly.

2. Can you recall when your daughter pretended to be a mommy when she was little? Do you remember pretending to be a mom when you were a girl? Talk about the qualities of a mother that this pretend play revealed as important to you and your daughter.

3. Has there ever been an occasion when you knew your daughter needed you or was in trouble, even though she couldn't tell you? Tell your daughter about this mysterious connection.

4. Spend some quality daydreaming time (lounging in the sun, lying in bed, riding in the car) to describe to each other "The Mother You've Always Dreamed Of." Give your daughter permission to talk about her needs and longings by expressing your own. Don't censor her description or take it personally, but consider what you can learn about your daughter and what changes you can make in your mothering based on her description or on your own longings.

Chapter 2

Your Mothering Style

*The daughter never gives up on the mother
just as the mother never gives up on the daughter.
There is a tie here so strong that neither can break it.
I call it the "unbreakable bond."*[1]

RACHEL BILLINGTON, *The Great Umbilical*

What kind of a mother are you? Your answer may come from the stage of mothering you're in right now—or afraid you'll soon be in: tired, scared, lonely, frantic. Maybe your answer is formed from the way in which you were mothered. Are you determined to be like your mom or afraid you'll be like her? However you characterize your mothering, one helpful way to evaluate it is to notice where you place yourself in relationship to your daughter.

We are going to examine four different mothering styles based on where the mother places herself in relationship to her daughter:

- above
- beneath
- at a distance
- hovering

The purpose of these categories is not to make anyone feel guilty. All four mothering styles are appropriate at times. But understanding your predominant mothering style will help you to recognize your weaknesses and strengths, see where you may be responding out of fear, and guide you in developing new ways of responding to your daughter to create the kind of relationship that will truly support her and satisfy you.

In the last chapter, you read part of Marilyn and Britney's story. When

Marilyn saw her mothering style as one of keeping her distance from Britney out of a fear that she couldn't handle her daughter, she was able to make changes that not only helped Britney with her eating struggles, but also cemented a much stronger mother-daughter bond. You'll get to read more about these changes at the end of this chapter. For now, take a look in the mirror at your own mothering style and see what you discover.

MOTHERING FROM ABOVE

DAUGHTER: I can't go to school today. I don't have anything to wear. Everything makes me look fat!

MOM: You are not fat. Now go upstairs and find something to wear. And hurry, or we'll be late.

DAUGHTER: You don't understand. I really hate the way I look. I just can't face everyone today.

MOM: You look fine. But what you don't understand is that whining and complaining make you ugly. While you're getting dressed, why don't you practice being grateful? I want to see you come down those stairs with a smile on your face.

The mother who places herself above her daughter is most comfortable teaching, correcting, and admonishing. She sees her role as one of dispensing rules and regulations, providing instruction, and shaping a productive member of society. She relies on her experience, knowledge, and authority.

This mothering style is especially effective during our daughters' early years. Young girls feel unloved without firmness and boundaries. The strengths of this mothering style are consistency, structure, and direction. However, if this style of mothering continues to be the most prominent as a daughter approaches and enters adolescence, it can become a barrier to a deepening relationship between a mom and her developing daughter.

For many parents, setting limits turns into issuing commands.
They back up those limits and rules with more commands—
heavily spiced with sternness and anger—

And when those fail they resort to punishment.
Typically, teens respond to these methods
with irresponsibility, resistance, and rebellion.[2]

Foster Cline, M.D., and Jim Fay, *Parenting Teens with Love and Logic*

The weaknesses of this mothering style are connected to its strengths. First, enforcing external consistency may force internal turmoil underground. For example, in the preceding vignette, this mom is teaching her daughter that appearance is everything and that she should hide anything negative or unpleasant. In the world of body-image struggles and eating disorders, this is a setup for disaster on many levels, as I will explain in later chapters. Second, providing a structure of rules and consequences can lead to a frustrating inflexibility. As our daughters enter adolescence and seek more independence, in the face of inflexibility they will resolve to find some power for themselves. If the only place they can find control is over their eating, the potential for

JUST FOR YOU

Your answers to the following questions will help you examine how you may use this style of mothering:

1. How important is it to you that your daughter's appearance reflects well on you? Begin to notice your response when your daughter is messy, tries different styles, or changes her appearance. What do you believe her appearance says about you?

2. Do you believe it is important that your daughter never embarrass you? What happens when she does?

3. When do you focus completely on your daughter? When you enjoy her? play with her? teach her? appreciate her? want to change her?

4. Is compliance a priority in your mothering? If so, how do you achieve this goal?

5. How often do you have an agenda in your conversations with your daughter?

6. When your daughter questions you, do you consider that rebellion?

problems is greater. They need us to be their allies as they seek independence. Third, having a rigid agenda might cause us to miss some crucial detours in relating to our daughters.

When our daughters begin to think about body image, ask questions about dieting, and experiment with exercise, our primary function is not to force, instruct, or demand. In fact, our daughters will quickly discover that this is one area in which they, and they alone, can have control. The mother who places herself above her daughter in the midst of eating and body-image issues will find herself in a perpetual power struggle. And she will ultimately lose. The place we long for our daughters to rest with regard to their bodies is an attainment of the heart, and we won't assist them in finding that place when we talk down to them, dismiss their feelings, and insist on our agenda.

THE ABOVE MOTHER

Goal: Compliance.

Role: Dispense rules and wisdom.

Fear: "If I'm not in control, everything will go wrong."

Response to Feelings: "You don't feel that way." "Stop complaining." "Just yesterday you were happy."

Response to Behaviors: Regulate, forbid, lecture, and punish.

Favorite Motherism: "I know what's best for you."

Daughter's Response: To fight back or resolve to gain power for herself.

MOTHERING FROM BENEATH

DAUGHTER: I can't go to school today. I don't have anything to wear. Everything makes me look fat!

MOM: Oh, honey, you're not fat. Just be thankful you don't have my legs.

DAUGHTER: You don't understand. I really hate the way I look. I just can't face everyone today.

MOM: Don't talk like that. I don't know what to say when you talk like that. I don't want you to have the problems I have with self-esteem. You are so beautiful and have so much more

than I ever did. Let me help you find something to wear. Maybe
I have something you'd like to borrow?

The mother who places herself beneath her daughter is most comfortable
when she is serving others and putting herself down. She sees her role as one
of providing everything necessary for her daughter to turn out better than she
did. She relies on what she is lacking as motivation to guide her in mothering
her daughter.

The strength of this mothering style can be a genuine servant's heart
and sense of appreciation. In the battle against poor body image and unhealthy eating behaviors, our daughters need lots of affirmation and kindness.
However, when affirming our daughters is attached to attacking ourselves,
we send a confusing message. When we combine a destructive behavior
(self-deprecation) with a healthy behavior (complimenting our daughters),
we signal that it's okay to use good things (like food and exercise) against
ourselves.

The weakness of this mothering style is once again connected to its
strength. The mother who places herself beneath her daughter may live only
through her daughter and not develop a life of her own. Anthropologist Ruth
Bennedict explains: "It's very simple: this is my daughter's life that's posing as
mine. It's my daughter's love life which shall be perfect; it's my daughter's abilities which shall find scope; it's my daughter's insight that shall be true and
valid. It is she who shall not miss the big things of life."[3]

The purpose of our daughters is not to add to our value or increase our
self-esteem. Our daughters need to sense that we can look at them closely, listen to them intently, and respond to them calmly out of a rootedness in our
own lives.

When it comes to body image and eating behaviors, the mother who
places herself beneath her daughter will not be in a position to help her
daughter navigate this tricky terrain. She may spend most of her time steering her daughter away from anything that is hard, and because she lacks self-
confidence, she cannot offer her daughter a sense of safety in the midst of
these confusing and often painful issues. This mother can also become manipulative, determined that her daughter will look a certain way or be a certain
size to make up for her own perceived deficiencies.

THE BENEATH MOTHER

Goal: Live her life through her daughter's.

Role: Provide a better life for her daughter than she experienced.

Fear: "If my daughter doesn't 'succeed,' I am worthless. I don't have what it takes to help my daughter."

Response to Feelings: "Please, don't say that." "I can't stand it when you're unhappy."

Response to Behaviors: Powerlessness, panic.

Favorite Motherism: "Make your mother proud."

Daughter's Response: Feels pressure to succeed for her mother and be responsible for her mother's well-being.

JUST FOR YOU

Your answers to the following questions will help you examine how you use this style of mothering:

1. Do you feel like your life is over? If not, what are you looking forward to, preparing for, and dreaming about that is not connected to your daughter?

2. When your daughter succeeds at something, what is your response? Do you ever feel competitive with your daughter?

3. In what ways does your daughter's appearance or behavior impact your self-esteem?

4. Do you often recall your own adolescence negatively while interacting with your daughter?

5. What is your mothering priority? For your daughter to be popular? make good grades? be thin?

6. Do you believe you and your daughter should contribute the same amount of effort to your relationship?

MOTHERING FROM A DISTANCE

DAUGHTER: I can't go to school today. I don't have anything to wear. Everything makes me look fat!

MOM: Please get ready. We're running late.

DAUGHTER: You don't understand. I really hate the way I look. I just can't face everyone today.

MOM: Well, if you really feel that bad, I guess you can stay home today. I just hope you don't get behind in your schoolwork. I've got a lot of things planned for today, so I need to get going.

The mother who places herself at a distance from her daughter is most comfortable when she is observing her daughter or immersed in her own activities. She sees her role as one of providing for the basic physical needs of her daughter. She relies on her daughter to find her own way in life.

The strength of this mothering style is that at times a hands-off approach can encourage a girl to develop independence and self-confidence. Knowing when to step in and when to step out is a skill that requires knowing your daughter's world and staying aware of your own. But if you are distant from your daughter for any other reason than for her growth and development, she will perceive that the distance is because something is wrong with her. As our daughters grow into adolescence, we need to give them more space, but they

JUST FOR YOU

Your answers to the following questions will help you examine how you use this mothering style:

1. Do you often feel disapproval for or irritation with your daughter?
2. Do you feel estranged from your daughter? Recall the circumstances of the times when you felt close to your daughter.
3. Are you willing to be inconvenienced by your daughter?
4. Do you believe your daughter is overly dramatic?
5. Do you believe teens are mature and should be capable of taking care of themselves? If so, think back on your own adolescence. Does this belief grow out of your own experience?
6. How often do you take time to focus completely on your daughter? What gets in the way?

also need to sense that our hearts are always open to them and that our commitment to a relationship with them is unwavering.

_____

But most of all, Mother, I want to know you love me.
I know you've had a hard day at work.
I don't want to bother you, but will you spend some time with me?
Please, Mother, I need someone there for me
when friends are just not enough.
I need someone to talk to, to trust with my deepest secrets,
someone to share in the pain of my losses
and join in the laughter of happiness.
Friends may come and go, Mother, but you will always be there.
Please be there for me to share my life with now,
while I need you most.[4]

CARLY SANKO, age 15, *Ophelia Speaks*

_____

A hands-off approach can be disastrous. When our daughters begin to ask questions about their bodies and experiment with eating and exercise, they need us. If they are like rudderless boats, blown by the winds of the culture and bumping into whatever comes toward them, the result can be devastating. A daughter left to find her own way in the flood of questions about body image can develop destructive eating behaviors and adopt unhealthy beliefs about her body that will haunt her for the rest of her life.

THE DISTANT MOTHER
Goal: Provide basic needs for her daughter.
Role: Observer.
Fear: "If I get involved, I will just make things worse."
Response to Feelings: No comment.
Response to Behaviors: No response unless behavior interrupts mom's
        priorities.
Favorite Motherism: "Act your age."
Daughter's Response: I am on my own.

HOVER MOTHERING

DAUGHTER: I can't go to school today. I don't have anything to wear. Everything makes me look fat!

MOM: Oh, honey, you're not fat. What about your new pink shirt? I could iron it for you. You look great in that shirt.

DAUGHTER: You don't understand. I really hate the way I look. I just can't face everyone today.

MOM: Honey, please don't feel so bad. You are so pretty. How about if we go shopping today after school and get you something new to wear tomorrow?

The mother who hovers is most comfortable when her daughter is happy and content. She sees her role as one of banishing misery and making everyone happy all the time. She relies on her own abilities to fix every problem and keep her daughter satisfied.

The strength of this mothering style is its abundance of nurture. And when it comes to preventing eating disorders, a healthy amount of nurture

JUST FOR YOU

Your answers to the following questions will help you see how you use this style of mothering:

1. Are you afraid to disagree with your daughter? If so, why?
2. When your daughter is sad or angry, do you try to talk her out of those feelings? If so, do you know why you are uncomfortable with these feelings?
3. When your daughter is unhappy, do you believe if you don't intervene she will remain unhappy?
4. When your daughter is sad, do you try to cheer her up?
5. When your daughter expresses negative emotions, do you dismiss or deny what she is feeling?
6. When things don't go right for your daughter, do you try to fix things?

nourishes and satisfies emotional hunger, keeping our daughters from looking for love in a bag of potato chips. We can never overestimate the sustenance of kindness, attention, and devotion to our children. But a healthy abundance can turn into unhealthy smothering. Suppressing all pain and discomfort eliminates a necessary context in which our daughters can grow and find their own internal resources for handling difficulties. We can also easily send the message that it's not okay to feel negative emotions, compelling our daughters to stuff, numb, or hide these emotions from us. And because the hover mother wants her daughter to be happy, she may ignore or dismiss behaviors that need to be addressed.

When issues arise with regard to body image and eating behaviors, the hover mother wants to take away the pain rather than help her daughter learn to use the struggle for good. When a mom won't enter her daughter's world of confusion and hurt and instead tries to fix it, she may end up alienating her daughter and provoking her to withdraw into her own world. Teenage girls are completely preoccupied with leaving behind their childhood fashions, bodies, and behaviors. Their struggle toward independence is healthy. When we "guilt" them into going underground with their struggles, we miss the wonderful opportunity to help them grow up. And when we ignore the foolish choices they make in the process because we don't want any conflict, we miss the chance for our relationship to deepen.

THE HOVER MOTHER

Goal: Make her daughter happy.

Role: Cheerleader, caretaker, problem-solver.

Fear: "I am responsible for everything that happens to my daughter, and if I can't fix things for her, I am not a good mother."

Response to Feelings: "What can I do to make you happy?"

Response to Behaviors: No negative consequences.

Favorite Motherism: "Please don't frown, or your face will freeze like that."

Daughter's Response: She may withdraw from the smothering with a mean-spiritedness or become self-absorbed in the absence of consequences and the need to take responsibility for herself.

Do you recognize yourself in one of these mothering styles, or in all of them? What prompts you to place yourself above, beneath, at a distance from, or hovering around your daughter? Is it fear or love?

Hand-in-hand mothering will look a little different for every mother and daughter, but three internal consistencies undergird it: faith-filled vision, hopeful acceptance, and well-formed love.

FAITH-FILLED VISION

What's a daughter for? For that matter, what are mothers for? How you answer those questions reveals your vision for mothering. If you believe your daughter is here to boost your ego, reveal your strengths, or make up for what you are lacking, your vision will be focused on external goals. If you believe you are here to produce a successful member of society, create a replica of yourself, or keep your daughter on the straight and narrow, your vision will be one of outcome-based objectives.

External goals and outcome-based objectives are not all bad, but they don't engage the heart. What do you believe will have a lasting impact on your daughter? Your rules, speeches, cleanliness, or achievements? In our heart of hearts we know what impacts *us* most significantly. *Real relationships.* Our daughters are no different than we are. A faith-filled vision of mothering is lived out in moment-by-moment decisions that support a real relationship between mother and daughter. This vision is of a relationship that lasts well beyond the "Mom, I feel fat!" stage. Author and sociologist Gina Bria testifies to the power of relationships: "Your relationships make you who you are, because they give you a chance to actually manifest yourself, and what you really believe in."[5]

Our daughters need our help, our listening ear, our empathy, and our feedback. But most of all they need *us*. They want to know how we feel, what we've learned, and even the mistakes we've made along the way. The best way to invite your daughter's confidences is to share your own. The purpose of disclosure is not to shock, frighten, or burden your daughter with your own problems, but to build a bridge of connection. Your growing relationship in this area will be determined by your daughter's age and maturity.

As she reaches the middle-school years, remember she is no different from you in her enjoyment of relationships. How do you feel in relationships when you do all the disclosure, have all the problems, and express all the needs? We are dissatisfied in relationships that are one-sided. Being vulnerable, however, is risky. We may be afraid we'll be judged or misunderstood. Many mothers are afraid to reveal their humanness to their daughters because they fear their daughters will use these revelations to justify their own bad choices. I have seldom seen it work that way. In fact, just the opposite often occurs. Daughters trust their mothers more and seek their guidance, and a real relationship develops.

When my daughter was in the eighth grade, I prayerfully decided it was time for me to tell her about my own adolescent and young-adult struggle with bulimia. When I finished, I said, "I didn't tell you these things before because I didn't think you were ready and because, quite frankly, I was afraid that you'd think less of me or be disappointed in me." Kristin quickly replied, much to my surprise, "Oh, Mom, I think it makes you so much more interesting!" Being real is what connects us.

A faith-filled vision for a real relationship not only holds on to who you are as you share yourself with your daughter, but it doesn't forget who your daughter is. This vision never loses sight of who your daughter can be even when she pouts, yells, disobeys, forgets, questions, and doubts.

Marilyn admitted that she had become so focused on her daughter's lettuce-eating behavior that she'd nearly lost sight of their relationship. She was conveying to Britney that all she cared about, looked at, and could focus on was the one thing she didn't like about Britney's current behavior. She'd become as obsessed as her daughter. Mustard on lettuce had obscured her vision.

Marilyn began to live with faith-filled vision by first of all remembering who she was. She shared with Britney that when she was growing up everyone sat down to dinner together and ate an elaborate meal that her mother worked all day to prepare. She described the full-course meals and recalled her own desires to have more control over what she ate. Marilyn and Britney laughed about their own family's fast-food dinners, eating on the run, and different likes and dislikes, and concluded that family life surely had changed since her mother's childhood days. Marilyn further disclosed that she really had become discouraged in preparing meals because it seemed that everyone in their family had such distinct tastes.

As Marilyn held on to a vision of a real relationship with her daughter, she was able to give of her true self to her daughter instead of focusing only on her daughter's behavior and her own "responsibility" to correct it. In her book *The Art of Family,* Gina Bria writes, "[Our children] come wanting us and instead are handed hours, days, and years of being told who they are.... This is generous, but too small for a family to make it through a life together.... In the end, who children are and what they become does depend on what we give them of ourselves."[6]

What we build into our kids' hearts
underpins what they live out in their lives.
It has little to do with how much we give them.
It has everything to do with how we make them feel.[7]

LINDA WEBER, *Mom, You're Incredible*

With a vision of their relationship firmly in view, Marilyn went on to remind Britney of who she was. When Britney fixed herself a plate of lettuce for dinner, Marilyn reminded her daughter of her creative and quirky projects from childhood and her disciplined tenacity to stick with something. She surprised Britney when she complimented her: "I understand your desire to eat healthfully and I'm amazed by this unique idea. I can't wait to see what else you come up with." Suddenly the kitchen was no longer a battlefield. Mother and daughter were no longer at war. Within a few weeks Britney was planning relatively healthy, creative, sometimes quirky meals, and preparing them for the whole family. She empathized with her mother's discouragement in cooking for a family of picky eaters.

Marilyn's renewed vision for creating a relationship with her daughter made them allies in the midst of the testing, tumult, and turbulence that often come with adolescence. When the "lettuce leaf test" became boring and the tumult and turbulence calmed, the relationship remained!

HOPEFUL ACCEPTANCE

A growing relationship between mother and daughter did not eliminate Britney's struggles with eating and body image. She continued to come up with strange ideas about dieting and to worry about her size and appearance. But Marilyn was no longer afraid, because she accepted that these struggles could become the very crucible in which their relationship was strengthened.

As Marilyn accepted her daughter's inevitable questions and experiments in the areas of eating and exercise, she found hope in the invigorating opportunity to grow and develop as a mother. Marilyn discovered the truth that every question our daughters ask, every mistake they may make, and every struggle they encounter has the potential to transform *us*. Of course, we pray for their transformation as well, but hope withers away when it is dependent upon the behavior of our children. Hope is fueled when we surrender to God, inviting him to use whatever is happening in our relationship with our daughters for our own growth and good.

Every time I give my daughter a piece of advice, I learn plenty.

ANONYMOUS

Hand-in-hand mothering is anchored in the hope that mother and daughter will change for the better, together. Trying to help our daughters change without changing ourselves won't work. We've lost hope when we resort to pat answers or manipulative phrases to pressure our daughters into change. Hope is restored when we accept our daughters' struggles as gifts and prayerfully and intentionally look for where *we* can change.

Of course, at different stages of mothering our daughters need us to set rules, give direction, and enforce limits. But when it comes to eating and body-image struggles, we cannot regulate a healthy body image or ultimately control our daughters' eating behaviors. We want our daughters to grow into accepting their bodies and caring for them with good nutrition and exercise. We won't guide them to this end if we resist, fear, or even hate the struggles that will take them there.

WELL-FORMED LOVE

We can learn as much as we can about helping our daughters develop a good body image and adopt healthy eating habits, but they will only be techniques if they aren't grounded in our love for our daughters. It's easy to lose sight of our heart for our children in the midst of the busy, complex, and scary challenges of mothering. But if "Well-formed love banishes fear," as 1 John 4:18 (MSG) claims, then we have great hope for becoming the moms we long to be.

We can consistently mother out of well-formed love when we know— really know—that we are loved. When we know that there is nothing we can do to make God stop loving us, we can be unwavering in our love for our daughters.

> Do you think anyone is going to be able to drive a wedge between us and Christ's love for us? There is no way! Not trouble, not hard times, not hatred, not hunger, not homelessness, not bullying threats, not backstabbing, not even the worst sins listed in Scripture.... I'm absolutely convinced that nothing—nothing living or dead, angelic or demonic, today or tomorrow, high or low, thinkable or unthinkable— absolutely *nothing* can get between us and God's love because of the way that Jesus our Master has embraced us. (Romans 8:35-39, MSG)

We can offer comfort to our daughters because we are in relationship with One who promises to never leave us comfortless: "I will not leave you as orphans; I will come to you" (John 14:18). In the face of mistakes and foolish behavior, we won't condemn our daughters if we ourselves have rested in the reality that there is no condemnation in Christ (Romans 8:1). We will live with an unshakable faith in who our daughters are and can be because we know that God is *for us.* "What, then, shall we say in response to this? If God is for us, who can be against us? He who did not spare his own Son, but gave him up for us all—how will he not also, along with him, graciously give us all things?" (Romans 8:31-32).

When Kristin was five years old, she could display her passion and stubbornness in dramatic ways. Once, when things did not go her way, she glared at me, stomped her foot, and declared, "Fine, I am just going to shut myself in my room and never speak to you again." I resisted the urge to retort, "Fine with me." I had recently been seeking answers from God about some disappointments in my own life. I wondered what he was up to in our relationship and was learning that he simply longed to love me. I'd spent a month reading and meditating on 1 John, and these words quickly came to mind while I considered how to respond to my daughter:

> This is how we've come to understand and experience love: Christ sacrificed his life for us. This is why we ought to live sacrificially.... If you see [someone] in need and have the means to do something about it but turn a cold shoulder and do nothing, what happens to God's love? It disappears. And you made it disappear. (1 John 3:16-17, MSG)

I was beginning to understand the lengths to which God was willing to go in order to reveal his love for me, and I wanted my prickly daughter to feel my arms of love around her as I'd felt God enfold me in his love.

After Kristin had been in her room for almost an hour, I peeked in on my stubborn daughter. I smiled at her and told her I was baking cookies. No response. A little later I brought her cookies and milk, and she took them from me sulkingly. I went into her room still later and picked up the empty

JUST FOR YOU

1. How do you know God loves you?
2. Write out a vision for your relationship with your daughter.
3. What questions or struggles is your daughter facing right now that trouble you?
4. How might these struggles be a part of your own transformation?
5. In what ways do you represent God to your daughter?
6. If you wanted to have a heart-to-heart talk with your daughter, how would you approach it?

plate and gently rubbed her back for a minute. Still no response. Finally her resistance wore down when I knocked on her door and asked her if she'd like to play a game. I'll never forget her answer: "Okay, Mom, I get it. You love me."

There are times to discipline, instruct, serve, back off, and affirm, but it is always good timing to love. Although I certainly cannot control my daughter's heart, I can endeavor to keep my own heart pure. Hand-in-hand mothering loves as God has loved us, and in so loving we invite our daughters to catch a glimpse of his love. What an awesome, sacred calling!

JUST FOR THE TWO OF YOU

Every girl is different—a world unto herself. But whatever her personality type, the questions below will help you understand the type of relationship you have with your daughter. You need to know what kind of relationship you have before you press forward to understand your daughter's world more fully.

Prayerfully consider asking your daughter these questions to help in evaluating your relationship. Use your daughter's answers to reevaluate where you place yourself in relationship to your daughter and the impact this placement has on her. As you consider asking your daughter to discuss the questions with you, keep the following in mind:

- Ask age-appropriate questions. Some of the questions may be too abstract for younger girls.
- Don't go on a guilt trip. These questions are simply a way of opening the door to a different and better relationship.
- Be brave. If your heart starts pounding, your palms start sweating, and you don't think you're courageous enough to ask, pretend like you are. You'll discover you are indeed a brave woman.

1. Do I interrupt you when you're trying to tell me something?
2. Do I make plans for you without asking or consulting your schedule or preferences?
3. Do I trust you? If not, is there a reason?

4. Do I lecture you?

5. Do I talk to you like you're a little girl?

6. Do I try to cheer you up every time you are sad or feel bad?

7. If you are upset, do I act like what you are feeling is important?

8. Can you tell me when you're sad, angry, or depressed?

9. Is there anything you can't talk about with me? Why?

10. Do you feel like I understand what you are trying to say?

11. Do I get angry if you disagree with me?

12. Do I criticize you? If so, about what?

13. Is there anything you want to ask me, but are afraid to ask?

14. Do you trust me?

Chapter 3

Being a Girl

Sugar and spice and everything nice;
That's what little girls are made of.

Nursery rhyme

Question: How can I recognize an adolescent?
Answer: You can tell the adolescent not so much by the way she looks
as by the way she slams the door in your face
after you have said something offensive, such as "hello."[1]

Lewis Burdi Frumkes, *The KGB Diet*

Our children had a remarkable conversation on their way home from church one Wednesday evening several years ago. Our son, Graham, who was six years old at the time, got into the car and slammed the door, moaning: "This was a horrible night…I didn't get anything…I didn't get a patch or a ribbon or a balloon. Our team didn't win any of the games. And I didn't like the cookies they had for the snack."

Kristin, then eight, began to set her brother straight. "Now, Graham," she pontificated, "you should be thankful. There are some kids who didn't even have anything for dinner, and they don't get to go to church. They don't even know Jesus."

I was torn between feeling proud of Kristin for the sentiments she expressed and feeling a little sick to my stomach at her self-righteous tone. She concluded the sermon to her brother: "You have so much to be thankful for. Now, me, *I* know what it is to suffer!"

Graham responded with a retort that would become one of his favorites in the years ahead. Shaking his head and spitting out the word, he shuddered: "Girls!" The father of psychology, Sigmund Freud, echoed my son's frustration when he wrote, "Despite my thirty years of research into the feminine soul, I have not been able to answer…what does a woman want?"

Entering the world of girls is an adventure of heroic proportions, daunting to many (including the founding father of psychotherapy) but a journey that mothers are specially equipped for by our female nature and our fierce love for our daughters. When entering our daughters' world, we have a unique perspective. We begin with the confidence that we have been in her world before, when we ourselves experienced the roller coaster of being a growing girl. We quickly realize, however, that this is uncharted territory. Being a girl today is different than it was when we grew up, and mothering a growing girl is a new and challenging experience every day.

ENTERING THE WHIRLWIND

Imagine waking up tomorrow morning and discovering that none of your clothes fit. You step on the bathroom scales, and, no wonder. You have gained ten pounds—overnight! You look in the mirror and can't believe what you see. You've grown taller by several inches. From somewhere in the long-ago-stored files of adolescence, you hear your brother's mocking chant: "Ho, ho, ho! It's the Jolly Green Giant!" You move in closer to the mirror, and your panic intensifies because your face has broken out in ways it hasn't since you wore braces and purchased Clearasil by the case. You are experiencing puberty all over again!

You finally find something you can wear and dash off to work, only to discover that your overnight changes have far-reaching effects. Your coworkers smirk at you, and you feel more self-conscious about your appearance than you have felt for years. You see them huddled together and know they're talking about your hair or outfit or body changes. By lunchtime you've had enough. All you want to do is run home, get back into bed, pull the blankets up over your head, and hope that when you wake up everything will be back to normal.

Welcome to your daughter's world! Of course, a girl doesn't go from being eight to adolescent overnight, but sometimes it feels that way to her—

and to us moms too! At age ten she may weigh in at 75 pounds, and just five or six years later she may tip the scales at 125! We have a shelf lined with pictures to chronicle her year-by-year changes—a toddler with a frilly dress and a pink bow in her hair, a cute, pudgy-faced kindergartner with appliquéd cartoon characters on her overalls, a second grader with missing front teeth and pigtails. All the years following blur until we get to the picture of a beautiful young woman in a formal standing beside a gangly teenage boy holding a corsage box.

It really does go by in a minute! And entering every phase of this whirlwind world with our daughters is an ever-changing and always challenging task—especially when it comes to helping her understand and honor what is going on in her physical development.

This challenge greets us earlier than it did mothers of previous generations. Recent studies indicate that for a variety of reasons, puberty, with all of its complexities, comes earlier for girls today than ever before. The most recent scientific studies list the triggers for this early onset of puberty as obesity, pollution, food additives, divorce, and sexualized advertising.[2] (In other words, the reason is not clear.) We can certainly strive to keep our daughters from excessive junk food, to buy organic foods, to keep our marriages strong, and to censor sexualized media, but we cannot escape the reality that our daughters

JUST FOR YOU

1. Can you recall your passage into puberty? What were your primary feelings? What did you discuss with your mother? What do you wish you could have discussed with your mom?

2. As a growing girl, how did you feel about being female? In what ways was it honored and celebrated in your family? Dishonored and shamed?

3. As a woman, how do you feel about being female? How do you honor and celebrate your unique physical and emotional design?

4. As you anticipate your daughter's entry into adolescence, are you filled with dread, fear, excitement? Why?

are growing up in a culture where young girls are more grown up. Dr. Michael Freemark, Chief of Pediatric Endocrinology at Duke Medical University, reports, "It's as if an entire generation of girls has been put on hormonal fast forward: shooting up, filling out, growing like Alice munching on the wrong side of the mushroom—and towering Mutt and Jeff–like over a generation of boys who seem, next to the girls, to be getting smaller every year."[3]

Childhood is short enough as it is, with kids bombarded from every
direction by sexually explicit movies, rock lyrics,
MTV videos, and racy fashions.
If young girls' bodies push them into adulthood before their
hearts and minds are ready, what will be forever lost?[4]

MICHAEL D. LEMONICK, *Time* magazine

Every girl is different, and no book can outline for you the exact progression of your daughter's physical, emotional, or spiritual development. But this chapter will explore three characteristics that I hope will help you to understand your daughter's unique world. Entering your daughter's world requires *courage, curiosity,* and a *commitment* to relationship that is unshakable. Without these three Cs, we make assumptions that may overlook who our daughters really are, we miss opportunities to guide them and develop our relationship, and we can easily get lost in the maze of questions and struggles that arise in the life of a growing girl. Entering your daughter's world with courage, curiosity, and commitment will give you and your daughter a much better chance of understanding and enjoying the process of becoming and being female.

COURAGE

Entering a daughter's world is not a task for the faint of heart. When our baby girl came into our lives, we never thought about eating disorders, body-image struggles, or the possibility that one day she might want to look like Barbie. What mother could anticipate her fourth grader coming home and reporting, "Boys are gaga over girls with breasts"?[5] When we looked at our sweet-faced little girl, we could not imagine the day she would storm through the house shouting, "I don't have anything to wear! Everything makes me look FAT!" Therapist Annie G. Rogers, Ph.D., empathizes that allowing girls their say can be "profoundly disturbing and disruptive."[6]

New hair styles and colors, body piercing, vegetarianism, bellybutton-baring heroes like Britney Spears: all are a part of the world of girls that we did

JUST FOR THE TWO OF YOU

I keep a list of "Questions I Will Ask My Daughter When I Work Up Enough Courage." I can't explain why some of these questions are hard for me to ask. Maybe it's because I know deep in my heart that they need to be asked and will likely provoke a difficult conversation. I add to the list while I'm sitting in the orthodontist's waiting room, while I'm watching sporting events, and while I'm waiting in the carpool line. It has become a challenge to see if I can come up with a question that surprises my daughter with my insight or even leaves her speechless with my daring!

Here are a few questions to get you started. Keep in mind that the goal is to invite your daughter to open the door to her internal world and to let her know that you can handle anything!

1. What do kids at school say about girls' bodies or even your body? How does it make you feel? Does it impact the way you want to dress?
2. What new hair style or color would you like to try?
3. Do you and your friends talk about bad foods and good foods? Is it hard to eat a certain food after it has been branded bad? Do you ever hide what you eat from your friends?
4. What do you hate about the pressures and expectations in your world?
5. If you could walk down your school hallways yelling one thing, what would it be? What about through our home's hallways?
6. Why do you think people like you? Why do you think they don't like you?
7. What change in your appearance do you think would guarantee that your peers would like you or dislike you more? How about adults?

not encounter while growing up. As our daughters traverse from eight-year-old innocence to worldly-wise adolescence, it takes courage to understand, engage, infiltrate, and be winsomely present in their world.

When it comes to body image and eating behaviors, our daughters will be tempted to experiment with conforming to the unique pressures in their world. One study at the Harvard Eating Disorder Center suggests that pre-teen girls *bond* over mutual body hate and food choices. Relationships are formed in conversations like, "I'm so fat. I hate my stomach. Let's be good and just eat a salad for lunch." The Harvard study suggests that girls who don't participate in this bonding ritual may actually experience social isolation.[7] (We will look more closely at peer pressure in the next chapter.)

Some girls may withdraw from or rebel against the "appearance is everything" culture and overeat or dress in radical styles, which can be just as scary to moms who aren't sure what is at the root of their daughters' behaviors. As girls measure their own bodies and how they fit in, they may become depressed or angry. At every turn, we must summon all our courage to walk hand in hand with our daughters as they make their way through this difficult time of life.

CURIOSITY

"My mom has all the answers," Janine lamented in my office. She quickly glanced at her mom and quietly added, "She doesn't even know the questions."

Janine was sixteen years old and struggling with bulimia. Her mother was caught in the nightmare of eavesdropping at the bathroom door to listen for sounds of an eating disorder and desperately searching for something or someone to help her daughter with her increasingly destructive eating habits. I knew that Janine's mom didn't have all the answers, and I also knew that she probably didn't know the right questions either.

[Y]oung girls want their mothers to be their main source of information about puberty. They appreciate mothers' stories about their own experiences, and they need to hear the same information again and again.[8]

JESSICA GILOOLY, *Before She Gets Her Period*

Curiosity is a skill that is neither taught nor encouraged in our culture. We read books about our daughters, listen to experts talk about female development, and even observe the culture that is creeping in and gaining a tighter grip on our growing girls. The result is that we carry around inside us definitions of a "normal" eight-year-old or thirteen-year-old girl, we fearfully memorize the statistics about eating disorders, and we get mad at a culture that sexualizes girls and glorifies thinness. We all too often interact with our daughters on the basis of what we know of the world, forgetting that our daughters are themselves a world apart to be explored and discovered with eager anticipation.

"What would you like your mom to ask?" I gently questioned Janine.

"I don't know" was her predictable adolescent response.

By the time Janine and her mother had arrived at this crisis, their pattern of relating was entrenched. Janine's mom used her wealth of knowledge and experience to passively make assumptions about Janine that may or may not have been true. She mothered primarily from above, and Janine responded with disdain for her mother's wrong assumptions and withdrew even further.

I asked Janine if she would be willing to give her mother another chance to learn how to ask her daughter questions. Janine reluctantly agreed. Of course Janine needed to make significant changes in her attitudes and behaviors as well, but the beginning of healing in their relationship would start with one of the most important principles of mother-daughter relationships: If you want a real relationship with your daughter—not just an obligatory one that comes from the fact that you're related—then you are going to have to do most of the work!

So why did I suggest that Janine's mom begin to tackle the crisis in their relationship with curiosity? Because when I ask girls what they want most from their mothers, I get one uniform response: "Understanding." Understanding can come from no other source than from our daughters. Because we wear many hats in caring for our children, it's easy to overlook the process that opens the door to the best mother/daughter relationship. Protecting, teaching, admiring, enjoying, guiding, and helping our daughters are all part of mothering, but unless we *understand* them, our relationship becomes superficial and may even wither away entirely.

Theologian Helmut Thielicke wrote, "The Gospel must repeatedly be forwarded to a new address because the recipient is repeatedly changing places of residence."⁹ Our "gospel"—whether it be about God's love and way of life or a healthy body image and good eating habits—must be continually shaped to fit our daughters' "place of residence." She is like a continual change-of-address form, asking us to "Please take note!" Unless we are curious, our message about love and life, and even our relationship itself, will get "lost in the mail."

---

*It doesn't matter how true our message is or how passionate and noble our efforts to communicate that message are. If we don't speak to [our children] from the vantage point of knowing them and their world, chances are they'll have little or no interest in what we've got to say.*¹⁰

WALT MUELLER, president of the Center for Parent-Youth Understanding

---

When your young daughter says, "Watch me, Mom!" what does she really want from you? After watching her, ask why she likes to show you things, what she likes best about your response, and what she likes least. What have you learned about your daughter that reveals her true nature? Is she nurtured by attention? Does she like to perform for others? Is she unsure of herself and seeking encouragement or direction? Curiosity will be squelched if you internally respond, "She just wants attention. I don't want her to become too self-centered." *Of course* she wants attention, and mothers are the ideal candidates to lavish the nourishment of attention on their daughters. The sustenance of maternal curiosity can prevent girls from looking for love in a bowl of ice cream—or worse.

When your growing daughter casts off a favorite dress, saying, "I hate this dress; it's stupid," what is she really saying? You might ask her, "What would you *like* to wear?" "What do you hate about this dress?" Keep a few age-appropriate clothing catalogs on hand and suggest that she circle some outfits she likes so you can get to know her changing sense of style.

Curiosity is circumvented when you focus on the negative words in her expression by chiding, "We don't say 'stupid,' and you should be thankful for the clothes you have." Your curiosity about what is underneath your daughter's questions and expressions teaches her to use her feelings and preferences to choose good behaviors. Eating disorders are a girl's way of expressing herself. We will examine this more fully in later chapters. When our daughters do not grow up learning to express themselves in healthy ways, they may use food for expression.

When your daughter exclaims, "I feel fat!" is there anything else going on? Ask your daughter about the stressors, expectations, or friendships in her life.

Just for You

You will be better able to help your daughter when she feels fat if you're curious about your own negative body feelings.

1. Take note of the times when you feel fat. Is there a context? What day of the week or time of the month is it?

2. Did something happen between yesterday and today that might be a part of your feeling fat? Do you feel obligated to do something you don't want to do?

3. When you feel fat, what other feelings can you uncover? Loneliness, anger, disappointment, feeling left out?

After I finished my first book, *Bravehearts,* I agonized over how it would be received by others. As I anticipated speaking engagements and opportunities to talk about the material in my book, all I could feel was fat. I kept telling myself that if I could just lose ten pounds, the book would be a greater success. As I write these sentences, I realize how foolish they sound, but feeling fat in connection with thinking about introducing my book to others was my internal reality. Once I became aware of what I was doing, I realized that what I was really feeling was scared. I was afraid people wouldn't like my book—or me. When I identified the emotion, I was able to express my insecurities to friends, to my husband, and to God, and to confront my fears humbly bolstered by the love and support of others.

4. How about you? Do you express your feelings in healthy ways or do you allow internal heaviness to be turned against your physical body? Can you think of any recent examples?

Can you help her uncover emotions she might substitute for the word *fat?* In her wonderful book *When You Eat at the Refrigerator, Pull Up a Chair,* Geneen Roth explains that "feeling fat" is a "shorthand for inner states of mind and heart. While there is obviously a physical reality of fatness or thinness, that reality is profoundly affected by the things we say to ourselves, the lack of respect or curiosity or kindness we are able to muster."[11] Curiosity about our daughters' world will spring most authentically from a curiosity and understanding of our own world.

COMMITMENT

I recently returned from a trip exhausted and frustrated by the many delays and cancellations during my travel. I called my husband as soon as I left the airport and began to detail my experiences. His quiet on the other end of the telephone unsettled me, and so once during my recounting I stopped and asked, "Dave, are you still there?"

"I'm here," he answered. "Go on."

When I finished my tale of travel woes, Dave began to kindly suggest some ways I might avoid the same problems in the future. I smiled as the conversation with my Mr.-Fix-It husband ended. And then I called my friend Joan.

Joan immediately made noises of empathy and sympathy, "Ohhh, I'm so sorry," and "Aaargh, that's awful." She then related to me a travel nightmare she'd recently experienced, and we ended the conversation with mutual pity for one another!

Understanding differences between my husband and me keeps me from being overly frustrated with his response to my struggles. For my husband and many other men, language is a tool for solving problems. He wants to hear the whole story before he comments. In contrast, for many women language is a process of creating connection. We interact throughout the story and provide sympathy and support, as well as identification. These differences between men and women often show up shortly after birth. Studies indicate:

- Girls are interested in people. Boys are interested in things.
- Infant girls spend almost twice as much time maintaining eye contact with adults as boys do.

- At four months, girls recognize photographs of familiar faces.
- Girls can hear as many as five different tones. Boys hear only three.
- Girls learn to speak earlier. Boys have better eye/hand coordination.[12]

Neither approach to life is superior, and there is certainly lots of room for individuality apart from these norms, but understanding the unique makeup of girls can help us offer what our daughters need *most* as they grow up. The majority of studies suggest that relationships are at the heart of female development.

Of course we don't need studies to confirm what we all experience. Watch girls leave a group to go to the bathroom—in pairs! What do girls and women talk about, read about, dream about? Relationships. We use our stories to confront problems and think through solutions with one another. The oohs and aahs of female conversation make us feel understood. The sharing of similar experiences allows us to feel connected. The empathy for our pain or joy assures us that we are not alone.

I am saddened by the report of clinical psychologist Catherine Pines of DePaul University: "True friendships—the kind based on interdependence and mutual respect, are very unusual between mothers and daughters. That's because it is really hard for mothers to love and accept their daughters as they are."[13]

Hand-in-hand mothering can eradicate this sad reality as we offer ourselves to our daughters with a commitment that is unshakable. I remind myself often that my daughter is no different from me. She wants a relationship. She doesn't need me to be an expert on everything or to fix her. She wants *me*. And she needs me to want *her.*

The best way to help your child avoid an eating disorder
is to stop it before it starts.
The younger a child has open communication with her parents,
feels loved regardless of her achievements, mistakes or looks,
the stronger she will [be].[14]

DR. TIMOTHY BREWERTON, director of the Eating Disorders Program
at the Medical University of South Carolina

As you ponder your commitment to relationship with your daughter—when she talks back, rejects your opinions, looks ridiculous, asks terrifying questions, complains about everything, and makes big mistakes—consider God's simple statement of unshakable commitment to us in spite of the fact that we certainly talk back, reject his opinion, look ridiculous, ask terrifying questions, complain about everything, and make big mistakes: "I'll never let you down, never walk off and leave you" (Hebrews 13:5, MSG).

PRACTICING THE THREE *C*s

Courage, curiosity, and commitment to our daughters will take on various forms during the many stages of her growth and development, specifically as she confronts questions and struggles with regard to body image and eating choices.

AGES EIGHT THROUGH ELEVEN

A girl between the ages of eight and eleven is on the cusp of significant changes. Developing curiosity about your young girl during this stage will prepare you for the more complicated years ahead. During this stage of development your daughter's interest in the outside world begins to grow. She realizes there are people, ideas, and experiences different from the ones she's known in her family-centered world. One of my favorite authors and poets, Annie Dillard, describes this stage of childhood: "Children ten years old wake up, and find themselves here.... They wake like sleepwalkers, in full stride...equipped with a hundred skills."[15]

---

*At nine, I can remember walking on a fence, all around a park,
thinking, I really liked being nine years old and I wouldn't mind
being nine forever.... I remember having a real sense of joy,
of confidence about negotiating the world on my own.*[16]

EMILY HANCOCK, *The Girl Within*

As you watch your daughter experiment, find joy, and participate in her world, you'll see glimpses of who she is and will become. Now is the time to watch her, take note of how she lives her life, and ask lots of questions. Your courageous, curious, and committed interaction with your daughter will allow you to know—really know—who she is. Write down things she says and does that reveal her unique gifts, her character, and her growing faith. Record experiences that the two of you enjoy in a journal or photo album. Document the development of your relationship. You may need to remind her that you two have indeed built a relationship when she forgets amid the storms of adolescence.

One of the biggest surprises I've encountered while working on this book is the response I've received from mothers of girls in the eight- to eleven-year-old age group. Many mothers have resisted looking at the subject of body image and eating at this stage in their daughters' lives, stating, "It's too early, and I don't want to give her any ideas." But a study by the Medical University of South Carolina of more than three thousand middle-class fifth to eighth graders found that:

- 40 percent felt fat and/or wished they could lose weight
- 30 percent had already dieted
- 8 percent had fasted
- 3 percent had pilfered parents' diet pills
- 5 percent had forced themselves to vomit[17]

May I suggest you gently begin to broach this subject now? The earlier onset of puberty, the bombardment of sexualized and thin-looking girls in the media, and the certainty that your daughter's young peers are thinking and talking about body-image issues make it necessary to discuss this subject early.

As you begin to interact with your daughter about her changing body, you don't want to overwhelm her. A series of casual conversations about her immediate concerns can naturally spring from your practice of being curious about your daughter. The eight- to eleven-year-old girl is developing in significant ways. She's getting taller and rounder as her body prepares for menstruation. One day she may feel confident and strong, and the next awkward and clumsy. She may want to be tall one minute, and to be a little girl again the next. Your curiosity about your daughter will help her to know herself, to understand her own development, and to not be completely shocked when she wakes up a teenager.

JUST FOR THE TWO OF YOU

Consider weaving the following questions into conversations with your daughter:

1. Have you ever seen me stand in front of the mirror and complain about how I look?

2. What do you think of my complaints? Have you ever done the same thing? Have you heard adults or friends talk about losing weight? Do you worry about your weight?

3. Do you think we need to have a perfect appearance, that is, hair, makeup, clothes, etc.?

4. Devise a "Getting to Know You" quiz to take periodically with your daughter. Go out for lunch, or walk in the park, and see how well you know each other. Watch for issues of body image and eating. Some questions might include:

   • If you had lots of money, what would you buy?

   • What's the best way for you to snap out of a bad mood?

   • If a friend offered you a Snickers candy bar, what would you say?

   • What is your favorite outfit?

5. Now is the time to create a library of books (see the Resources section) that answer questions, provide pictures, and detail development about female growth. My husband often teases that women buy women's magazines to find out if they're normal. Our daughters are no different than we are. Especially in this age range, girls want to know if they are normal, and we are their best and most reliable source of information.

6. Begin to prepare your daughter for menstruation. What she learns about this important event and how you interact with her can have a significant impact on how she feels about becoming female. Don't abdicate the privilege of discussing God's sacred design of women in favor of the school's sex education video with animated ovaries. (See suggested resources on this subject in the Resources section.)

Ages Twelve Through Sixteen

Not long ago our daughter came home from an evening with her church youth group. She slammed the front door, ran up the stairs discarding coat and shoes along the way, and slammed her bedroom door. The silence that followed was ominous. My husband and I looked at each other, and he expressed my sentiments exactly: "I don't even want to know."

The emotional roller coaster that an adolescent girl rides can make us want to stay as far away from this ride as possible. But there is no other time when a girl will need her mother more.

As our newly adolescent daughters find themselves in the midst of a whole range of physical changes, equally significant mental and emotional development is going on as well. This is the stage during which a girl begins to make sense of her world and to look for models to show her how to look and live. She is looking for discrepancies between what she's been taught and what she's experiencing. She longs to make relationships more intimate, to find a way to fit in and yet be unique, and to take risks and achieve independence.

Girls this age seek justice and fairness. They look for a cause, and if they don't find a good cause, they often take on a bad one—which could be attaining thinness at any cost. As we encourage our daughters to love their bodies and treat them honorably, we must examine our attitudes and behaviors, because our girls most certainly will be scrutinizing us! In later chapters we will examine our own attitudes in more detail, but begin now to look at any discrepancies you may present to your daughter. The old adage "Do as I say, not as I do" can reap disastrous consequences in your relationship with your daughter.

In households where moms talk about feeling fat,
81% of their teenage daughters said they felt fat too.[18]

Young and Modern magazine

We often create an impossible bind for our daughters. We want them to have a healthy body image, even when we don't. We don't want them to worship the media models, but we don't believe we have something better to offer. And if we do, we don't creatively, attractively, and purposefully present it to our daughters.

One of my friends became fearful as she watched her daughter teeter on the brink of destructive eating habits. Rather than resort to fear and judgment, this wise mother approached her daughter with curiosity and discovered a passion in her daughter's commitment to low-fat, low-calorie eating. She wondered if her daughter's zeal could be channeled elsewhere.

This amazing mother researched teen mission projects and presented several options to her daughter. She sparked her daughter's passion for travel and interest in people from other countries and directed her zeal toward planning a trip of a lifetime. They agreed on a plan to raise support together for her daughter to participate in a month-long mission trip to India. One of their most memorable support-raising efforts was serving a gourmet breakfast in bed to mothers of small children. At the same time they cared for or entertained the babies and toddlers in the home. One morning they changed thirteen diapers during the course of one breakfast!

When her daughter returned from India, her compassion for these impoverished people transformed her eating behaviors radically! She no longer focused on her own weight and compulsive dieting but began to crusade for support for relief work in India. And her gratitude for her own abundant lifestyle invaded her eating habits and resulted in a healthy relationship with food.

During this stage of development, your daughter will be searching to find her place in her world. She wants to fit in. She wants to be unique. If you want to be a part of this sometimes crazy process, you've got to grab her hand and let her know you're not afraid of her world, you don't think it's stupid, and you support her in her efforts to find her place. As your daughter seeks to make sense of the world, she needs to express her opinions and test her ideas. According to Dr. Ava Seigel at the Family Institute at Northwestern University, "A daughter may have her mom's eyes, smile, and sense of humor, but she has her own ways of thinking, feeling, and doing that are different from her mom's. That has to be seen by the mother as valid and deserving respect. From the beginning, mothers who dream of adult friendships with their female children should allow daughters to make age-appropriate decisions, encouraging them to express their own opinions and allow disagreements."[19]

JUST FOR THE TWO OF YOU

1. Practice noticing the ways in which your daughter is different from you, and let her know that you *enjoy* the differences. I constantly remind my daughter of how wonderful it is that she is much more athletic than I will ever be. Kristin also knows how to apply makeup, and I just never got the hang of that art. I admire her artistry and ask for tips.

2. Allowing your daughter to grow up involves seeing beyond some of her clothing choices that strike you as ridiculous. Ask your daughter if there are any changes to her appearance, including fashion styles, that she'd like to make. Remember that how you interact about her appearance may be far more important than the clothes she chooses.

3. Does your daughter want to change her eating patterns? Become a vegetarian? You can honor her questions and interests by asking her to spend two weeks researching a particular eating plan, learning how it can be healthy. After she learns what is good for her, let her write her own shopping list and prepare food for herself and the whole family occasionally. When she discovers recipes she likes, honor her by preparing "her food" for her.

4. Begin to make a list of available service projects. Find out details, times volunteers are needed, and costs involved. (One organization that provides challenging teen mission trips is Teen Mania Ministries, 1-800-299-TEEN or http://www.teenmania.com.) Present your ideas to your daughter and ask if she has any of her own. Sometimes our ideas will spark our daughters' imagination. Along with your daughter, come up with a plan for her to be involved in a ministry or community project. If she is reluctant to go alone, volunteer to go with her or to help her enlist a friend to participate.

After a lifetime of work, Freud claimed that he didn't know what a woman wanted. *We know.* We want relationships. We want someone who sees, knows, encourages, supports, forgives, remembers, believes, and understands us. On a very practical level, we need someone we can ask "Am I fat?" one thousand times and know we'll hear from them "You're not fat. You're beautiful" one thousand times. Our daughters want no less than we do.

Chapter 4

Your Daughter's Culture

*Although the purpose of "entertaining" is usually seen
as mere amusement or just moneymaking, its real purpose is education.
The teenager goes to the school of adolescence
with entertainment as friend and teacher.*[1]

QUENTIN J. SCHULTZE, *Dancing in the Dark*

Saturday night our daughter attended her first high school homecoming dance. She awakened at 9:00 A.M. in a bit of a panic. After all, she had only nine hours to get ready! She spent the day pampering herself, painting her nails, and experimenting with all sorts of glittery makeup applications. Finally, one hour before she was to meet a group of friends for dinner before the dance, she put on her velvety dress and high-heeled shoes. She twisted her hair into a freestyle bun that only a high school girl could think of, much less maneuver. And she was ready.

Before we took pictures, her father wondered if Kristin was going to put on a sweater! Her exasperated look told him, *Don't tease me tonight. This is too important.* As if we didn't already know.

We prayerfully drove our daughter to meet her friends and wondered how we had arrived so quickly at this rite of passage. It seemed as if it was only a few short months ago that she loved to play with her American Girl doll and read her favorite book, *Heidi,* over and over again. The stakes seemed astronomically higher as she entered a world filled with high school hormones, music beating with sexuality, and peers dressed in clothes we would have never dreamed existed, much less thought our parents would consider letting us wear.

All evening long I thought about Kristin, I prayed for her, and I found it difficult not to give in to a rising panic. Only mothers of high school girls know that it's possible for a three-hour dance to seem three weeks long! During my evening vigil I had a lot of time to think about the teenage girls in their slinky dresses moving to music that only highlights their new female curves. Would Kristin compare herself to others and feel too big or "dorky"? I wondered for a moment if my Baptist forefathers and foremothers were right in believing that dancing should be feared and avoided!

I knew there would be a group of students in dancewear more gothic than glitzy, with black accouterment. Should I worry about their intentions to go against the high school mainstream with more than just alternative fashion? What about the clean-cut boys with ties and boutonnieres who listen to contemporary music that refers to girls as whores and encourages sex with no limits? Would Kristin be able to spot honorable boys and turn down the dishonorable? What if no one asked her to dance? Would she assume she wasn't asked because she didn't "look right"?

Kristin's high school was recently cited as the school in our area with the highest rate of marijuana use. She'd already told me that rumors were flying that some kids were going to try to sneak alcohol into the dance. What were we thinking in letting her attend such a dangerous event? I was ready to grab a flashlight, drive to Kristin's high school, and rescue her from enemy territory. I decided Mark Twain was right when he said, "When a child turns twelve you should put him in a barrel, nail the lid down, and feed him through a knothole. When he turns sixteen, plug the hole."

In lightning speed, I devised a plan. We could sell all we own and move to a remote area of Nebraska. With no television, radio, magazines, or peers, perhaps my children would be safe. It was only when I began to envision making our own clothes that I knew I needed a reality check! I needed to return to a truth that is freeing in my mothering of a teenage daughter.

THE CULTURE IS NOT THE ENEMY

How can I say that? I know that music, movies, magazines, and fashion designers conspire to make us believe that thin is in, that bodies are commodities, and that no price is too high to pay to look good. The culture of skinny has produced seven million American girls and women who struggle with eating disorders.[2] The culture is an easy target of our disdain, outrage, and even hatred. We want to believe that if we can tame teenage music, fill the movies and magazines with wholesome young girls and boys, and return fashion to the 1950s, then our children will be safe.

Our family lives in a community (Littleton, Colorado) that has dissected the culture during the past two years. On April 20, 1999, a high school tragedy in our suburb rocked our world. Two seniors entered their school, Columbine High School, and opened fire, wounding and killing twelve of their peers and one teacher. Our community has desperately sought to identify the enemy that caused this unthinkable event. We've considered violent video games, dark heavy-metal music, a gothic subculture, careless teachers and administrators, racism, cruel peer groups, alcohol abuse, antidepressants prescribed by one of the gunmen's psychiatrist, liberal gun regulations, and negligent parents. Despite hearings, research, and testimony by experts, no one can pinpoint the specific reason that two boys, immersed in a culture similar to that of so many other adolescents, responded with such horrific behavior.

When it comes to body-image struggles and eating disorders, there are likewise a plethora of suspects: glossy magazines with unrealistic images of body size; a fashion and beauty industry that spends millions of dollars advertising an ultraslim look; movies where all the pretty, popular girls look more like Barbie than real girls; music sung by skinny, sexy girl heroes or by handsome boy heroes clearly in search of the perfect date; and a diet industry that is ever ready to sell the cure for the body-image blues. When we add peer pressure to the cultural pressure, it seems foolish to think our daughters can avoid succumbing to body-image struggles and eating disorders.

Adolescent girls are saplings in a hurricane.
They are young and vulnerable trees
that the winds blow with gale strength.[3]

MARY PIPHER, *Reviving Ophelia*

I recently attended a seminar on adolescent struggles and spent several hours listening to thoughtful experts pinpoint the causes of teenage trouble. During a question-and-answer session one attendee asked a panelist: "But what if it was *your* daughter in trouble? How would you respond to her?" The expert's answer stunned me. She explained that she would never be caught off guard by problems with her daughter because she knew all the warning signs, understood the causal links to adolescent struggles, and would be able to "nip trouble in the bud." My heart broke for this expert's false confidence and for the mothers in the audience, with daughters in trouble, who were propelled into shame because they had not been so "insightful."

The danger of tracing complex problems to specific root causes is that we begin to believe we can be in control. We hold on to false and potentially damaging guarantees that if we follow a certain set of rules and eliminate all dangerous temptations from our daughters' worlds, then they will be safe. We forget the lesson in the book of Genesis about the first woman who thought she could control her world by knowing everything. Genesis 3:1 records the chilling words, "Now the serpent was more crafty...."

THE CULTURE IS NOT THE ENEMY— BUT THERE IS AN ENEMY

When we use all our energy to fight the culture, we may not only be lured into a false sense of control, but we also can alienate our daughters who might join the culture to fight us. Most significantly, we can miss the real Enemy.

The apostle Peter warned: "Your enemy *the devil* prowls around like a roaring lion looking for someone to devour" (1 Peter 5:8, emphasis mine). Of course that "someone" includes our daughters. He is a crafty enemy with many devices to capture our daughters—body, soul, and spirit—for his purposes (2 Corinthians 2:11). The culture is a powerful device that the Enemy is skilled in using against our daughters and us.

If we want more than control (which we will never have anyway), then we must give up trying to control. If we want connection with our daughters in powerful and sustained relationships, then we must cultivate a passion to understand the culture, engage with our daughters about the culture, and learn to *use* the culture to invite our daughters to growth and to God.

I know this sounds like an overwhelming task. We don't understand the words to their music, we'd never pierce our bellybuttons, and *Seventeen* magazine makes us a little sick to our stomachs. But remember that our enemy is God's enemy as well. We are not in this alone. In the New Testament, God promises us that he is greater than the one who manipulates the culture for evil (John 16:33), and in the Old Testament he encourages us in this very task of using an evil culture for good. The words of the prophet Jeremiah speak directly to our mother hearts: "Therefore thus says the Lord...: If you return..., then I will give you again a settled place of quiet and safety, and you will be My minister; and if you separate the precious from the vile,...you shall be My mouthpiece" (Jeremiah 15:19, AMP).

Jeremiah wrote to people who were filled with distrust and despair and reminded them that they would find rest in returning to their relationship with God. What a wonderful insight for mothers who survey the culture with suspicious and uneasy hearts! We find rest in navigating these tumultuous times for girls when we hold on to the truth that *relationships are central*—our relationship with God and with our daughters, and their relationship with God and with us. If we ourselves have been harmed by the failures of our mothers or if we have already blown it with our daughters, then we know that relationships can harm. But if relationships can harm, they can also heal. We can rest in that truth.

First, we can rest in our relationship with God. Dean Borgman, Professor of Youth Ministries at Gordon-Conwell Theological Seminary, writes: "Christ is the key to our interpretation of culture. The divine nature permanently identifies with human culture. The eternal Son takes on a physical body in a particular culture. While retaining his divine identity, Christ relinquishes so many prerogatives. This mystery of the incarnation offers us a grand and useful model.... The Word becomes flesh that we may find spirit.... Culture is the transient stage of an eternal drama."[4]

Christ's humility in entering our culture for a chance at relationship with us encourages us to go into the culture of our daughters for the sake of a relationship with them and ultimately to model God's love and longing for them as well.

Second, we can rest in our desire for a wondrous relationship with our daughters. Walt Mueller, president of the Center for Parent-Youth Understanding, warns that "attacking culture creates a climate for our kids to respond in bitterness and an unwillingness to open up and doesn't nurture intimacy."[5] Creating a climate that fosters openness and nurtures intimacy requires "clear focus, humility, and a tolerance of differing opinions."[6] The surest foundation for a heart that is shrewd as a serpent and innocent as a dove (Matthew 10:16) is a courageous commitment to the relationship with our daughters. Remembering the power of this relationship is what we must always come back to.

We may be tempted to feel overwhelmed by, angry with, or even jealous of the culture. And with good reason. Youth specialist Tom Piotrowski explains that we should "never discount the *relational* factor that many young people have with the media they consume, whether it's music, TV, film, or print" (emphasis mine).[7] When we feel the culture pulling our daughters away from us, *we* must do the work of creating a relationship that offers more than the culture.

There is no better way to do this than by actually using the culture we too readily try to separate ourselves, and our daughters, from. Dean Borgman instructs: "The elements of youth culture are as precious to them as the language and rituals, music and dances are to tribal societies."[8] We can take what is precious, separate it from the vile, and use it to create a relationship with our daughters that will be less vulnerable to the attacks of the Enemy.

THREE RULES FOR USING THE CULTURE

1. Know your daughter's culture.
What's out there? What books, music, movies, and magazines does she like? What books, music, movies, and magazines do her friends like? We really need to know our girls' culture better than they do.

When one of my friends discovered that her fifth-grade daughter's circle of friends was reading a series of books called The Baby-Sitters Club, she bought several of the books in the series and read them herself. After her daughter read a book, they'd plan a gab session. My friend developed a series of questions that allowed her to use the culture to know her daughter better and to open the door to important conversations:
- What did you like/dislike about the story?
- Is any of this true in your life?

- Why do you think the characters did or said certain things?
- Has this ever happened to you before?
- What did you think of what the characters did or said?
- What do you think you might do in a similar situation?
- If you could rewrite the story, how would you do it?

My friend wisely and winsomely opened the door to conversations about culture during a time of relative innocence in the hope that the door of communication will remain open when her daughter's world becomes more complicated.

2. Look for something positive first.

No one is ever judged, criticized, or pressured into changing. If our daughters believe that we're on a witch hunt, they will wall off parts of their hearts from us. If instead they see us approach their culture with curiosity and a sense of humor, they will be watching and waiting to hear our response.

One of my clients took her sixth-grade daughter and three friends to see teen pop idol Britney Spears in concert. This mother could barely look past the unbelievably skimpy outfits of the performer. But when they went out for ice cream after the concert she said, "Wow! Britney sure has a lot of energy and passion when she sings." Her comment led to a conversation about passion and what each of the girls felt passionate about. At the end of the discussion my client casually remarked, "I sure didn't like some of Britney's outfits." The girls quickly chimed in, "Yeah. They were embarrassing. Gross." Enough said. This mother's one negative comment was received and will impact her daughter because it was cushioned by many positive remarks.

3. Connect the culture to stories.

If your daughter has a favorite musical performer, try to find out about the performer's life and connect the lyrics of her songs to her personal story. If your daughter likes to look at teen magazines, learn something about the models in the advertising. If you watch a movie together, connect part of the plot of the movie with your own or your daughter's story. Relationships are a continuing story, and stories are the lifeblood of relationships. You can wisely use stories in ways that go beyond words to speak the language of the heart.

Listen! Listen to stories!...stories convey the mystery
and the miracle—the adventure—of being alive....
[Stories] speak to the limits of our endeavor...suggest hope
and, ultimately, the promise of our shared journey.[9]

Ernest Kurtz and Katherine Ketcham, *The Spirituality of Imperfection*

The following three "stories" can be told effortlessly while observing the culture with your daughter:

- Model Kate Moss is 5' 7" and weighs 100 pounds. When Kathy Bruin was twelve, she began a rebellion against advertisers who portrayed only thin, thin women in their ads. Using a real perfume ad, she created a thousand posters with the picture of Kate Moss lying almost naked on a couch. Instead of the words "Obsession by Calvin Klein" her posters said, "Emaciation Stinks, Stop Starvation Imagery." Friends and family helped her put up the posters all over their community. Her efforts resulted in an organization called About-Face, which fights negative and distorted images of women.[10]

- Columnist Margie Boule tells the story of sixteen-year-old Megan Gerking's fight to overcome anorexia: "I read magazines by the handful when I was younger. Looking at magazines and watching TV, you always get this need to look prettier or better. It's a struggle. You think, 'Why aren't I that thin?' Now I flip through those and it's like, let's check out which models have eating disorders."[11]

- Our culture's ideal standards (as determined by Miss America's weight) grew even skinnier between 1979 and 1988. By 1992, Miss America's weight was 13 percent to 18 percent below the average expected weight of women.[12]

Before we look at more practical ways to use the culture to walk hand in hand with our daughters, let me share with you the always-relevant advice of eighteenth-century pastor Henry Venn. A concerned mother wrote to Pastor Venn about her child, asking for any further suggestions to save her child from trouble. His answer should permeate all that we mothers do today: "[Consider] your own weakness and inability to give a single ray of light, or to excite the faintest conviction of sin, or to communicate the least particle of spiritual good, to one who is dearer to you than life. How ought this to take away every proud thought of our own sufficiency, and to keep us earnest; importunate suppliants at the door of the Almighty's mercy and free grace."[13]

JUST FOR YOU

1. How do you view your daughter's culture? As an enemy? A threat? A tool?

2. How did your parents view your culture? How did their viewpoint impact your relationship?

3. In what ways does the life of Jesus challenge the way you think about your daughter's culture?

4. How does the culture influence your life? In what ways is it enriched or impoverished by the media?

5. How significant are music and movies to you?

6. How do you listen to music or watch television and movies with your daughter?

7. How do you pray for your daughter's culture? Consider praying every day for one aspect of your daughter's culture, that God's presence might show forth in some way. One mother and daughter I know read the acknowledgments on CD jackets, and whenever they read that an artist thanks God and is strengthened by his or her faith in Christ, they thank God for this and pray that it might be reflected even more brightly in the artist's life.

8. How do you pray for your daughter? Make a list of the cultural influences you fear. Pray for your daughter with regard to each of these and begin to pray about how you can use these fears to strengthen your relationship with your daughter.

USING THE CULTURE: A PRACTICE SESSION

My daughter loves to look at teen magazines. We have many wonderful rituals connected with these magazines. Most of these rituals take place in my bedroom. We keep a stack of magazines in a basket by the bed, hoping for a few minutes to use these magazines in some of our favorite times together. With Kristin's gracious permission, I'd like to let you in on one of our memorable magazine evenings.

Earlier in the day I had jotted down three principles about body image that I wanted to delve into for my sake as well as for Kristin's:

- The Body Is Important
- The Body Is Not All There Is
- The Body Is a Temple

I chose these categories as a result of previous conversations with Kristin about the teenage culture's approach to body image. If you want to incorporate this practice with your daughter, you can make it age appropriate, using *her* culture. You can come up with your own principles to look for in her magazines, books, music, or movies that apply to what she's thinking about and confronted with at her age. Don't hesitate to use Christian magazines, music, or books; these are part of our collection as well. In the next "Just for the Two of You" section there are suggestions that will help you come up with your own magazine night.

I briefly explained to Kristin my agenda and asked for her help. I asked Kristin to pick her favorite recent magazine so we could see what we could learn about these three principles. I told her I wanted to know what her magazine said about the importance of the body, the body's impact on the rest of our life, and the body as a dwelling place for God.

Kristin and I call my bed "The Throne." We pile it with pillows, light candles, sometimes play music, and post a Do Not Disturb sign on the bedroom door. We take turns bringing the snack. This particular night was Kristin's turn, and she brought licorice and Dr Pepper. (Kristin's snacks are usually far more interesting than mine are.)

So, you have all the elements: my daughter and me; The Throne; *Seventeen* magazine, December 2000; licorice and Dr Pepper; candles and Christmas music in the background (although it was early November, we decided it was time to jump-start the Christmas spirit). These humble elements provided the context for a night we will never forget, as well as insights into three important principles that have become part of our thinking and behavior regarding eating and body image.

THE BODY IS IMPORTANT

We quickly flipped through the magazine and saw bodies everywhere. On the first three pages we noted sultry blondes in black leather pants and midriff-baring tank tops advertising Sheer Blonde shampoo; a sexy young model with midriff bared again, complemented by stiletto heels advertising Levi's; and a hip looking young couple—both with midriffs bare—in red and black leather jackets advertising Wilson's Leather. That prompted us to count how many young women were depicted in the magazine with their stomachs showing. Twenty-seven!

I asked Kristin what she thought this midriff-revealing trend is all about. She said, "I guess if you feel good about your stomach, you want to show it off!" We did note that all the girls pictured had flat or even concave stomachs. We decided to see for ourselves what this trend might do for our look. We each pulled on a pair of tight jeans and experimented with a T-shirt revealing various degrees of our stomachs. We laughed so hard I'm sure we burned as many calories as we would have doing fifty sit-ups. It is not a fashion style you will be seeing on me anytime soon.

"What is the big deal about the body?" I asked Kristin. Her answer seemed obvious: "I guess it's what everyone sees first." We talked about how our bodies represent who we are, whether it's right for others to judge us by our bodies, and if it's okay to believe that the body is really important.

I complimented Kristin on how she has encouraged me to care for my body. There are so many wonderful body-pampering products available today, and Kristin loves to luxuriate in different scents and lotions. She knows that whenever one of her favorite lotions is missing, it's probably in my bathroom.

Seventeen magazine knows that the body is important. Advertisers know that the body is important. And the Enemy knows that the body is important. Our daughters wonder if it's okay for the body to be important. I explained to Kristin that as I was growing up I was confused about my body, afraid at times that it was scary and out of control, and sadly convinced at other times that it was a terrible, treacherous enemy. Kristin's response was one of compassion, with an element of self-assurance that she would never be as messed up as I was! Silently I prayed that Kristin would continue to grow into a healthy relationship with her body that would inform her choices about eating and exercise, as well as baring her belly!

THE BODY IS NOT ALL THERE IS

This particular issue of *Seventeen* was divided into twelve sections: Fashion, Beauty, Guys, Quiz, Features, Eating, Bodyline, Day in the Life, Backstage Pass, Fiction, Columns, and Who Knew? I asked Kristin if she thought these topics pretty much represented the concerns of girls her age. She thought they did. I couldn't resist commenting on the lack of spiritual content. Kristin politely responded, "Uh-huh."

We each decided to pick one section and find everything in it we liked. Kristin picked Fashion, and I picked Who Knew? (because I didn't!). Kristin pointed out several outfits, styles, and accessories she liked. Without any prompting from me, she also pointed out some of the incongruities of teenage magazines. We've been looking for these mixed messages for a long time, and this habit comes naturally now. We laughed at the Cheez Whiz advertisement only a few pages apart from one of those midriff-baring models and a few more pages away from an article on weight watching during the holidays. Kristin's discernment encourages me that she is developing the skills of picking and choosing among the many conflicting messages her culture hurls at her daily.

Humble pie was my snack for the night after I read the article I'd selected. The article in the Who Knew? section was entitled "The Praying Fields"— about the battle for school prayer at sporting events. This article reported on a recent poll taken on http://www.seventeen.com that found that 81 percent of teenage respondents disagree with the Supreme Court's decision to keep prayer off school playing fields. I admitted to Kristin that this magazine did take into consideration the spiritual and that I was wrong in assuming it would not. We talked about how adults unfairly put teenagers into a box, making inaccurate assumptions about who they are and what is important to them. Kristin came up with a great metaphor: "It's like whenever people want to paint teenagers, they have only one color."

I agreed with Kristin that teenagers are connected to a wide variety of ideas, passions, beliefs, and plans. I couldn't resist the impulse to bring the conversation back to the body and use Kristin's own metaphor—that when we focus *only* on our bodies, it's like painting with one color. Obsessing about body image and weight loss keeps us from experiencing so much more! The body is important, but Kristin agreed it's not all that's important to teenagers, no matter what the culture tries to tell us.

THE BODY IS A TEMPLE

I have to confess that I expected to find more "vile" than "precious" with regard to the subject of treating one's body as the temple of the living God (1 Corinthians 6:19). Kristin and I have talked often about the careless and even profane attitude toward the body that is prevalent in her culture. While scanning *Seventeen's* table of contents, my heart leaped and my voice exclaimed, "Yikes!" at the Sex and Body column entitled "Can I get pregnant from semen on a washcloth?" When Kristin was younger and began to look at teen magazines, I always screened them first, tearing out anything inappropriate for her to read or discuss at her age. I still read all of Kristin's magazines, but we talk about all subjects now because, as Kristin so aptly stated, "This stuff is all over the halls of my high school."

Kristin noticed where my eyes settled on the table of contents and reminded me of my own rule to look for something positive first. So we began the daunting task of looking for some encouragement to treat our bodies as temples of the Holy Spirit. Kristin reminded me that good grooming and beautiful adornment is honoring to our bodies and to God. And I agreed. We read a great article on the need for sleep and concurred that protecting our sleep is sacred.

Page 145 seemed like an unlikely place to connect the body to an important spiritual principle. It featured an article about the popular boy-band 98 Degrees. This band reminded Kristin of a story that provided a wonderful conclusion to our evening.

JUST FOR THE TWO OF YOU

Here are a few suggestions to guide you on your own magazine night with your daughter.

1. Buy some of the magazines marketed to girls. Read them first yourself, and tear out anything you're not comfortable with your daughter reading.

2. Load up on your favorite snacks, and choose a special place in the house for just the two of you.

3. Do specific issues come to mind that you'd like to address with your daughter using her culture? If not, try some of the following ideas. The more you practice using the culture, the more skilled you'll become.

   - Let your daughter look through one magazine and pick out everything she thinks you will like or won't like while you look through another magazine picking your daughter's likes and dislikes. Be specific to the topic of body image. Compare your choices.

   - Look for the hypocrisy. For example, an article on one page about eating disorders and a picture of a size 0 model on the next page. (Did you know that Gap actually sells a size 0?!)

   - Make a collage of all the body shapes in a magazine. Are they all identical? If so, what does this message send to readers?

   - If possible, get some old magazines from your adolescence. Look at these together, noting the styles, trends, and messages of the time. When my daughter and I did this exercise, we had so much fun! We laughed at the styles while I defended my era (*everything* wasn't ugly in the seventies, was it?). We had a great discussion about the transience of styles, the ever-skinnier models, and changes in advertising. We agreed that hairstyles look much better now, that today's clothes are starting to look more and more like yesterday's, and that models keep getting skinnier and skinnier. At the end of the evening, the power of the ever-changing, fickle, and often foolish culture was diffused, while our relationship was strengthened.

One of the members of the band (Nick) dates pop music star Jessica Simpson. Kristin told me she'd read about their commitment to remain sexually pure because of their faith and dedication to God. She longingly asked me, "Do you think I'll ever find a guy that good looking who loves God too?" I asked her to describe the perfect guy for her fifteen-year-old life. Then we prayed specifically for her requests. I asked her to describe exactly who *she* would want to be when that guy came along. With simple elegance she described her longings to love God, look good, have friends, get good grades, play lacrosse, and write poetry. She quickly agreed that she would need to take loving, diligent care of her body to be the young woman she wants to be. And then we decided to get the recommended eight hours of sleep!

As I said good night to Kristin, she sleepily mumbled, "Thanks, Mom, for caring about the things I care about." I have to admit that there were many moments in our evening together that I wanted to lecture, rip out pages, and suggest we read *Heidi* together again instead. I suspect Kristin knows that I don't care for midriff-baring shirts; left to myself I probably wouldn't read about "energizing shower gels" and "shimmering lip lacquers"; and I find some of the material in *Seventeen* offensive. But I know in her heart of hearts that Kristin knows I care about *her*. And her culture is a powerful tool for me to use in communicating my love for my daughter.

"BUT MOM, EVERYONE ELSE IS...!"

The culture can seem overwhelmingly difficult to use well on our daughters' behalf when their peer group so often seems bent on using it destructively. We may learn to use the culture, but is that enough to overcome the pressure of "everyone else's" dieting, obsessing about weight, and trying with all their might to look like their cultural heroines? It is painful and scary when our daughters begin to replace us as the central influence in their lives. It's hard not to be offended when a girlfriend's, boyfriend's, or teen magazine's opinion matters more than what we have to say.

We cannot discount the power of peer pressure. As the research cited in the last chapter suggests, girls bond early with each other over concerns about body size and eating. And unfortunately, they don't always give each other the best advice or example to follow. Eating disorders have been called contagious because girls give the ideas for harmful behavior to one another. As you begin to use the culture to strengthen your relationship with your daughter and to point her in a healthy direction with regard to body image and eating choices, be aware of all her friends who might be steering her in a completely different direction.

---

*In the 1960's a majority of teenagers were citing their parents
as the most important influence in their lives.
By 1980 a majority of teenagers named their friends
as the chief influence in their lives.
Parents had slipped to second, and the media showed a remarkable rise.*[14]

DEAN BORGMAN, *When Kumbaya Is Not Enough*

Rather than throwing our hands up in despair over the power of peer pressure or locking your daughter in her room until she turns twenty-one, you can respond to the reality of peer influence in ways that can strengthen your relationship with your daughter rather than tear it apart.

First, *don't take it personally.* The importance of your daughter's peer group is not about you. Let your daughter know over and over again that you want a good relationship with her but that you value her other relationships. Remind yourself, when you feel left behind or forgotten, that developing her peer relationships is a necessary and important part of growing up. Youth specialist Dean Borgman writes: "We should remember how much adolescent growth goes on outside the family and the church. Significant development of self-image takes place among friends; we need to understand peer groups as a very influential social system."[15]

Second, *watch for positive peer influence.* Congratulate your daughter or her friends when they give each other good advice or ideas about body image and weight loss, or when they criticize the hypocrisy of the media. Look for every opportunity to validate and compliment your daughter's peer group. Just as with the culture as a whole, when you make your daughter's friends into the enemy, you run the risk of your daughter joining her peers just to be against you.

Third, *make room for peer influence to join your own.* When you ask your daughter to disregard everything about her peer group, you risk your daughter disregarding everything you believe and advise. Dr. Barbara Stagger works with teenagers at Children's Hospital in Oakland, California, and gives this advice to parents:

> We don't get very far by just telling teenagers not to take risks because it scares us. When we demand to know why they've screwed up, the kid says, "I had to. Everybody else was doing it." The adult replies, "If everybody else jumped off the cliff, would you, too?"
>
> The honest answer to that question is *yes*. It's really, really important that we understand this. For the teen at that moment, being down at the bottom together feels better than being on the edge of the cliff alone.
>
> What we need to engage our teens in discussing is the question: What else can you do to be part of a group and still survive, while taking reasonable risks? If you've got to jump off the cliff, can't you choose one that's not 50 feet high? Can you jump off the cliff that's 2 feet high instead?[16]

When one of my friend's daughters asked to get her bellybutton pierced (because "everyone else" had a bellybutton ring), she wondered about the health risks and worried what "everyone else" in her own adult world would think—immediately revealing that moms are vulnerable to peer pressure too! She asked her daughter to come up with one other good reason to get her bellybutton pierced.

Two days later her daughter said that she'd been thinking about recent conversations they'd had about dating. They'd discussed getting her a purity ring to symbolize her commitment to reserve sex for marriage. The daughter explained that she wanted a bellybutton ring to symbolize her commitment to sexual purity. She said that a bellybutton ring seemed more symbolic to her of a decision to honor her body in this way than a ring on her finger.

Her mom admired her creativity and individuality in expressing her values while at the same time wanting to identify with her peer group. She significantly strengthened her relationship with her daughter by leaving room for peer influence to complement her own. To her, a bellybutton ring seemed like a two-foot jump compared to the fifty-foot leap of sex before marriage.

Finally, *compassionately fight negative influence*. When you are with your daughter and her friends (and do take every opportunity to be the chauffeur, to host the parties, and to make your home slumber party central), you will intuitively recognize the girls who might have a negative influence on your daughter. When you have the opportunity, away from her friends, suggest to your daughter that you are aware of the possible negative influence, but suggest with compassion. Teenagers are intensely loyal to their friends, so wisdom and kindness must guide any conversation about friends.

Compassionate intervention could look something like this:

- "I wonder if Maureen and her mother can talk openly about Maureen's obsession with her weight? I'm glad she has a wise, good friend like you."
- "I'll bet Jessica doesn't even know how foolish she sounds when she calls herself fat. I hope there's someone in her life who is complimenting her on how pretty she is."
- "I've noticed how little Katie eats. I hope she's not dabbling with an eating disorder. I'm afraid she's going to lose her bubbly personality and energy for life."
- "I overheard Meagan say that she doesn't eat anything with fat in it. Do you know how she came up with that idea? She must be putting a lot of pressure on herself. I hope that you and Meagan can do something really fun together and get her mind off this obsession with fat."

One of the greatest moments for me in mothering came a few months ago when I overheard my daughter talking with her friend Alyssa. They were discussing an upcoming event, and Alyssa said, "I'm just going to starve myself. I've got to lose ten pounds." Kristin replied, "I don't think starving yourself is a good idea. You could talk to my mom about it. She could help you."

Our daughters need to know that we care about their friends and that we want to be their ally in their friendships as well as in their struggles with eating and body image.

JUST FOR YOU

1. How important was your peer group to you when growing up? Think about its positive as well as negative influence. How important is it today? Take note of the times you find yourself wondering what others will think or are thinking.

2. List the ways your daughter's peer group is encouraging healthy growth and development in her.

3. Begin to pay attention to your daughter's friends. Think about the unique talents and abilities of each friend and find ways to affirm your daughter's friends when you are with them. Pray for each friend regularly.

4. Is your home the hangout for your daughter's friends? How can you make your home more central for their get-togethers?

5. Get to know the parents of your daughter's friends. Our daughters will be blessed if they are surrounded by moms who know them and know each other. If some of the girls in your daughter's peer group don't come from healthy, supportive families, then you have a wonderful opportunity to give them a taste of parental involvement.

6. Encourage your daughter's friendship with adult or older friends. I have consistently prayed that God would bring older friends into my daughter's life to provide positive influence. Kristin has a college-aged friend that she admires and loves to be with. Occasionally I've called Amber and let her in on some of Kristin's struggles and concerns, knowing that Amber's advice will only add to and strengthen my own.

Part II

Building a Bridge
Between Your Worlds

With bandaged knee and a paint-stained dress, [my daughter] met me with a smile.
Hungry arms wrapped themselves around me, as she whispered in my ear, "I love
you so, Mama...." For the first time in months I felt a sense of balance return. The
weight of my deadlines, my illusionary race with time, my tired and burdened real-
ity were each a result of my blindness, not my vision. I didn't need to reduce the tasks
at hand. I didn't need to pour more sand into the hourglass. All I needed was to
remember what mattered most. Love was the purpose behind everything. Love for
my daughter, my family.... This was the golden thread of my passion, the source
of my peace and my strength—the very conviction of my soul. This is what made
the impossible possible.[1]

LISA WEEDN, *Across the Porch from God*

Chapter 5

"Mom, You Just Don't Understand!"

Enter the teenage girl …
After years of your attempting to be sensitive to your daughter
and to stay in tune with her emotions,
to be told you 'don't have a clue' about her is devastating.
Even when you know deep down that her accusations aren't particularly rational,
when she tells you that you failed horribly as a mother and slams the door in your face,
it is difficult not to second-guess yourself.
Your very sense of self-worth is at stake.[1]

RONI COHEN-SANDLER AND MICHELLE SILVER, *"I'm Not Mad, I Just Hate You!"*

Do you remember when your daughter couldn't get enough of you? She followed you from the bedroom to the kitchen, and even into the bathroom. She watched you dust, make dinner, and put on your makeup. You cuddled and giggled together and sometimes spoke a language no one else understood. And then, seemingly overnight, things changed. She wanted time alone, slammed her door, told her secrets to her friends instead of you, and seemed offended, at times, by your very presence.

You may or may not have watched your little girl transform into an alien life form—yet. But when your daughter goes through the natural progression from girl to teenager, you might mistakenly conclude that you are now raising a scary ghost of her former self, or a petulant, chaotic whirlwind you'll be lucky to survive!

Witness this all-too-typical exchange between fifteen-year-old Sarah and her mom:

Sarah's mom knocked tentatively on her daughter's bedroom door. She whispered a prayer, "Lord, help me," as she walked into the bedroom.

"Sarah, can we talk for a minute?"

Sarah looked up from the book she was reading without answering.

"I'm concerned about you. You come home from school and stay in your room all night. You're either on the computer or the telephone, but you never have time for your family. When you do eat with us, you don't talk and you barely eat anything. You never eat breakfast anymore. You seem tired and you have dark circles under your eyes. I want you to start eating better and spending more time with us."

"Well, Mom," Sarah began with sarcasm dripping from her words, "you sure know how to make a girl feel good."

"Sarah, I don't mean to make you feel bad, but I'm concerned about you."

"Mom, I'm fine. You just don't understand my life right now."

"Well, why don't you explain it to me?" Sarah's mom said with a hint of agitation.

"I couldn't if I tried. You wouldn't get it, and you'd still end up wanting me to eat your stupid dinners and try to make conversation with a brother who's a dork and a father who understands even less than you do." Sarah closed her book and got up from her bed.

"I'm not finished with this conversation," her mother pleaded.

"Well, I am," Sarah spoke with finality.

"If that's the way you're going to be, then I'll tell you how it's going to be," Sarah's mom spoke with increasing frustration. "You will eat with us and enjoy a family dinner or you won't go out with your friends this weekend. And that's final."

Sarah's mom shut the bedroom door a little too hard, and Sarah turned on her stereo a little too loud.

As we consider the issue of conflict about eating between mothers and daughters, I believe we must begin with a foundation that is different from the bedrock of much that currently defines teenage girls. Our daughters are becoming women, and that means they are testing the wings of passion, emotional expression, intuition, and independence.

When Kristin first began to walk, she did it in her own time and her own way. Sometimes she'd fall immediately and cry, not wanting to try again; other times she'd take a few faltering steps and sit down; and still other times she'd walk with a gait that would leave us all laughing hysterically. We never looked at each other with exasperation, wondering how we'd survive such an awkward child. We saw every step and fall as a sign of hope for our daughter's healthy growth and development.

How sad that when our daughters begin to walk into adolescence, we so often view their awkwardness with despair, fear, or even shame. I wonder how our infant daughters' growth and development might have been affected if they'd sensed that we were repulsed by them, afraid of them, or determined to control their every move. When we view our daughters as embarrassing, hysterical, difficult, or manipulative, they are more likely to become as we see them. In the first part of this book, we looked at how girls develop themselves *in* relationships. If, in the mirror of their relationship with us, our daughters see themselves as chaotic messes, who can blame them for complying with the image we reflect back?

When Kristin began to enter puberty, Dave and I immediately experienced her moment-by-moment mood swings, her irrational expressions, and her sometimes irresponsible choices. We also noticed that she began to make independent and sometimes strange choices with regard to eating. She decided she wouldn't eat red meat, and she started commenting on the "gross, fatty" foods we'd always enjoyed together before. Friends told us to brace ourselves for a tornado that would last for a few years but assured us that we would survive with our sanity intact if we just remembered that teenage girls are crazy.

But be honest: Was everything perfect between you and your daughter until she crossed the threshold of adolescence? Take off your rose-colored glasses for a moment and remember what it was really like when your daughter was little.

CONFLICT IS INEVITABLE

Researchers suggest that normal and healthy infants are in sync with their mothers only about one-third of the time. They are out of sync another third but get back together. During the remaining third of their interactions, healthy infants and mothers are out of sync and stay out of sync.[2]

Think back. Just when you thought your baby was sleeping through the night, she started waking up at 3:00 A.M. When you thought your toddler would sleep in her own bed, she started coming into your room in the middle of the night, asking to sleep with you. One day your six-year-old loved veg-

JUST FOR YOU

As you prepare to address conflict with your daughter, it will be helpful to think about how conflict was dealt with in your family of origin. When one mother came to see me for help with conflict between herself and her daughter, I asked her how conflict was addressed when she was growing up. She explained, "Oh, my parents never fought. They didn't speak to each other for days at a time, but we never had any conflict in our home."

Conflict is inevitable. It may be like the proverbial elephant sitting in the living room that no one will acknowledge is there, but it is there nonetheless.

1. Did your family members discuss together thoughts and feelings? Or were emotions "underground"?
2. How and when was affection expressed?
3. When there were differences between family members, was it resolved together? Individually? Never resolved?
4. Which best describes your family's approach to conflict?
    * Avoid conflict at all costs.
    * Let it all hang out.
    * Conflict is bad.
    * The most important thing is that we all get along.
    * No one likes a pushy or hysterical girl.
5. Did someone have the final word in your family? If so, what was the response of family members who disagreed?
6. What kinds of conflict did your family have about food or eating behaviors?
7. Write out a memorable conflict you had with your mother. What was said? What was unspoken? How was it resolved? Looking back, what do you wish could have been different?

etables, and the next day she spit them out like they were poisonous. So take a deep breath of relief: Conflict is inevitable. Harmony is fleeting. It always will be this way between two distinct individuals.

How did we handle the first conflicts with our young daughters? And how did our daughters handle them? *We each learned to self-soothe and to reestablish connection.* Do you recall when you decided not to respond to your baby's midnight cries and let her learn to soothe herself back to sleep? If you were like me, you needed to soothe yourself as well! I prayed that Kristin would fall asleep quickly, I asked my husband to peek into her room to make sure she was okay, and I promised myself that I'd take her to the park in the morning. When morning came, we reconnected with joy and hope that long nights of good sleep lay ahead.

Self-soothing and reconnection are the cornerstones of walking through conflict with our daughters at any age. If we enter conflict always wanting to discipline, instruct, and control our daughters, we will dwell in misery. Trying to control or banish conflict when everything within our growing daughter is shouting, "Become your own person!" is like telling a crawling toddler not to pull herself up on every piece of furniture she comes across.

Naturally, there are times when discipline and instruction are necessary— but these should not be during times of conflict. We have been conditioned to believe that conflict with teenagers should be filled with negativity, shouting, and slammed doors. *It doesn't have to be that way.* How you handle conflict with your daughter will give your relationship its form and flavor. I hope this chapter will encourage you that there is a way for you to actually *enjoy* your daughter during this necessary part of growth and development, just as you did when she was taking her first faltering steps.

---

*If you find that you are squeamish about facing conflict with your adolescent
because you will feel hurt by her anger at you,
it's helpful to remember that an adolescent needs to know
that your relationship bond is strong enough
to withstand her—and your—anger at each other.*[3]

JUDI CRAIG, *You're Grounded Till You're Thirty!*

Conflict, Body Image, and Eating

Let's take a moment to address the importance of understanding conflict with regard to body image and eating disorders. If constructive conflict involves self-soothing and reconnection, consider what destructive conflict might provoke. When our daughters do not learn healthy ways to self-soothe, they might turn to food in unhealthy ways. When leftover lasagna or not eating anything becomes the balm for conflict, our daughters are set up for unhealthy or addictive eating behaviors. If conflict in our relationship with our daughters does not become an opportunity for reconnection, our daughters might bond solely with peer groups or media images. Of course, it is inevitable they will identify with their friends and media heroes to some degree, but when that identification is juxtaposed *against* us, we lose our chance to be a powerful presence in our daughters' lives.

Destructive Conflict

Our family tries to take advantage of the privilege of living in Colorado by going skiing a few times every year. We each have very different styles of skiing. My husband is athletic and able to conquer almost any terrain. Our son, Graham, points his skis downhill and takes off! Whatever gets him down fastest is his choice. He may fall, slide, and be covered with powder at the end of the run, but he's taken on the mountain his way. Our daughter is graceful and adventurous. She's willing to try a new run, a ski jump, or ride up the chairlift with a new friend she meets in the lift line. I like to take it s-l-o-w. I enjoy easy runs, beautiful scenery, and am proud to say that I seldom fall!

A few weeks ago we all stood at the top of a somewhat challenging run (read: *very* challenging for me). We started down the hill, I quickly lost sight of my family, and I was almost immediately at war with this mountain. I began worrying about Graham skiing down this steep hill and wondered if he'd put on his helmet. I realized I was a little outside my range of abilities on this run, and I tensed up. I started to anticipate what was around the bend, willing the hills to become less steep, and spending a lot of time looking for the easiest part of the mountain. I was acutely aware of all of the other skiers zipping by me and kept slowing and stopping to stay out of their way. Halfway down the mountain, I spied my family waiting for me. My frustration mounted. "Don't wait," I yelled, as I fell into a pile of powder.

I pulled myself up and continued slowly down the mountain, worrying about all the elements of this steep hill, including the weather. I noticed the wind pick up and starting worrying about toes and fingers too cold to maneuver even awkwardly down the hill. As I neared the last part of the run (it looked like the steepest so far), I glanced at the chairlift overhead. I spied my daughter sitting next to an older teenage boy, chatting away. I called up to her, "Why didn't you wait for me?" Kristin, of course, didn't hear me, and I didn't see where I was headed. I slipped, more than skied, down the hill, unable to slow down, and finally plowed into the line of people waiting to get on the ski lift. My son and husband quickly stepped into another lift line and acted as if they didn't have the slightest idea who I was!

My run down the mountain is a good metaphor for a destructive approach to conflict. Instead of focusing on self-control, using and improving my skiing skills, and enjoying my run, I worried about and tried to control the weather, the slope, the other skiers, and my family. The end result was that I didn't control anything or anyone—including myself—and I missed the opportunity to develop my skiing ability as well as to enjoy a challenging, beautiful run down the mountain.

Not only do mothers despair over feeling that their relationships
with their daughters have been lost,
but they become terrified about surrendering any lingering threads of control
they may have held.[4]

RONI COHEN-SANDLER AND MICHELLE SILVER, *"I'm Not Mad, I Just Hate You!"*

In the same way, conflict becomes destructive when I try to control my daughter's emotions, beliefs, or values during a conversation. In the process of trying to control her, I inevitably lose control of myself, resorting to yelling, lecturing, or withdrawing. And I miss the opportunity to enjoy the process. Yes, I said *enjoy.* There is no better opportunity to gain understanding of our daughters than during conflict. And there isn't a better time to develop our own insight, self-control, and communication skills than during conflict. We really ought to *relish* the opportunities to collide!

Let's translate this skiing metaphor into a common conflict that occurs between mothers and daughters early in their relationship. One of my friends expressed to me her distress over her daughter's picky eating habits. Her daughter was only eight but already had a decided dislike for a lot of foods. I asked my friend how she responded to her daughter's likes and mostly dislikes. "Not very well, I'm afraid," was her answer. "We usually end up in a fight that ruins the whole meal, and I make her sit at the table until she's eaten a few bites of everything."

My friend went on to explain that she'd tried fixing only her daughter's favorite foods, which caused problems with other family members. She'd

JUST FOR THE TWO OF YOU

This might be a good time to evaluate where you are and are not in sync with your daughter. How do you view the differences between you? As your strengths and your daughter's weaknesses? How do you honor the differences? I have suggested several questions to get you started in evaluating the differences. Make this a time of mutual sharing to get to know one another better, to understand what is uniquely soothing to each of you, and to discuss how you can *use* these differences to strengthen your relationship.

1. Would you rather stay home or spend time away from home?
2. When you stay home, what invigorates or comforts you?
3. When you come home from an activity, how do you like me to ask about it?
4. Do you prefer time alone or time with friends?
5. When you're alone, what do you like to do? Do you want interaction with me?
6. When you're with friends, I want to know what you're talking about and doing. What would be the best way for us to discuss this?

taken her daughter to the pediatrician, who told her that her daughter was in the lower percentiles for her weight but not to worry. "Kids have a way of eating what they need when they need it," he assured her.

"So, what are you afraid of?" I asked.

My friend replied, "I'm just afraid she won't learn to eat and like good foods."

I knew a little about my friend's childhood, and we talked about her family of origin. Her mom was single and had to work a lot. My friend often fended for herself when it came to eating, and she was determined to provide well-balanced, home-cooked meals for her family. There was a pause in the conversation.

"But I'm most afraid," my friend confided, "that all my children will remember about me is that I was mad at them and made dinner a miserable

7. Would you rather play games or watch television? What games do you like and why? Who do you want to play with?
8. What television shows do you like? Which do you like to watch by yourself, and what programs do you want to watch with others? Why?
9. Do you like home-cooked meals or fast food best? What do you like about eating as a family? dislike?
10. Do you like to eat in the car? by yourself? Why?
11. How do you like someone to show his or her love for you? With a gift? a hug? a note?
12. Would you rather go to the movies or to the park?
13. What do you like about the movies? about going with friends and/or family? Does it bother you when your family is at the same movie as you and your friends? Why?
14. What do you like to do at the park? Do you like to do this with family, friends, or by yourself? Why?
15. What do you enjoy about cooking or baking? Do you like doing it more by yourself or with someone else? Do you like cleaning up? Why, or why not?

time for everyone." My friend's insight was the beginning of hope for her in this conflict with her daughter.

"Why don't you start with what you *can* control?" I suggested. She was spending so much energy trying to control her daughter, her family, and even trying to rewrite her own life story, that she'd lost control of herself and was becoming a nagging, negative mother. My friend quickly noted that conflict had become destructive because of *her* response to the inevitable out-of-sync condition that occurs between mothers and daughters.

"Wouldn't it be amazing if we could actually *enjoy* meals together?" my friend asked. Using conflict, even at mealtimes, to understand your daughter and to develop your relationship can make dinnertime enjoyable even with the most picky of eaters.

YOUR RESPONSE TO CONFLICT

Let's take a closer look at three of most common destructive responses to conflict. It takes courage to look at your own troublesome patterns. It will be easier to recognize your daughter's self-defeating responses to conflict, but recognizing your own choices is the beginning of learning a new way of relating in the midst of conflict.

TAKING IT PERSONALLY

I list this first because it's the hardest reaction for me to overcome. When my daughter is angry, sad, or worried, I take her emotions and expressions personally. Being inclined toward being a "hover mother," I want to fix Kristin and make everything okay. But I am learning that she doesn't need to be fixed and that I need to accept that sometimes life is painful and disappointing.

Kristin was a competitive gymnast for seven years. She had to quit gymnastics at the age of thirteen because of a back injury. Grief over the loss of her sport resurfaced many times during the next year. When friends wouldn't call, she'd long to be back at the gym. When other hobbies didn't work out, she'd express frustration at having to quit. She'd even look in the mirror and complain, "I'm getting so fat. I need to get back to gymnastics. I'm nothing but a big blob without it."

My response to her emotional angst was to remind her of how painful gymnastics had been, list all of the remedies and things we'd tried, and renew, yet again, my grievances with this sport that glorifies little bodies and can cause such devastating injuries. I took her complaints and pain personally, and we'd usually end our discussion by retreating to our own corners.

One afternoon I found Kristin in her room looking over all her gymnastics memorabilia and crying. She recounted her sorrow and second-guessing about quitting the sport. I responded, "It must be so awful for you to revisit this loss again and again. I'm sorry for the pain this is causing you." I hugged her and left the room. A few hours later Kristin found me and congratulated me: "That was the best you've ever been with me about my quitting gymnastics!"

When we take our daughter's expressions and choices personally, we

Just for You

1. Go back and review the different mothering styles in chapter 2. In what specific ways does your mothering style affect the way you handle conflict? How does it allow or encourage your daughter to self-soothe or reconnect with you?

2. When your daughter has a bad day, how do you encourage her to soothe herself?

3. If your daughter doesn't like what you fixed for dinner, what is your response? Does it put a wedge in your relationship? How do you reconnect?

4. Do you believe the best decision your daughter can make is the one you suggest? If she decides differently, how do you assure her of your love and support and reestablish relationship, if necessary?

5. Do you overextend yourself or do anything you can to accommodate your daughter? If so, how does this keep her from learning to solve her own problems and comfort herself?

6. Are you embarrassed by conflict? If so, why? How often has conflict resulted in the end of a relationship for you?

deny her the very goal she is attempting to achieve in these expressions—the development of her own person. Even when her words are directly aimed at you, it is good to realize that "many times, when girls are upset, especially with themselves, they prefer to pin the blame on someone else. Of course, their favorite targets are their mothers."[5] Learning to sidestep the attacks and discover what is beneath them will be more helpful to your daughter than simply reprimanding her for her words.

By taking the comments and the conflict personally, we miss the potential benefits of conflict. First of all, our daughter learns that the only soothing that works is to agree with us. She, of course, is not soothed, but we are. Second, any reconnection that occurs is often superficial because our daughter's grievances have not been allowed, heard, or validated.

The daughter who lives with a mother who takes conflict personally is more likely to develop a struggle with overeating or not eating at all. A number of researchers report that eating disorders result from a developmental snag when girls are neither allowed nor encouraged to develop an identity separate from their mothers.[6] "Daughters and mothers lock horns over many issues. They are caught in a struggle, with the daughter attempting to find out who she is so that she can establish her individuality yet maintain a bond with her mother."[7] Eating is an act of personal expression. Overeating may be your daughter's expression of trying to make something—namely, food—about her, and all about her. Not eating at all may be a subconscious validation of your making everything in your daughter's life about you. She begins to believe she doesn't even deserve food.

BECOMING OPPOSITIONAL

An oppositional response is most often used by the mother who places herself above her daughter in relationship and believes that conflict is simply an opportunity to instruct and discipline. When our daughters become emotional or make foolish, irresponsible choices, our first response may be to set them straight. Think back to your last argument with someone who dissected your thoughts or feelings in order show you how wrong you were. How well did you respond?

Communication with our daughters is not undermined by a generation gap or all the pitfalls of the "terrible teenage years." Rather, communication is undermined most significantly by *our* desire to be right. Once we become defensive or argumentative, every word out of our daughters' mouths becomes ammunition for us to prove our point.

Better to apologize a thousand times
than let one poisonous remark remain without an antidote.
Your apology means everything.[8]

Joyce L. Vedral, *My Teenager Is Driving Me Crazy!*

If you are genuinely concerned about your daughter's behavior, the greatest gift you can give her is to *hear* what she has to say, not debate her. When the friend I mentioned earlier began to ask her eight-year-old daughter what she didn't like about certain foods, she discovered her daughter's sensitive palate. Certain smells, textures, and colors actually made her daughter feel

Just for You

1. Reflect on your family of origin. Was there a lot of yelling and slammed doors? When we grow up in a combative home, we begin to view this behavior as normal.

2. Ask your daughter if she has heard you yell at her and how it makes her feel.

3. In the midst of discussions, notice how often you are listening and how often you are formulating your own arguments.

4. Chart the cycle of your own anger. Note when you feel distressed, frustrated, or mad. Do you calmly deal with those emotions or swallow them? How long can you keep them in?

5. When you explode, how do others act toward you? Respectful? contemptuous? mocking?

6. Reflect on Ephesians 4:26: "In your anger do not sin: Do not let the sun go down while you are still angry." How might you apply this to conflict with your daughter?

nauseous. This opened the door for my friend to acknowledge and begin to help direct her daughter's sensitive personality. She explained to her daughter that not everyone is so sensitive, and it would be wonderful for her to learn to use her sensitivity to help others, enjoy beauty, and discover the smells, textures, and colors she really liked. Even if the conflict over green beans had continued until her daughter turned eighteen, it would have been relatively short-lived. But the opportunity to help her daughter use her sensitive nature for good will impact her child a lifetime!

An oppositional response to conflict can also result in yelling, slamming doors, and stomping out of the room. The damage that results from those behaviors lingers long after the argument is over. Our daughters learn to self-soothe by exploding. The adrenaline that is released in an explosive argument is calming. After an outburst, mother and daughter may retreat to their rooms, underscoring for the daughter that conflict results in disconnection.

USING THE SILENT TREATMENT

The mom who places herself beneath her daughter as well as the mother who places herself at a distance from her daughter may choose the third style of dealing with conflict. We withdraw, sulk, or keep our thoughts to ourselves. We force our daughters to guess what we are feeling and to wonder what we believe about them. We may smolder underneath but act as if everything is okay on the surface. Occasionally we can't help ourselves, and we may snipe at each other with a sarcastic remark. Or, the same kind of explosive scenes that are common to an oppositional approach to conflict will result. When we suppress our feelings and don't verbalize our opinions in healthy ways, eventually we explode.

One of my clients who struggled with bulimia told me that when she began to experiment with bulimia, she knew that her mother knew something was going on. Although her mother never asked any questions, my client suspected that her mother spied on her. This mother and daughter made a silent pact to avoid conflict and keep all their concerns to themselves. My client continued to soothe herself with destructive binging and purging behaviors. We will discuss this further in the chapter on bulimia, but eating (especially foods high in carbohydrates) produces chemicals in the brain that calm. Purging also results in a calm after the violent act is done.

When my client came home from college during the summer of her sophomore year, she went to see their family doctor for an annual checkup. She learned that her mother had expressed her concerns about her daughter's eating behaviors to the doctor, and he confronted my client. She felt two things simultaneously: the awkward kindness in her doctor's eyes and the stab of betrayal from her mother. (Of course, she'd betrayed her as well.) She left that examining room more sure than ever that her mother couldn't handle all that was in her and that it must be pretty monstrous. Reconnection was not an option for her at that time

Just for You

1. When your daughter is angry, sullen, or sad, do you feel at a loss for words? Do you avoid eye contact? If so, why? What are you afraid of?

2. Do you resolve conflict by keeping your mouth shut? How often do you see those same conflicts resurface?

3. Can you think of a conflict you have been able to resolve? What allowed the resolution?

4. Did you grow up in a family that believed children were to be seen and not heard? If so, how was this message conveyed? How did it affect you?

5. Do you often go through times of not speaking to family and friends? If so, are you more often afraid or angry during these times?

6. Do people often ask you, "What's wrong?" The next time someone asks you this, courageously ask how you are acting that makes the person want to ask this question.

7. When your daughter is going through a difficult time, do you feel it's better to just stay out of her way? How do you feel about yourself when you avoid her or her problem?

8. When you withdraw, what do you withdraw into? When you withdraw, what does your daughter withdraw into?

The amount of creative, intellectual…energy that is trapped by the need
to repress anger [or other emotions] and remain unaware of its sources
is simply incalculable.[9]

HARRIET LERNER, *The Dance of Anger*

The daughter who lives in a home under the strain of the silent treatment is left to imagine the worst about herself and find ways to soothe herself that may not be healthy. She may become vulnerable for any connection that eases the pain of the disconnection with her mother. Or she may learn to isolate and withdraw as well. She becomes vulnerable to a host of secretive eating behaviors.

CONSTRUCTIVE CONFLICT

Most of us don't have a lot of experience with constructive conflict. Some couples go through an entire marriage and never truly resolve a single issue. Many children leave home, hoping they can leave the conflict behind and avoid it in the future. *It doesn't have to be this way.*

I offer you three truths that can expand your understanding of conflict and open the door to a better relationship with your daughter. This isn't a methodology; it is a way of approaching conflict that can help *you* grow while staying in a close relationship with your child.

Perhaps we should begin by asking ourselves if that's what we really want: personal growth and deepened relationship. I must admit that all too often I just want to be right, take control, or achieve my agenda. But if I choose, conflict can be a crucible in which I grow in important ways and develop a wondrous relationship with my daughter.

There are only three things you need to let go of:
judging, controlling, and being right.
Release these three and you will have the whole mind
and twinkly heart of a child.[10]

HUGH PRATHER, *Letting Go*

CONFLICT IS HOPEFUL

When your daughter says, "I can't eat that" or "You just don't understand," it's time to feel hopeful. She's learning to walk! Look beneath the immediate conflict for her positive intention, the stretching of her wings, and the expression of her unique personality. If your heart is gripped with fear or anger, dig deeper for the root of your concern.

Last week Kristin got her braces off! We celebrated the big day with a bag of taffy and our own photo shoot of her beautiful, nonmetallic smile. Today we went to the orthodontist to get her retainer. Kristin came out of the office with a pink plastic box and an unpleasant look on her face. She threw the box containing her three-hundred-dollar retainer to the ground and said, "I can't believe I have to wear more metal, twenty-four hours a day. And now I talk with a lisp!" She dissolved into tears.

I picked up the pink plastic receptacle and jammed it into my purse. I got ready to unload on Kristin about her ungratefulness, her overdramatization of a fairly insignificant hardship, and, of course, the thousands of dollars we had spent to ensure her perfect smile. I briefly thought about this chapter on conflict I'm in the midst of working on, but quickly dismissed any thoughts that an emotion-laden conversation about her retainer contained any *hope* for Kristin's good or the development of our relationship. I was ready to lecture. And I did.

Kristin responded to my speech by staring stonily out the window of our car. One tear ran down her cheek, and I felt a moment of compassion for her but quickly dismissed it. When we pulled into her school parking lot, another mother was dropping her daughter off at school. She was being lowered from her van by a lift as she sat in her wheelchair, covered by a homemade afghan. She breathed through a white, plastic tube connected to a machine at the back of her chair.

I looked at Kristin and could not hold back one more point to my speech as I remarked, "Now *that's* a hardship." Kristin glared at me and then got out of the car and made her way into the school.

All afternoon long I thought about how my response to Kristin's concerns killed hope. I took her angst about the retainer personally, I dismissed her feelings, and I lectured her with very little compassion.

Two hours after I dropped Kristin at school, she called and left a message.

"I'm sorry I wasn't grateful, Mom," she apologized in a rush of words. "I know I have so much to be thankful for and that I have a great life. See you later this afternoon. Bye."

My daughter! She is tender-hearted and so open to seeing her own short-comings and making changes. But I missed the opportunity, this time, for change to occur *in the context of our relationship.* Kristin came to a wonderful resolution of her complaints about her retainer on her own. I feel sad that I missed the opportunity, in the midst of her fears and complaints, to take her hand and walk with her. While I was so busy pointing out the hardships of the other daughter being dropped off at the school, I overlooked my own opportunity to be grateful—grateful for a daughter who can express herself, speak her fears, and listen to my thoughts. I pray I never forget the joy—and great hope—of mothering a daughter who is willing to enter into conflict.

YOU CAN RESPOND RESPECTFULLY

Begin by controlling what you can: yourself. As I enter a conflict with my daughter, I try to recall a passage from Scripture: "[God] brings gifts into our lives…things like affection for others, exuberance about life, serenity. We develop a willingness to stick with things, a sense of compassion in the heart, and a conviction that a basic holiness permeates things and people. We find ourselves involved in loyal commitments, not needing to force our way in life, able to marshal and direct our energies wisely" (Galatians 5:22-23, MSG). I cannot control my daughter, but with the help of God's Spirit, I can respond respectfully. I use the attributes in the preceding verses to measure my response.

Perhaps a time apart will be required when a conflict intensifies. You or your daughter might need some time alone to reflect. You will have to deter-mine when too long is too long and take upon yourself the responsibility for reconnecting. It may feel like a sacrifice and be humbling to reconnect, espe-cially if your daughter behaved badly, but this is how we reflect God's parent-ing style to our children: "He didn't, and doesn't, wait for us to get ready. He presented himself for this sacrificial death when we were far too weak and rebellious to do anything to get ourselves ready.… But God put his love on the line for us by offering his Son in sacrificial death while we were of no use whatever to him" (Romans 5:8, MSG).

You Can Have a Good Fight

Many mothers cannot think about conflict with their daughters without envisioning screaming, slammed doors, and unresolved issues. The residue that builds between mother and daughter often spills out into subsequent conflicts, ensuring that conflict is never resolved and almost always destructive.

I encourage you to examine your conflicts and discover what might be getting in the way of healthy conflict. Perhaps it is where you choose to talk, the tone of your voice, your tendency to interrupt, or your rehearsal of past problems. Dissect your conflicts and come up with a few guidelines that will enable you to be allies even in the midst of a fight.

Listed below are some guidelines Kristin and I have developed for having a constructive conflict. You can use our rules or come up with your own,

Just for the Two of You

1. Part of responding respectfully involves being able to soothe our own anxiety and resist becoming infected with our daughters' angst. Make a list of self-soothing behaviors you can use during a time of conflict. They could include taking a walk, listening to music, sipping a cup of tea, calling a friend, or praying with someone.

2. As you resist merely going tit for tat with your daughter, you will model self-soothing and reenergize yourself for the relationship. You can help your daughter devise her own list of self-soothers. The best time to work on this list is during a calm time in the relationship.

3. Above all, take your concerns to God. He has promised, "I will not leave you comfortless: I will come to you" (John 14:18, KJV).

4. Come up with a phrase you can use to indicate that you are feeling it would be a good idea to take a break from the current conversation. A phrase like "It's getting a little warm in here" could be a nonthreatening way to agree to temporarily halt the conflict.

5. When you decide to take a break to self-soothe, always part with a promise of reconnection. You might say, "It's getting a little warm in here, so why don't we talk about this again tomorrow after school?"

using self-soothing and reconnection as cornerstones. If your daughter is not old enough or mature enough to engage with these guidelines, use them yourself until she is ready.

- Wait for the right time. For us, that means not at night, when we are both tired.
- Avoid taking things personally by repeating to yourself while the other is speaking, "She really means this. This is about what she is feeling and thinking; it is not about me."
- Don't say no until you have heard everything the other wanted to say and thought about it and prayed about it for at least an hour.
- Never attack.
- When you get stuck or things begin to deteriorate, agree to put the talk on hold for a specified time. Be specific about when you will resume the conversation, and use the time apart for self-soothing.
- When you resume talking, begin by sharing with each other one thing you are grateful for in the other. This is just one way that conflict becomes an opportunity for reconnection.
- If you remain stuck, find one thing you are each willing to give in this discussion. This way, your relationship is deepened. For example, if your daughter doesn't want to eat breakfast with the family any longer, you might agree that she can skip family meals on school days so she has more time to get ready, as long as she agrees to eat something healthy.
- If things are still unresolved, specify a time to begin again. Once again, make self-soothing and reconnection your guidelines.

Recall for a moment all the hopeful hours you spent holding your daughter's hands as she learned to walk. It's time to take her hand again in hope, as she walks (and sometime stumbles) through additional stages of development. Conflict is the inevitable process through which she will grow up, you will grow, and your relationship will be cemented in new and meaningful ways.

Chapter 6

"Mom, I Hate My Thighs!"

We are so busy obsessing over what is wrong with us—
whether it's our weight, misproportion, wrinkles, pimples, excess hair,
or functional limitations—that we fail to develop our potential as human beings.
If we could harness a tiny fraction of the energy and attention wasted in body hate
and use it as fuel for creativity and self-development,
just think how far we could travel toward our life goals.[1]

MARCIA GERMAINE HUTCHINSON, *Love the Body You Have*

Body image often has little to do with our actual physical body. In chapter 1, I defined body image as the way we see our size, shape, and proportions, as well as how we feel about our bodies. Girls and women who have normal, healthy bodies often believe they are fat.

Consider the following exchange between a girl and her mom. Sound familiar?

"Mom, I hate my thighs! They are huge. Why can't I have straight, skinny legs like everyone else?"

"Everyone else?" her mother asked. "There are all sizes and shapes out there, honey. Besides, your legs are shaped like mine. There's very little we can do about it."

"Oh, thanks a lot, Mom. You're not taking me seriously. Summer is coming, and I'll have to stay in my room all summer long." The girl's tone revealed the very real pain she felt.

"Look at the styles out there," the girl continued. "Short shorts. Two-piece swimming suits. They don't make clothes for girls with thunder thighs."

Her mother suppressed a smile but noticed her daughter's eyes well up with tears.

"I'm sorry you're so worried about this," her mother began, not quite knowing how to console her daughter. "When you're my age," she continued, "the size and shape of your legs won't matter so much."

She quickly glanced in her daughter's bedroom mirror to see if her nose was growing.

Although the mother in the story above had moved past the "thigh trauma" of her teenage daughter to some degree, she had to admit to herself that she, too, continued to struggle with her body image. She was caught in the dilemma of trying to respond to her daughter's concerns about the way she looked and felt while suppressing her own concerns and conflicting feelings.

In this chapter we will examine three different ways to untangle the body-image dilemma—first for yourself, and then for your daughter. You can become your daughter's ally in forming a healthy body image by understanding her biology and helping her to embrace it; by inviting and welcoming her emotional expressions; and by equipping her to confront the cultural forces that sabotage a healthy body image.

One of the pioneering researchers in the field of body image states: "We live constantly with the knowledge of our body. The body image is one of the basic experiences in everyday life."[2] That's really not news, is it? We've all felt fat, obsessed about different body parts, and compared ourselves to others. Now is the time to put a lifetime of living in our own bodies to work on behalf of our daughters. And along the way we might gain a healthier body image ourselves!

You may consider disordered eating and poor body image an emergency
(and it is) and immediately try to give first aid to your daughter—
but your efforts will mend your daughter's injured body image only temporarily
because you have to have a healthy relationship with your own body first.[3]

DEBRA WATERHOUSE, *Like Mother, Like Daughter*

UNDERSTANDING YOUR DAUGHTER'S BIOLOGY

Instead of denying or dismissing your daughter's worries about her body, really listen for her areas of concern. Like it or not, dissatisfaction with body image has become the norm for girls. Today girls worry about clothes, makeup, hair, friends, and boys. But most of all they worry about weight. It is inevitable. During the years when our daughters are growing and changing from little girls into young women, they *will* worry about the size and shape of their bodies. Researchers at Iowa State University found that 60 percent of ten-year-olds were weighing themselves daily.[4] Responding well to your daughter's body-image concerns requires that you understand her biology and invite her to befriend her body.

During middle school most girls gain 15 percent to 20 percent of their adult height and up to half of their adult weight. Their bone structure, heart, lungs, liver, spleen, pancreas, and various glands double in size. Yikes! No wonder girls feel out of control and worry about their body size. They think, *If I keep growing at this rate, I'll be huge!* By the time your daughter reaches seventh grade, she will likely be supersensitive about her body, and whenever she looks in the mirror, the image reflected will seem to her like the distorted image in a fun house mirror.

I wish I really looked the way I did on the magazine covers.
I was airbrushed.

POP STAR JESSICA SIMPSON, *J14* magazine

Although she might not articulate or even be aware of the roller coaster of emotions she is feeling with regard to her body, whenever she says, "I feel fat!" or "I hate my thighs!" she is probably wondering, *What am I going to look like next week, next month, or next year? Will I keep gaining weight? Do I look normal?* At no other stage of human development are we so confused and insecure about our bodies. How you respond to your daughter during this time of great vulnerability can have a significant impact on how she feels about her body and will likely be intricately woven into her body image for the rest of her life.

Before we can coach our daughters to respect and enjoy their bodies, we must examine our attitudes toward our *own* bodies. What is your body image? Which parts of your body don't you like? Why? In what ways do you feel strong and confident in your body?

When my daughter began to express concerns and contempt for her body, I knew I needed to look at this complicated and confusing part of my own life. Kristin's questions and struggles turned the light on my own insecurities, destructive ideas, and unhealthy attitudes toward my body. I realized that my daughter had a slim chance of developing a healthy body image if I was constantly critiquing and criticizing my own body.

So, put on your favorite comfort clothes, wrap yourself in a soft blanket, make yourself a cup of tea, take a deep breath, and take a good look at your body image.

Revisiting our own struggles with body image can be painful, but the payoff will come in a strengthened alliance with our daughters. One of my friends connected powerfully with her daughter when Kim expressed contempt for her "bulging stomach." My friend told Kim about her own conviction in adolescence that she had huge legs. Although she had normal-size legs, she criticized herself often enough that she could not see the truth. She never wore shorts, refused to go swimming, and decided not to try out for the track team even though she loved running. She concluded, "It wasn't until I was forty years old that I realized my legs were fine. I cheated myself out of a lot of fun and carried a terrible burden of self-hatred." Her daughter was able to see the danger of her self-criticism because of her mother's self-disclosure.

If your daughter hasn't entered adolescence and is not yet feeling fat or expressing concerns about her body, then now is the perfect time to begin coaching her toward a healthy body image. As your daughter grows toward puberty, she begins as early as age six to acquire fatty deposits that will help her develop her wonderful female form. She will almost certainly entertain fleeting questions and concerns about her growing body whether she articulates them or not. Studies suggest that girls in kindergarten begin to worry about their bodies. A 1998 survey of girls ages eleven to thirteen found that over half were worried about the flatness of their stomachs and the size of their thighs; 45 percent of these girls wanted to be thinner; and 37 percent

Just for You

Although you may eventually want to do some of these exercises with your daughter, you will be more authentic and effective with her if you've done your own work first.

1. Pull out photos of yourself at different ages. What photos are you drawn to? Why? Organize them chronologically. How has your body changed? When did you become aware of your body? When did you like your body? When did you not like your body? What was going on in your life at these times?

2. Read books about feminine growth and development. (See suggestions in the Resources section.) How much did you or do you know about your own body? How do you think this has influenced your body image? How did you learn about and first experience menstruation? How has this contributed to your body image?

3. Evaluate your own care for your body. Is it fun, sensual, and positive, or critical and negative? As you apply lotion, do you say, "This lotion smells and feels wonderful," or, "I can't believe how old, wrinkled, and ugly my skin looks"? When you exercise, do you lament, "I've got to do something about all this fat," or, "It feels so good to move, stretch, and get my heart pumping"?

4. Write down everything you think or say about your body. Is your body image fundamentally negative or positive? Work on creating the most positive body image you can. If you say (as I have), "I have flabby arms that jiggle like Jell-O," consciously say instead, "I am grateful for my arms that can hug the people in my life with comfort, strength, and caring." Second Corinthians 10:5 instructs us to "take captive every thought to make it obedient to Christ." Hatred for our body and a complaining spirit go against God's heart for us and keep us from engaging in life with compassion and gratitude.

5. Write down all the ways your body serves you and all the things you could not do if you didn't have your body. Give thanks.

had already tried dieting.⁵ This is the time to intentionally teach your daughter to live in her body with gusto and gratitude.

One of the most precious gifts we can give our daughters is a positive view of their bodies. How do we give this gift? Not all at once, but slowly, experience by experience. Celebrate different features of the body with your daughter—eyes, arms, sense of smell, hands, and feet. Look together at these different body parts and senses with curiosity, amazement, and thanksgiving. Treat them with special lotions, activities, or massages. Pray together: "We thank you, God, for exactly how you made our legs, our hands, and everything about us." As you engage in these activities with your daughter, your sense of wonder and gratitude for your own body will increase as well. Our daughters are a gift to us as we learn that it is never too late for God to redeem destructive experiences and attitudes we have toward our own bodies.

Touch is especially important to integrate into your relationship with your daughter during this important time in her development. Taking every opportunity to touch her demonstrates that *you* like her body.

Oh yes, you shaped me first inside, then out;
you formed me in my mother's womb.
I thank you, High God—you're breathtaking!...
You know exactly how I was made,
bit by bit, how I was sculpted from nothing into something.
Like an open book, you watched me grow from conception to birth;
all the stages of my life were spread out before you.

PSALM 139:13-16, MSG

As your daughter gets older, she may be less receptive to overt activities to develop a positive body image. Teenagers usually become increasingly self-conscious and sensitive about their growing and changing bodies. But you can subtly continue to guide your teenage daughter toward a positive body image in the following ways.

- Compliment. Compliment. Compliment. Compliment her looks, accomplishments, and character traits. All three are important.

- Every time your daughter says, "I feel fat," or "My body is gross and disgusting," remember that there is a lot going on in her mind, heart, and body. You won't be able to address it all at once. It is important, however, to reassure her every time she expresses those statements of self-contempt. Even when your words seem to fall on deaf ears, don't stop saying, "You are not fat. Your body is beautiful." Your affirmations won't address all that is going on for your daughter, but your failure to affirm her will encourage her to imagine the worst and sink even deeper into despair.
- Don't tease. Enforce a moratorium at your home on any teasing about body size or shape. When I was growing up, every time I walked into a room my brothers would mimic a cartoon character from that time and say: "Hey, hey, hey. It's fat Sharon." I'm sure my parents did not guess that those words would haunt me for the rest of my life, or they would have put a stop to them right then.
- Model physical activity. According to the President's Council on Physical Fitness and Sports, girls who participate in sports and exercise have positive feelings about their bodies, improved self-esteem, tangible experiences of competency and success, and increased self-confidence.[6]
- Don't disregard specific appearance issues such as acne and dental problems.
- Don't point out faults—yours or your daughter's.
- Don't use your daughter as a mirror for yourself. ("Thank goodness you didn't get my legs.")
- Don't underestimate the power of your example. As you befriend your body, you will be modeling the formation of a healthy body image for your daughter. Treat your own body well with good food, fun-filled activity, and nurturing self-care. As you engage in activities with your daughter, make positive references to your body and your gratitude for it. For example, say, "I'm grateful for my strong legs so that I can keep up with you while we Rollerblade!" Express thanks for the strength and flexibility of your body after a day at the swimming pool. How long has it been since you took care of

your physical body by exfoliating, moisturizing, and giving it extra pampering? When you let your daughter know that you are paying attention to your physical needs, she'll see the message that the body is worthy of care.

Just for the Two of You

1. Encourage your daughter to take a luxurious bath. Shop for bath oil and lotion, facial masks, and skin soothers, or make your own. Gather fragrant candles and relaxing music. Teach your daughter to celebrate all her senses by encouraging her to feel the water soothe her tired muscles, to smell the fragrances, to really hear the music. Take a luxurious bath yourself!

2. Dance together. (Yes, this is especially hard for those of us who have seen ourselves as awkward and uncoordinated!) Pick music you both like. Move your arms and legs, twirl, sashay, and spin—just for the joy of it!

3. When her body feels out of control, it is essential that your daughter learn to experience a sense of control in healthy ways. If you neglect being her guide and support, she *will* find control on her own. Encourage your daughter to make a list of all her body features that she doesn't like. Look at the list together. What can easily be changed? For example, if she's concerned about acne, look into skin care and medical treatment. What can be changed or refined with work and dedication? If she hates her thighs, find exercises that can tone and tighten those muscles (and then would you please send them to me!). What can't be changed? Help your daughter to make peace with those aspects of her body that she can't change (height or basic body type).

4. Affirm your daughter's changing body. Whether or not she says, "I feel fat," compliment her when appropriate. "Your hips are developing, and you're getting breasts. That's normal and the way God designed the female form, and it happens to every girl."

Our children, especially our daughters, watch us.
They look to us to see what their own future may be like and what is possible.
Even more important than what we tell our daughters
is what we show them.[7]

Harriet Lerner, *The Mother Dance*

As you can see, working with our daughters to understand and honor our bodies is a daily, intentional, prayerful, and creative task. In taking it seriously, we will be freeing ourselves and our daughters from pointless and destructive preoccupation with self-criticism, comparisons to others, and superficial concerns. Have *fun* building a positive alliance with your daughter! Don't hold back your own feelings and experiences. And when you fear that your own issues with regard to body image are keeping you from walking hand in hand with your daughter through these concerns, remind yourself that your daughter doesn't need you to be perfect. She just needs you to be real.

When my daughter entered seventh grade, I discovered two things about her: She was beginning to develop a bad habit of criticizing her body, and she longed for a T-shirt from the expensive department store Abercrombie and Fitch. One day I splurged and bought two T-shirts from this store. I showed her the first shirt and asked her if she'd like it. She eagerly reached for the shirt, and I pulled it out of her grasp. I explained that I needed to make a few adjustments to my gift. With the largest pair of pinking shears I could find, I began to cut this shirt into shreds.

My daughter shrieked and begged for me to stop. I asked her why she was so upset. She explained, "I thought the shirt was my gift. And besides, that's an expensive shirt!" I then presented her with the second, intact shirt, and while she was breathing a big sigh of relief, I explained that when she criticizes her body, she is shredding God's gift to her and that her body is a gift far more valuable than a store full of clothes!

Inviting Your Daughter's Emotional Expression

What do *feelings* have to do with body image? Everything. Paul Schilder, in his pioneering work *The Image and Appearance of the Human Body*, instructs us that "Every emotion changes the body image."[8] We all know what it's like to carry tension in our shoulders, to hold in excitement, or to clench our jaw in anger. Your daughter is also growing in her experience of the world, and that means she feels new, changing, and intensifying emotions daily. She has no idea what to do with these feelings. Her rapidly changing internal world isn't always logical; it's scary, it makes her sad or excited, and she is constantly assessing how others receive or interpret her expressions of emotions.

The female brain responds more intensely to emotion.
Feelings activate neurons in an area eight times larger
in the female brain than in the male.[9]

DEBORAH BLUM, *Sex on the Brain*

One young woman I see in my counseling practice told me how her emotional life began to influence her experience of her body. When she was in the fourth grade, she made it to the finals in a poetry recitation contest at school. She practiced and practiced for the final competition. When she came in second, she was deeply disappointed and cried to her mother, "I'll never be good at anything. I wanted to win so bad!" Her mother responded with good intentions. "You did your very best. Winning isn't the most important thing, and there's always next year."

By ignoring the intensity of her daughter's anguish, this well-meaning mother signaled to her daughter that her intense desires and disappointment were not acceptable. After a few more similar interactions with her mother, this daughter began to keep all her deepest desires and negative emotions hidden.

When a girl learns that she should not express anger, jealousy, disappointment, longing, hurt, fear, or sadness because she will be punished, judged, ignored, or labeled, then all of those feelings get stuffed in the body. And often those stuffed emotions are transferred to feelings against the body. Kathryn J. Zerbe, M.D., Vice President for Education and Research at the Menninger Clinic, explains: "Eating disorder patients often talk about their bodies as hideous receptacles.... As a protective container, the body harbors our experiences and feelings."[10] The body is concrete. It is something we can see and try to understand. Its inevitable imperfections (highlighted by the glossy, unrealistic pictures of "perfection" in the media) are easy targets.

When my client entered adolescence, she developed bulimia and found relief for all her stuffed feelings by purging herself. She didn't believe her body deserved nourishment, care, and positive attention because she'd told herself for years that she was fat. The problem, she believed, was her body, and she was willing for it to pay the price of a serious eating disorder.

It is critical to remember that the feeling of fatness often has little to do with whether we are fat or not fat, but everything to do with how we handle our inner world of emotions. Some studies suggest that as many as 30 percent of eating disorder patients have not learned healthy ways of emotional expression.[11] A growing girl and adolescent feels a multitude of emotions in one day. Inviting her to express her emotions keeps them from being stored in the body and contributing to an unhealthy body image. Zerbe concludes her discussion of body image by emphasizing the link between emotional expression and the development of a healthy body image: "In summary, the struggle with body image faced by patients with eating disorders derives from their difficulty with expressing feelings and in developing a full emotional life."[12]

Just for You

1. How did the people in the family you grew up in express their emotions? How did you know if your father or mother was angry? What did you argue about with your parents?

2. Practice expressing your emotions. If you don't feel comfortable expressing the emotion to another person, then try talking out loud to yourself about what you are feeling. Write a letter describing the emotion, or draw a picture that represents the emotion.

3. Which feelings are easy for you to feel? Which are more difficult?

4. Notice how various feelings affect your body. Where in your body do you feel anger, sadness, or loneliness? What happens when you hold the emotion in?

You won't be able to encourage your daughter to express emotions in healthy ways if your own emotional life is suppressed, distorted, or out of control. Before we examine how to help our daughters with their emotions, take some time to courageously peer inward at your own emotional life.

To be truly healthy, we need access to our full menu of emotions and the freedom to learn to express them all. In their book *Raising a Daughter,* Jeanne and Don Elium write, "The feeling life is a girl's soul life, her heart—her intu-

Just for the Two of You

1. Set aside time and look for opportunities to ask your daughter how she is feeling about herself, her friends, school, her siblings, etc. As you are listening, don't look for inconsistencies or irrationalities. Don't plan your response to her feelings. Remind yourself, "She really means this." Care about what she cares about.

2. As your daughter expresses her feelings, give advice sparingly. You don't have to agree with the feeling, but you can listen with focused attention. Don't problem solve, patronize, or try to talk her out of the feeling.

3. When she says, "I feel fat," you might say, "That sounds like an important feeling. Tell me more." If your daughter can talk more about what she is feeling, help her identify the emotions she is *really* feeling. (Keep in mind that "fat" is not a feeling.)

4. After your daughter has an emotional outburst, find a good time to talk about it. Ask your daughter what she liked about your response to her and what she didn't. Ask her if she'd prefer to be left alone to sort things out during a hard emotional time, if she'd like you to simply sit with her, or if she wants you to talk her through it.

5. Chart the cycle of your emotions together. You can do this in two ways:
    - For two months, keep track on a calendar of whether each day was a hard emotional day or an easy one. You can do this by evaluating it on

ition, her emotions, and her feelings. Acknowledging these ways of knowing is vital for the development of a whole, healthy woman."[13] Every emotion tells us something important: what we like or dislike, what excites us, what scares us, or what we need. Most of us are more uncomfortable with or intolerant of negative emotions, and this attitude can do great damage to our alliance with our daughters. "With this partial awareness, a girl is destined to say 'Yes,' when she means 'No,' 'No,' when she means 'Yes,' and 'I don't know,' when

a scale of one to ten. Notice how your emotions reflect your hormonal cycles, how they change on weekends or Mondays, whether they are more intense at night or in the morning, and how they are affected by your activity level. (My daughter and I are both sensitive and more emotional according to our menstrual cycles. When we discover that this time of the month is going to coincide for us, we make plans to be extra kind to one another, pamper ourselves, encourage one another, and warn the males in our household to give us a little extra space!)

• Notice the cycle of one emotional event. Most women experience intense emotions in the following way (and remember, most emotions are intense in adolescence):

—Something triggers the emotion (begin to notice your triggers).

—The emotion builds and becomes more intense.

—The emotion clouds judgment, perception, and rational thinking.

—The emotion gives way to greater clarity and understanding.

When you note this cycle in your daughter's experience of emotions, you can stop trying to fix her emotions and let her go through them, enabling her to discover that she has the resources to handle her emotional life. Congratulate your daughter when she works through intense emotions and gains new insights. Don't try to control her when she wavers between confusion and clarity. Simply offer calmness as she learns to steer her own course.

she really knows but is afraid to say. Our daughters need to know their whole hearts."[14]

Part of your daughter's healthy maturing process is the development of a critical mind, which helps her discern what is right and wrong, recognize danger, and grow in her individuality and independence. It may seem for a time that she complains about everything, combats all your suggestions, and views everything negatively. If your reactions suggest or dictate that she stuff this part of her developing emotional life, then her negative mind will take on a life of its own and may swallow her completely—or at the very least seek out and destroy her body image.

A friend once told me that the best way to understand teenagers was to think of them as constantly on LSD.[15]

MARY PIPHER, *Reviving Ophelia*

Don't allow negativity to make you your daughter's adversary. Become her ally in encouraging her to identify what she is feeling and to learn to express it effectively. Remember that effective expression often comes after trial and error in blowups, meltdowns, and hissy fits (as my mother called them). Be allies in the school of emotional expression!

EQUIPPING YOUR DAUGHTER TO CONFRONT HER CULTURE

We cannot underestimate the power of the media to sell our daughters on seeking a thinner body at any cost. Even if our daughters are sheltered from teen magazines, music videos, and television commercials, their peers probably aren't. Like a steady IV drip, the influence of the culture seeps into our girls' minds and hearts and can turn them against their own bodies.

In chapter 4 we examined creative ways to use the culture for our daughters' benefit, but we cannot deny that the culture has some pretty awful pictures and ideas about body image. What more can we do to become our daughters' allies in confronting the forces that sabotage a healthy body image?

When our daughters express that they are feeling fat or dislike something about their appearance and we begin to quake before the looming shadow of the culture, we give it more power than it should have. When we spend all our energy sheltering our daughters from the culture, we miss opportunities to guide them to develop their own inner wisdom when confronted with hypocrisy, shallowness, and foolishness. When we determine to forbid the culture from tainting our daughters, we may make it more enticing, or at the very least more interesting than it really is. The culture actually offers us many opportunities to engage productively with our daughters to discern truth, develop values, and deepen our relationship.

I recently sat down with a group of twenty-five middle-school-aged girls. I asked them to imagine the perfect girl. Their responses, in order of importance, are listed below:

- thin
- blond
- popular
- beautiful
- athletic
- has big breasts
- has a boyfriend
- confident
- straight white teeth (no braces!)
- has her own car
- doesn't have zits
- has her own phone

Does their description sound familiar? I immediately thought their perfect girl sounded a bit like Barbie. Of course, Barbie doesn't only have her own car and telephone; she also has her own gym, salon, house, beach home, motor home, and boat! When I pulled out a Barbie and showed the girls their perfect girl, they all groaned. They didn't want to be like Barbie, they explained, because they knew she wasn't real.

Their response thrilled me and reminded me of how I can confront the skinny, slick, and glossy images of our culture. I can help my daughter discover that these images are false while I continue to be creative, joyful, persistent, and intentional in a real relationship with her.

*There are three billion women who don't look like supermodels
and only eight who do.*

When was the last time you flipped through a teen magazine or watched MTV? Teen magazines and MTV producers believe they are experts on our

Just for You

1. Go back and pull out all those old photographs of yourself again. Do any of them reflect your efforts to meet the beauty and body ideals of different times?

2. Evaluate how you are influenced by the culture. Have you ever bought something based on advertisers' promises about weight loss or body shape and size, only to be disappointed?

3. Begin critiquing commercials and what they say about body image. (You will eventually want to do this with your daughter, but it's good to practice first.) What lies do commercials tell? What is the truth? What does the advertiser want us to believe about the women's or girls' bodies in the ad? What does the advertiser want you to believe about *your* body? What about this ad makes you feel good or bad about yourself?

4. I believe that every mother needs to order *Slim Hopes: Advertising and the Obsession with Thinness* (available from Media Education Foundation, 26 Center Street, Northampton, MA 01060). This video reveals the secrets and lies in the advertising world. You will learn about the techniques for creating the perfect girl through computer alterations. It is astounding to learn that although most models weigh 20 percent to 25 percent less than average girls and women do, they are still not good enough! They are airbrushed and altered to look perfect.[16] But they are no more real than your daughter's plastic Barbie! When the time is right, watch this video with your daughter.

daughters. In order to unravel the hypocrisy and reveal the lies of the culture about body image, we need to be experts on it. By the time the average girl finishes middle school she will have been exposed to over 350,000 television and magazine advertisements. Over half of those ads stress the importance of being beautiful and thin.[17] As overwhelming as the task may seem, we need to dive into the world of *Seventeen,* MTV, and pop culture to become skilled allies in guiding our daughters through the seductive world around them.

Once you know the names, styles, labels, and sales pitches of the contemporary culture, you will be ready to become detectives together in exposing the saboteurs of a healthy body image.

Girls younger than thirteen need lots of protection and guidance. This is the time for girls to develop their own inner guidance system and for moms to be by their daughters' side as they learn to see and decide for themselves

Just for the Two of You

1. Watch movies and music videos together. Discuss what you enjoyed, felt uncomfortable with, disliked, and would have done differently if you had been the producer—all specific to the issue of body image. How many different body sizes were represented? If larger girls are in the movie or video, what role do they play? How representative of real life is the movie or video? Remember that the goal is not to like the same things and be in complete agreement, but to engage together in finding what is good in the culture and sharpening skills for discerning what could sabotage a healthy body image.

2. If possible, get some movies that were popular when you were a teenager. Watch these together, noting the styles, trends, and messages of the time. What has changed since then? How have these changes influenced our ideas about the perfect body?

3. Normalcy is what is often lost in advertising. Together, choose and tear out advertisements depicting thin supermodels. Take the ads to the mall or the airport, and as you people-watch, notice how many real women look like the unreal models.

when it comes to cultural messages about body image. Although it is always good to keep television viewing to a minimum, when your daughter does find a program she likes to watch, take the time to watch it with her often. Encourage questions. Ask her what she likes and dislikes. What size are the girls/women in the program? How do they honor or dishonor their bodies? Are their bodies for living in, or just for show? Begin to view commercials together critically. Teen magazines should also be limited and censored during this stage. If your daughter does ask to buy a magazine, look at it with her and discuss the messages about body image throughout the magazine.

By the time your daughter reaches middle school, it is inevitable that she will be curious and bombarded with the culture. Besides using teen magazines to confront the harmful messages in the culture, you can use movies and music videos as well.

By understanding your daughter's biology, inviting her emotional expression, and equipping her to confront the cultural forces that can sabotage the development of a healthy body image, you can help your daughter befriend her body, live in her body, and relish being a real girl with a real life!

Chapter 7

"Mom, I Can't Eat *That!*"

Hunger should be cherished and respected
just as the impulse to breathe is cherished and respected.[1]

MARY PIPHER, *Hunger Pains*

While providing nutritional guides and good food for our children is an essential part of mothering, the purpose of this chapter is not to give a nutritional framework to guide your daughter's eating choices. There are many wonderful resources (see the Resources section) that provide guidelines and recipes for a well-balanced diet. This chapter will attempt to provide a *relational* framework for using your daughter's inevitable declarations of personal likes and dislikes in the area of food to enhance your understanding of her and to equip yourself to be proactive in fighting eating disorders.

Eating disorders do not develop from an occasional Coke for breakfast or a penchant for French fries. Although these choices might not be the best nutrition, in themselves they won't result in an eating disorder. Eating disorders develop when emotions, fears, desires, hurts, and confusion go underground, and eating becomes a substitute form of expression for emotion. As hand-in-hand moms, we have a good chance of preventing eating disorders if we learn to interpret our daughters' early eating expressions and guide them to greater self-awareness and self-expression.

Let's listen in on thirteen-year-old Anna and her family at the dinner table one evening.

"Mom, I can't eat that! Nobody eats red meat anymore. Please don't make me put that disgusting stuff in my mouth." Anna looked at the meat loaf on her plate as if it might contain toxic waste.

"Eating meat loaf will not kill you. I worked hard to fix a nice dinner for us all." Anna's mom looked at her pleadingly.

Anna and her mom were on the edge of familiar terrain, and the whole family watched tensely to see if the dinner table would become a battleground again.

"I'll just have cereal," Anna announced as she poured herself a bowl of Captain Crunch.

"I'll have cereal too!" Anna's nine-year-old brother jumped up from the table excitedly.

"You can't have cereal for dinner," their mom said. "That is nothing but sugar." Anna's mom began to serve the meat loaf.

Anna's father interrupted the family skirmish with a tone of finality. "Everyone will eat what your mother has fixed for dinner or you won't eat anything at all."

"Fine," Anna answered resolutely. "I'll be in my room."

It's easy to read about this family's food fight and see a rebellious teenager who is ungrateful for her mother's dinner preparation, who harmfully influences her younger brother, and who makes foolish food choices that do not reflect a well-balanced diet. When Anna's father steps in and determines that beef is what's for dinner, it's tempting to feel relief that someone is going to save this family from a nutritional nightmare. However, although Anna's parents' responses are reasonable, they miss an important opportunity for connection in the midst of their daughter's eating behaviors.

THE LANGUAGE OF EATING

As girls enter adolescence, their food choices are not so much based in reason or nutrition as they are in self-expression. Anna was declaring her desire for independence, disclosing her passion, and expressing her individuality. Although she communicated with all the elegance of a bull in a china shop, her message was worth listening to nonetheless.

When our daughters begin to experiment with food, choose certain foods over others, and customize their individual diets, we have a wonderful opportunity to get to know them in new ways. We can encourage them to grow into their independence while guiding them toward healthy and positive choices.

When we miss what our daughters' food preferences and eating choices communicate, when we criticize and mock their expressions or forbid them completely, we risk having those various forms of self-expression turn into secretive and dangerous eating disorders.

The language that was spoken in my house when I was growing up
was the language of achievement: excellence, accomplishment, performance....
There moved within me a hidden yearning to speak...to share a child's anger,
wonder, sadness, and joy with another human being.
But I could find no one to hear me.
More and more often I numbed myself, stifling, choking,
expressing all my longings, all my feelings, with food.[2]

MARGARET BULLITT-JONES, *Holy Hunger*

My children cannot believe that when I was in middle school we were not allowed to talk during lunch period. School administrators believed that lunchtime was for eating and that talking would only be a distraction. Unlike today's middle school and high school cafeterias, we were given one choice for our meal if we bought a hot lunch. Vendors from Taco Bell, Pizza Hut, and Subway did not offer us the variety that kids enjoy today. Teachers monitored closely to make sure we ate everything on our plates and in our lunch bags. I even had a teacher in the third grade who called my mother to tell her that I was trading my sandwich for a friend's chips during lunch. Eating was serious business, and adults closely monitored our eating choices.

At home we ate everything my mom prepared, even if we didn't like it. After all, my mom worked hard to include something from all the food groups in our meals, and it wouldn't hurt us to eat something we didn't like. I recall sitting at the dinner table for hours trying to finish my meal so that I could leave the table. We lived next door to a family with two girls. When I ate dinner with this family, I confirmed the normalcy of my own family. Mrs. Anderson carefully measured all our portions and served us just the right amount, because "you don't want to start putting on weight now, you know."

Mrs. Anderson's concern seemed justifiable to me because at about this time my brothers had begun to tease me about getting fat.

By the time I reached high school, I had come to three dangerous conclusions about my eating:

- I can't make good choices for myself.
- What I want is probably bad.
- I'm already fat. If I eat what I want, I will be really fat.

When I got my driver's license and was able to drive by myself, I stopped one day at our local 7-Eleven. I bought a small bag of a new product called Doritos and ate the whole bag before I pulled out of the parking lot. In that

JUST FOR YOU

1. Recall your own food history as a growing girl. Did you eat meals as a family? What happened when you didn't like the food served? Could you pack your own lunch? How did you eat when no one else was around?

2. Examine your relationship with food today. What are your favorite foods? How do you regulate your eating? How do you eat today when no one else is around?

3. Evaluate your own beliefs about hunger and eating. Do you tell yourself you are bad when you're hungry? Do you eat in secret?

4. Do you feel guilty when you eat dessert?

5. Do you use phrases like "pigging out"?

6. Do you refer to your eating with phrases like "I shouldn't have this, but…" or "I'm going to be bad this one time."

7. When do you enjoy eating? How do you eat? Quickly, experientially, gratefully, guiltily?

8. As you recall your childhood and adolescent eating experiences, what specific conclusions and choices did you make with regard to hunger and eating?

9. If you have struggled with an eating disorder, write down the story of the development of your eating behaviors.

instant I knew my mother wouldn't approve of the cheesy junk food and it probably was bad, but I loved it. I relished the delicious thought, *I could buy these every day and no one would know.*

Months later I began experimenting with an eating disorder I recognize now as bulimia. All I knew then was that it made sense out of my three conclusions about eating:

- I want something bad, but because I can't make good choices for myself, I need to keep my eating choices a secret.
- I should not be hungry for this food and fill myself with something bad.
- I have to purge myself of my bad choices to keep from getting fatter.

Sadness overwhelms me as I think about the destructive conclusions and choices I came to with regard to eating. For the next several years I struggled with bulimia and its tangled web of consequences. Because any independent expression through eating was forbidden in my world when I was growing up, my eating language was so secret that no one could help me.

When I was a sophomore in college, a chapel service addressed eating disorders. The well-meaning speaker explained that eating disorders are sin, only propelling me further into shame and secrecy about my eating choices. It wasn't until my junior year in college that I began to hope that I could change.

A girl in the room across the hall from me disclosed in a dorm prayer meeting that she had struggled with bulimia all through college but had recently received counseling and help. She asked us to pray for her. The next day I asked her about her counseling and eventually disclosed my own struggle. We became partners in praying for one another and encouraging one another to make healthy eating choices. We started jogging in the evening (the first time I'd ever exercised in my life) and talking about our struggle. I am so grateful for this ally God graciously gave me in my journey toward overcoming bulimia.

How to Interpret Your Daughter's Eating Language

We will discuss eating disorders in more detail in part 3, but in this chapter we'll focus on how to interpret your daughter's eating language and look at ways to encourage healthy, positive eating choices. In her enlightening book *The Secret Language of Eating Disorders,* mother and therapist Peggy Claude-Pierre tells of her own education in the field of adolescent eating:

> The true dawning of my understanding of eating disorders began with my struggle to save the life of my daughter Nicole. I recall sitting on the bathroom floor, counting the one-inch black-and-while tiles to distract myself. My back was—literally and figuratively—against the wall; fear and helplessness numbed my mind. I held a pen and notebook in my hands.... I had read every book I could find on anorexia.... After desperate months of searching, I finally understood that no one I had contacted or interacted with could offer a viable solution to reverse Nikki's condition. My thirteen-year-old daughter was not herself. I started to chronicle her behavior and then to compare it to the girl I knew. With the first word I wrote, sitting on those cold tiles of the bathroom floor, I stepped into a foreign land without benefit of passport or road map—only my good intentions.[3]

Peggy literally became a detective to decipher her daughter's eating language. Her vigilance, curiosity, and commitment saved her daughter's life. My prayer is that we won't wait until our daughters' lives are at risk to learn their eating language and encourage their expression in life-giving ways. There is something about this desperate mother's observation of her daughter, note taking with regard to her daughter's expressions, and belief that no one was equipped to understand her daughter more than she was that fills me with a passion to speak my daughter's language—fluently!

Our daughters are a complex world unto themselves and will express many things through their eating choices. Let's examine three foundational principles that can help us to interpret their most unique expressions.

HUNGER IS A GIFT FROM GOD

Deuteronomy 8:3 articulates that God is the One who causes us to hunger, and that he provides our ultimate satisfaction. Physical and spiritual hunger are divine gifts that force us to realize our dependence on being fed; we are not created to be self-reliant. Our culture of thinness and calorie counting, on the other hand, has produced a generation of girls who do not know that it's okay to be hungry. Worse, too many girls are convinced that they must micromanage their food consumption and rely completely on themselves to feed their hungry bodies and hearts.

Our daughters are learning early that their hunger is an enemy to be controlled, and by the time they reach the age when they are naturally the hungriest (adolescence), they believe they should eat the least. If they are to look like normal (thin) girls, they must be forever watchful of the wild hunger inside. All the tantalizing foods that provoke hunger—chocolate, French fries, cinnamon rolls—should be feared. Girls learn early that boys can be hungry and chow down with vigor, but girls need to be ambivalent or even ashamed about food and eating. The media only encourages this confusion with food commercials that say "eat!" while the actress advertising eating is skinny!

As parents, our best intentions can often be distorted by the same culture our daughters face every day. "Today's kids are the first generation to be raised

Just for the Two of You

1. Enjoy your daughter's hunger—and your own! Affirm that physical appetite is a positive and God-given reality. Talk about the joys of eating and being nourished.

2. Periodically ask each other questions about food:
   - What is your favorite/least favorite food?
   - Describe a good eating experience. Where were you, what did you eat?
   - Describe the perfect meal.

3. Take a cooking class together.

4. Have feast nights where you prepare and eat your favorite foods. Honor one another's preferences.

5. When you catch each other demeaning the sensation of hunger or feeding your hunger in unhealthy ways, challenge each other to talk about what you are really feeling and what might bring you real satisfaction.

by parents who target their heart rates, analyze their body fat, and purchase fat-free cookies. If Mommy moans that she can no longer zip her jeans, berates herself for having eaten that whole corn muffin, or precisely monitors every last morsel that her child puts in her mouth, she's not teaching healthy attitudes about food."[4]

Dr. Susan Sherkow points out that "many kids with eating disorders are children of women who suffer from clinical or still undiagnosed eating disorders. And these women overtly and covertly transmit a preoccupation with thinness and dieting to their offspring."[5] If you want to be your daughter's ally against the culture's barrage of distorted messages about eating and hunger, then you must deal with your own distorted thinking. Your daughter's need for a healthy role model can propel you in positive ways to work *with* her on challenging and correcting distorted ideas and behaviors.

FOOD IS NOT THE ENEMY

As mothers we want our daughters to like green vegetables and stay away from candy. We encourage a balanced diet and forbid Dr Pepper for breakfast. But it won't be long (if it hasn't happened already) before our daughters will discover new foods and different ways of eating than we encourage in our households. When we talk about bad food and forbidden food, either for us

JUST FOR THE TWO OF YOU

1. Together, evaluate your attitudes toward food. Make a list of all foods you consider bad. Reevaluate. Could you change your categorization to these being "sometimes" foods instead of "bad" foods?
2. Make a list of new foods you would like to try together.
3. Give your daughter a fun cookbook and let her pick and help prepare what sounds interesting to her.
4. Occasionally have an "If You Could Eat Anything You Want" meal, and let your daughter choose every course!
5. Allow your daughter to pack her own lunches.

or for them, we may inadvertently send them on a scavenger hunt to find out what they're missing.

When food becomes an enemy, we inevitably feel a sense of deprivation, which can lead to giving in to binge eating. We then not only begin to fear certain bad foods, but we fear our very hunger, because it might compel us to eat forbidden foods.

The fear of food can lead our daughters to secretive eating, guilty eating, overeating, or not eating at all. We give our daughters a great gift when we give them permission to *enjoy* eating. When we forbid foods, we set in motion a response of fear and guilt for this enjoyment. If our daughters are encouraged to enjoy their food, then they will feel more comfortable and satisfied when they eat. They will be less likely to hide their eating habits or search for satisfaction through binging.

Experimenting with foods is inevitable. Secrecy is not. When we allow our daughters to talk freely about their preferences, choices, and ideas about eating, we are providing a safe environment for them to learn about themselves and, ultimately, about how to care for their bodies with a zest for healthy nourishment.

Adolescence Is a Stressful Time of Life

Just as our daughters are making more independent choices about their eating behaviors, they are also entering one of the most stressful times of life. Their bodies feel out of control, peer pressure intensifies, and responsibilities increase. Your daughter innately senses what *your* priority is for her during this stressful time of life. Is it to be popular, make good grades, be a good athlete or cheerleader, be organized, be obedient, be polite to other adults? As your daughter experiments with eating choices, if you guide her toward your agenda, then she will more than likely rebel in the area she has control over— her eating choices. If, on the other hand, you enjoy, accept, love, and gently guide your daughter because you *know* her and believe in her, you both can relax a bit.

In a stressful season of life, what do you need? I need someone to believe in me, to remind me of my gifts and abilities, and to encourage me to trust God. Our daughters need no less than we do. One mother and daughter came to see me because the mother was concerned about her daughter's breakfast habits. This fifteen-year-old wanted to eat a Snickers bar and drink a glass of orange juice for breakfast. Her mother was appalled and fearful. The daughter ate healthfully at other meals and simply liked this breakfast combination.

I asked the mother, "Do you really believe your daughter will be eating Snickers for breakfast when she's forty?" "No," her mom answered. And before she could continue, the daughter chimed in, "Well, you sure act like you do. Do you know what it's like for me to start out the day knowing that you not only disapprove of me today, but you're afraid I will never make the choices you want me to?"

As is so often the case, this mother and daughter were caught in a power struggle about something more significant than candy for breakfast. The daughter wanted her mother's approval and confidence during this significant and stressful time of her life (and used a distasteful behavior to test her mother), and the mother wanted her daughter's compliance to family norms to ensure that she would turn out okay during this stressful time of life.

When we parent out of a fear of what might happen in the future, we miss the opportunity that is before us right now. When this mother began to enjoy her daughter's individuality in regard to this odd breakfast combo, to

Just for You

1. Take a moment to remember when you were a teenager. Write down the ways you dressed and behaved that concerned your parents. What did you eat that concerned them? Did any of these choices last longer than a few years?

2. What helps you most when you are stressed out?

3. When you notice that your daughter seems agitated, worried, irritable, or withdrawn, take note of all that could be stressing her. Let her know that you realize she's in a stressful period and ask how you can help. Offer her some of the encouragement that helped you as a teenager.

4. Do you take your daughter's stressors seriously? What would she say about the way you react to and treat her during her times of stress?

compliment her daughter on drinking orange juice, and even to surprise her by setting the breakfast table one morning with a Snickers already unwrapped on her plate and a chilled glass of juice on the table, the power struggle evaporated. Mom relaxed. The daughter relaxed and felt enjoyed. (You can't enjoy someone you disapprove of.) And the girl rarely chooses Snickers for breakfast anymore!

HEARING WHAT SHE IS REALLY SAYING

When I visit my daughter's high school cafeteria, it is quickly apparent that the primary function of the lunchroom isn't nourishment. Everyone has a can of soda. Some girls eat nothing, while others eat French fries and pizza slices. Groups are formed, romances are sparked, and homework is finished. I can't help but compare the noisy chaos to the orderly, silent cafeteria of my middle school days. We ate our fish sticks and creamed corn and quietly filed back to our classrooms. Kristin's high school cafeteria is a good reminder to me that eating is not just about eating. *Eating is a form of expression,* an important clue as to what we are feeling and needing when we choose a particular food.

We are going to consider three common forms of expression through eating, but there are many internal realities our daughters may express through their eating choices. We must take notes, listen carefully, and be aware of our own language of eating in order to communicate with our daughters.

COMFORT

Have you ever eaten a chocolate chip cookie, a bowl of ice cream, or a hot, frosted cinnamon roll when you weren't hungry? Has your daughter asked for French toast for dinner or wanted nachos while she did her homework? Why do we tend to seek food when we're stressed, lonely, tired, or anxious?

When stress hits, various brain chemicals are released that produce a chemical called cortisol. Cortisol is a powerful appetite trigger. We seek out foods, usually sugary carbohydrates, that give us immediate relief from stress. Unfortunately, these foods often cause our sugar-producing hormone, insulin, to go into overdrive and intensify our appetites, sending us on an unhealthy episode of overeating. *Young and Modern* magazine surveyed thirty-three hundred adolescent girls and discovered that 48 percent eat to cheer themselves up, 69 percent eat fast food when blue, and 32 percent eat to reward themselves for an accomplishment.[6] We can help our daughters, and ourselves, if we understand comfort eating.

JUST FOR THE TWO OF YOU

1. Discuss together your triggers for eating. (Some common stressors are relational tension, loneliness, an accomplishment, a failure.)

2. Recognize that a need for comfort is okay. Jesus often comforted those in distress (Luke 8:48) and encourages us to comfort one another (2 Corinthians 1:3-4). God gives us the Holy Spirit to comfort us (John 14:16).

3. Agree that when you eat to comfort yourselves, you will do it openly and without shame. Geneen Roth writes, "Now, imagine treating yourself the way you treat people you love. This means actually sitting in a chair when you eat. So, when you eat at the refrigerator, pull up a chair. Sitting down at the refrigerator not only allows you to be kind to yourself, it also allows you to be conscious. On a practical level, it keeps your teeth from being broken by fossilized cake."[7]

4. Make a list of comfort food that can also be relatively healthy. Here are some on Kristin's and my list:
    *   fat-free steamers (steamed milk) with flavored syrup (hazelnut, vanilla, raspberry)
    *   frozen fruit sorbet
    *   steamy oatmeal, with a sprinkle of cinnamon and brown sugar
    *   whole grain breads, toasted with honey
    *   grapes (and they are so fun to eat!)
    *   popcorn

5. Talk about other ways to de-stress. Listen to music. Take a nap. Soak in the tub. Go for a walk. Learn deep-breathing techniques. Make a list of possibilities with your daughter. I was surprised when Kristin explained that painting her nails relaxed her. My unpainted nails are a testimony to the stress of this activity for me!

One of my clients who has struggled with weight all her life described her unhealthy pattern of finding comfort only in food: "I would come home from school and go straight to the refrigerator. I wanted my mother. I wanted my mother and father to get along. I wanted good grades and friends. But instead I ate Pop-Tarts, cereal, cookies, potato chips, and cold lasagna."

As mothers, it is our job to observe our daughters closely and help them see when they are using food to keep from looking at their problems, asking for help from others and God, and learning different coping strategies for the inevitable struggles and disappointments in life.

Control

When life is stressful, it's easy to focus all our attention on one area we believe we can control—eating. Eating disorders develop when we fixate on eating and weight control. When life narrows down to cookies and fat-free yogurt or losing the next five pounds, it is a symptom of a potential eating disorder and an attempt to find control in an uncontrollable world.

Something is wrong when we find ourselves reeling in despair from eating a piece of garlic bread or three chocolate eclairs.[8]

Geneen Roth, *When Food Is Love*

All our daughters are at risk for unhealthy eating behaviors and potentially life-threatening eating disorders, no matter how safe and loving a home we provide for them, because of the chaotic world they live in outside of their home and the inevitable chaos this creates in their hearts and minds. Statistics measure the increase in teen sexual experiences, drug and alcohol use, and suicide, and these factors certainly contribute to a climate of fear, uncertainty, and even violence. But statistics cannot measure the infinite number of concerns that a girl grapples with on a daily basis, propelling her toward a determination to find some sense of control.

I asked ten of Kristin's friends to list what they worry about most. Their concerns are clues about the chaos in the heart of a teenager:

I'm worried that…my teeth are too crooked, my chest is too flat, my hips are too wide, I dress too sleazy, my feet are too big, my friends will laugh at me, my parents will get a divorce, my brother is on drugs, I'm too shy, my dad will yell at me, something bad will happen at our school, my boyfriend will stop liking me, my arms are too big, I'm not very smart, everyone thinks I'm a goody-goody, my grandmother will die, my clothes aren't very nice, my mom will lose her job, someone will find out my secret, no one will care about my secret.

JUST FOR THE TWO OF YOU

1. Make a list together of strategies for eating that give you control in a healthy way. Here are some conscious choices Kristin and I try to make:

    - Eat slowly. Put your fork down between bites.
    - Stop when you're full. It takes the stomach about twenty minutes to figure out what your mouth has been doing!
    - Don't waste calories on soda.
    - Keep peeled carrots, cubes of cheese, grapes, and nuts available for snacking.
    - Don't weigh yourself every day. (We don't even own a scale.)
    - Don't skip breakfast.
    - Blot your pizza with a paper napkin if it looks oily.
    - Brush your teeth when you want to put something in your mouth.
    - Don't watch television food commercials, unless you're going to watch them thoughtfully.

2. Discuss the fact that there are things, people, and situations you can't control. What do you do when a friend doesn't call you, a boy doesn't like you, peers tease you, or your day falls apart? If you eat because you can control what you eat and forget the painful feelings for a while, try praying instead—or journaling, exercising, deep breathing, talking about your feelings—in order to let go of what you cannot control.

Because of our daughters' need for growing independence and individuality and their inevitable desire to control part of their chaotic world, we must learn to interact with their expressions of control through eating.

Crisis

Sometimes a daughter's eating behaviors indicate a crisis. Perhaps she begins binge eating, purging, not eating at all, or becomes secretive in her eating behaviors. This is not the time to panic; this is the time to investigate. Listen more closely. Look more intently at your daughter's life.

Remember, eating is not just about eating. When your daughter's eating behavior changes dramatically, indicating there might be a crisis, be persistent in learning the roots of this crisis. Ask questions, investigate, be tender, be fierce in your love for her.

Encourage Your Daughter's Individuality

Our daughters' expressions of individuality in eating choices and experiments with eating behaviors should not be relegated to a category of crazy teenage behavior or adolescent nutritional nonsense. Our responsibility is to use our daughters' choices and experiments to affirm their growing individuality, better understand their internal world, and become their ally in navigating what can be, at times, a dangerous world.

When our daughters were babies, we took care of their every need—including food. As they began to eat table food we chose their foods, told them when to eat, introduced them to new foods, and kept them from sugary foods with empty calories. As our daughters grow into adolescence, it is healthy for them to become more independent of our care, and that includes their eating. As our daughters grow up, they cannot stand to be treated like little girls anymore. What they liked when they were four, they may hate when they're fourteen.

When we require our daughters to be dependent upon us and conform to the mold of how we think they should eat, we may be setting them up for unhealthy eating behaviors. In her comprehensive book about eating disorders, Dr. Kathryn Zerbe explains, "One can view an eating disorder as a way for the

JUST FOR THE TWO OF YOU

Understanding the roots of the crisis can help as you begin to interact with your daughter about her dangerous eating behaviors. Be gentle but diligent in asking her questions.

1. Have your daughter's friendships been stressed in any way? Help her describe behavior that has been hurtful to her.

2. Has a boyfriend relationship been stressed? Hopefully along the way you haven't had your head in the sand and have been aware of growing friendships with members of the opposite sex. Ask questions: What kind of boy are you interested in? Describe your ideal boyfriend. How do boys in your class make you feel? How would you like to be treated?

3. Be informed about bullying and sexual harassment. I was prepared for many things in our daughter's high school world, but I was shocked at the cruel profaneness of the culture. Boys call girls names like "bitch" and "slut," and comment openly on their bodies. Girls can be equally cruel. Help your daughter put words to what she might be experiencing by asking her questions, such as:

   • What's the most hurtful thing you've heard someone say to someone else at school? Has anyone said something similar to you?

   • What kind of names and words do you wish could be banned from school? Has anyone said these words to you?

   • What is the most shocking thing you've heard at school? Has anyone said something similar to you?

   • Are there some phrases and words you would tell your brother to never say to a girl? Why?

4. Be vigilant in keeping up with your daughter's academic and extracurricular activities. Ask her if she is having a hard time with a teacher or coach. Does she feel pressure or a sense of failure?

body to speak about issues of concern that were raised early on, when words were not available. One concern is the struggle for autonomy."[9]

It is difficult to be a healthy eater in our culture. Unhealthy food is everywhere, unrealistic images of thin girls and women bombard us, and a new fad diet comes on the scene every year. If we try to control our daughters' eating behaviors until they leave home, they may easily get lost in the maze of eating choices when they are on their own.

Adolescence is your daughter's time to experiment and make mistakes. While she is in the shelter of home, she should be encouraged to experiment, develop, and enjoy her own eating style. Believing that your daughter can grow into her own person—and is not against you and you don't have to be against her—is one of the rewards of hand-in-hand mothering.

Just for the Two of You

1. Discuss your daughter's food quirks. Kristin loves hearing about how she tried my creativity and patience with her picky eating preferences as an infant (she would only eat peaches!). She's still a picky eater, and we both understand her gift for knowing what she likes and her need to be sensitive to others as she honors her preferences.

2. Talk about your own unique food preferences, or those of other family members. When our children learned that their uncle liked soy sauce on mashed potatoes, they reluctantly agreed to try it. Now they won't eat potatoes any other way.

3. When you observe your daughter making her own choices with regard to eating—good or bad—comment on her individuality, creativity, or adventuresome spirit. Ask her what her choices are about for her.

4. Watch for the media's hypocritical messages regarding girls, hunger, and eating. During one recent teen television show, Kristin and I

decided to consciously analyze the commercials. Ironically, the program was about a girl with an eating disorder. She looked fabulous. We talked about the mixed message of a girl with a serious illness who looked really good. The first commercial was for Levi's and showed a boy in comfortably fitting corduroy pants. Kristin ran to her room and brought down a magazine advertisement for the same product with a girl in tight-fitting pants. We discussed the message to girls about comfort and style. The next commercial was for a hair-color product advertised by a waifishly thin model. The next commercial was for Taco Bell chalupas. What a confusing source of information about hunger, eating, and body image. Kristin and I decided that the culture was crazy and we didn't have to conform!

Chapter 8

"Mom, Why Can't I Use Slim-Fast?"

More mothers are dieting; more daughters are dieting.
More mothers are disordered eaters; more daughters are disordered eaters.
More mothers are overweight; more daughters are overweight.
This sequence is not coincidental.
Dieting is the primary cause of all our weight and eating problems.[1]

DEBRA WATERHOUSE, *Like Mother, Like Daughter*

Slim-Fast, Weight Watchers, Jenny Craig, Dexatrim, Metabolite, the Atkins diet, the Ab Rocker, Buns of Steel—the possibilities and promises for weight loss and toned bodies are endless, for our daughters and for us.

Have you ever had an exchange like this one with your growing daughter?

"Mom, I really hate how I look in these shorts. Look at me from the back. I look like a hog. I have to do something!"

"You look fine," Kelly's mother replied.

"No, Mom, I look horrible. Please let me get Slim-Fast so I can start a serious diet today."

Kelly's mom looked up from the book she was reading and spoke firmly, "We've had this discussion before. No, you cannot buy Slim-Fast. It's not healthy for a growing girl."

"Please, Mom. Lots of the girls at school drink it for breakfast or eat the snack bars for lunch. I'll buy it with my own money. If I can't try Slim-Fast, I'll just have to stop eating completely. I cannot face another summer looking like this."

Her mom shook her head and returned to her book.

When I stand in the checkout line at the grocery store, I often scan the titles on the magazine covers: "Lose Five Pounds in Five Days," "The No-Fail Diet," "Lose Weight Without Exercise," "Flatten Your Stomach by Summer." I must admit, I occasionally find a title that is irresistible. I buy the magazine and read it, only to discover that this diet or exercise scheme probably won't work for me either. It requires purchasing an entirely different list of grocery items, adhering to a schedule of eating that might work if I didn't have anything else to do or think about, or eliminating nutritional essentials like M&M's and cream in my coffee.

While I'm confessing, I'll go ahead and tell you that I actually have an Ab Rocker, guaranteed to give you a flat stomach in thirty days. I also have a StairMaster, a NordicTrack, a rowing machine, a weight set, and a stationary bike. I haven't used any of them in the past five years. But I bought them, based on the promise that in just a few short days I could achieve dramatic results. The problem is that they all require work—hard, consistent, and long-term work (not to mention coordination), and no diet or exercise will change the basic truths about my body structure.

NO MORE SECRETS, NO MORE LIES

My daughter was searching for a recipe in our stack of cookbooks last week when I heard her burst into laughter, shouting, "I can't believe this. Mom! You've got to be kidding!" She was holding a little booklet I'd wedged between cookbooks. I don't remember why I stuck it there, but the irony of it struck both of us. The book is called *Thin Thighs in Thirty Days*. Years ago my friends and I bought this book, determined to follow it religiously. Its final resting place between *Betty Crocker's Cookbook* and *Simply Scrumptious Desserts* reveals its significant impact on my life and thighs.

Face it. We've all tried diets, exercise plans, health club memberships, and pills and supplements to lose weight and reshape our bodies. We've bought into false advertising, grandiose promises, and unhealthy habits. We are the experts here. We are the ones to help our daughters navigate this world of promise and peril.

So why do we freeze, like the mother in the vignette that opened this chapter, flatly forbid diets and weight-loss schemes, and keep our mouths shut about our own trials and errors? There is probably no single part of the female experience more enmeshed with secrets and lies than the categories of body image, eating, and weight loss.

As a counselor, I have discovered that when women begin to talk about their lives in a therapeutic setting, they will discuss significant struggles and problems, but the last area many women will disclose is shame about body image or destructive eating behaviors. Why? Because from the time we are quite young, what we believe about our bodies as well as how we relate to food is usually a private experience. It might begin with a careless word on the playground—"Your stomach is fat!"—that results in body shame that is stored internally for years, even if it is completely invalid. That shame may lead to unhealthy eating choices or weight-loss schemes. No one else may know of the hurt and subsequent choices, and so secret builds on secret and lie on lie.

The very act of eating is about as intimate of an act with ourselves as possible. To disclose our choices and the things we believe that compel those choices is to be naked before another. In the story just mentioned, the girl courageously stood before her mother, disclosing her beliefs and fears about her body. She wondered if she looked gross, ugly, and fat, and if Slim-Fast might soothe her worries. The mother's clipped response may only help push her daughter inward into the labyrinth of secrets and lies that often accompany body image, eating, and weight loss.

We can help our daughters navigate this complex maze by exposing the lies and winsomely expressing the truth in three arenas: our daughters' vulnerable disclosures about their body image; our knowledge about diet and weight-loss schemes; and our own experiences with body image, dieting, and weight loss. As you begin to practice ferreting out lies and telling your daughter the truth, you will want to pick and choose. We will examine many different responses, specific facts, and possible projects to do together with regard to these subjects, but you will want to be careful not to overwhelm your daughter and to select what best fits where she is right now.

YOUR DAUGHTER'S DISCLOSURES

When your daughter discloses her fears and questions about her body image and weight-loss hopes, how do you respond? We laid the foundation for a life-giving response in chapter 6. Beginning early to understand female growth and development and enjoy and appreciate the body is essential. In this chapter we will dig a little deeper to consider what might be at the heart of your daughter's questions and statements. Unless we bring certain secrets and lies into the open, they are likely to take root in our daughters' hearts and result in unhealthy eating habits and weight-loss ideas. Nancy J. Kolodny warns, "So, having difficulty accepting your physical self, having problems accepting a discrepancy between your ideal body-image and the real one, and being misinformed or underinformed about the physical side of life before entering the teen years are some of the factors that can put you at risk of developing an eating disorder."[2]

A mother of a twelve-year-old girl sat across from me in my counseling office and expressed a common concern among mothers of nearly adolescent daughters. "My daughter is constantly asking me if she's fat, expressing despair that the boys will never like her because of her weight, and complaining that she hates herself. I don't know what to say to her."

I asked this mom how she viewed her daughter's questioning—as an irritant, a cry for attention, chronic whining? She explained that she'd never really categorized the questions, but that they would probably fall into all three of my possible categories. I asked her to consider her daughter's questions about body image as sacred disclosures. Yes, sacred disclosures. We live in a cynical age in which people often resort to self-contempt to cover insecurities and fears. We resist compassion, afraid that it will coddle or encourage a victim mentality.

I stood in the hallway of my daughter's high school one morning and just listened to the students passing by on their way to class. Some of the sentences I heard shocked me. Others broke my heart.

"Did you see what Brittney has on today? She looks like a slut."

"Hey Terri! You think your pants are tight enough?"

"Did you see that new girl in third period? What a cow!"

When our daughters dare to disclose a question or a fear about their bodies, they are hoping for a haven from the cold, cruel world out there. Their simple question "Do I look fat?" is an opportunity for us to expose the lies of this cynical and contemptuous culture and bathe them in a kindness and dignity that is all too often lacking in their world.

Cruel comments and harassment take place once every seven minutes in school today. It usually lasts about 30 seconds. The emotional effects can last much longer.[3]

Gesele Lajoie, Alyson McLellan, and Cindi Seddon,
Take Action Against Bullying

Listed below are some of the common lies we believe about body image as well as some ways in which you can interact with your daughter when she asks questions or discloses her concerns.

THE LIES
1. I'm not "normal."
This is a wonderful time to reinforce to your daughter that every girl struggles with her body image—that you did and also perhaps still do. Remind her of the natural female development and the chaos that comes as she approaches and experiences adolescence. Get out old photos of your own development and take note of genetic traits. Sometimes when I do this with my daughter, she gets more discouraged. We have the same thighs, which leads right into the next lie.

2. Thin thighs (or a flat stomach or being a size four) will make me happy.
Where does happiness come from? This is another good opportunity to examine the culture that wants us to believe and literally buy into the idea that happiness comes from things, from the way we look, and from how much we weigh. I can share with Kristin that losing five pounds never changed my life. Where does happiness come from? From being kind, which opens the door to discuss the next potentially deadly lie.

3. *Hating my body won't hurt me.*

With great compassion and kindness, we can use our daughters' body complaints to explain that hating our bodies or parts of our bodies is like constantly hitting ourselves. This self-contempt bruises self-esteem and weakens internal strength. It also paralyzes us from making healthy changes in eating and exercise to support our bodies. The environment we live in shapes beliefs about beauty and body image. We have to help our daughters proactively examine these beliefs and make conscious choices that fit the truth. Hating our bodies diminishes our capacity for joy and keeps us in the dark about who we really are. And who are we really? This question opens the door to examine another lie.

JUST FOR THE TWO OF YOU

Following are some truths about body image and weight loss and different ways to interact with your daughter when she discloses her concerns.

1. Family problems, relationship problems, or someone's casual remarks about weight and physical appearance can trigger questions about body image and ideas for weight loss. Your daughter's disclosures are a wonderful opportunity to ask if anyone has said anything hurtful or negative. Encourage her to share the details of her experience. Although this can be difficult and initially shameful, you can help dispel the shame. Express your concern and even anger over the thoughtless and cruel comments. Explain that these remarks are about the other's lack of self-esteem and desire to wield some sort of power. Girls need to know that hurtful comments about body image have nothing to do with their character or even how they look. Ask your daughter how she wants you to support her and if she wants you to intercede.

2. Ask your daughter if the way other girls dress and talk about their bodies and weight loss is adding to her concerns. You might share your own experiences with peer pressure. I recently had the opportunity to speak at a women's Bible study group in our community. I knew many of the women, and thinking about their slim figures and stylish

4. What I believe about my body only affects my body.
God made us a trinity (body, soul, and spirit) just as he is a trinity (Father, Son, and Holy Spirit). Believing that hating my body doesn't affect my mind, emotions, and spiritual life is like saying that God the Holy Spirit has nothing to do with God the Father or God the Son. You might share how hating a part of your body has affected your emotional life or desire to be involved in relationships.

Practically speaking, bringing lies into the open might have allowed Kelly's mom in the story at the beginning of this chapter to initially respond to her daughter in very different ways:

clothes made me want to lose weight and buy a new outfit. When I got up to speak, I was so nervous about my appearance and acceptance by this group that my mouth became so dry I could hardly speak. I finally just confessed my fears to the group, which took away the fear's power, and I was able to continue speaking with a lot more joy and passion. I shared this with my daughter, and she wisely replied, "Oh, Mom, they were far more interested in *you* than they were in your clothes or weight." I've filed Kristin's kind response away for future use with *her* when inevitable peer pressure tempts her to reduce herself to externals only.

3. This can be a good time to talk about your memories of when someone made you feel uncomfortable about your body. How did you handle the situation? What do you wish you would have said or done differently?

4. Becoming obsessed with a body part or weight loss can change one's personality. Thinking only about big legs or a flat stomach or weight loss kidnaps your daughter's brain and takes the joy out of her life. What would be the loss if your daughter's personality changed? This is a crucial time to remind her of who she really is. Tell stories about her childhood, her unique personality quirks, and the ways she has joyfully, creatively, or passionately experienced life.

- "Oh, honey, I'm honored that my opinion of your appearance matters to you. Thanks for sharing your concerns. Whose body are you comparing yours to?"
- "Is there anything going on in your life right now that has made you more conscious of what you don't like about your body? Do

Just for You

1. Take the following quiz, answering true or false, to gain a little insight into your own beliefs about eating and weight loss:
   - Fat people eat more than thin people.
   - Having a slow metabolism is just an excuse for being overweight.
   - Being fat is bad, weak, and disgusting.
   - Anyone can become and remain thin.
   - I don't trust myself to make decisions about eating.
   - Dieting is a good way to control weight.
   - The best reason to exercise is to lose weight.
   - Depression has nothing to do with what I eat or don't eat.
2. Recall your own dieting and weight-loss schemes. What were the long-term and short-term consequences, both good and bad?
3. When you feel uncomfortable about your weight, do you:
   - skip meals
   - begin a diet
   - overeat, since you already weigh too much
   - fast
   - begin an exercise program
   - use laxatives or some other method of purging
4. How do you define a diet? Any pattern of eating that you cannot sustain for a lifetime is a diet. Are you on a diet right now?
5. If you are unsure of the futility of dieting and its negative consequences, read and evaluate *Outsmarting the Female Fat Cell* by Debra Waterhouse or *The Diet Trap* by Pamela M. Smith. (See Resources.)
6. If your daughter is dieting, arm yourself with facts, pray about the right time to talk about her dieting, and model healthy eating choices.

you and your friends talk about this? What about the guys? Do they say things?"

- "I understand your concern, because as you've probably noticed I have the same body type. I went through a period when I hated my body too and tried everything to change it. I learned I can tone my muscles and subtly shape my body, but I can't change my basic body structure. Do you want to do some research on exercise programs that might help or consult a personal trainer for a session or two?"

- "When I hated my body—especially my legs—I never wanted to wear shorts, exercise, or swim. My self-hatred kept me from an active life, which contributed to some loneliness and boredom in middle school and early high school. Have you noticed any changes you've made or activities you've stopped doing because of your concern about your body?"

- "My self-contempt also affected my relationship with God. When I hated parts of my body, it was like taking one of the wonderful art projects you made in elementary school and cutting it to shreds. I hurt both me and God, my Maker. Have you thought about praying about how you feel about yourself? What would you pray and ask God for?"

Our daughters need to understand that no matter how much they diet, they can't change their basic body structure. True beauty is developed when we accept ourselves the way we were created. Some of us were built with a bigger bone structure. Others are more naturally slight. Some of us naturally carry our weight in our hips, others in our abdomens.

I have watched my daughter wrestle with this reality in the most awesome way. Kristin decided to take my word for it—that her life wouldn't change dramatically if she lost a few inches on her thighs. She committed to drop the major brain drain of obsessing about her legs. She entered high school determined to be kind to everyone, to ask God's help to be outgoing and self-assured, and to act like she's confident (even though there are days when she's not). She's discovered that people respond positively to kindness, passion, and self-confidence. She really is my hero. She would tell you that she loves her life, and it has nothing to do with her thighs!

Any movement toward self-improvement must be propelled
not by disgust and self-rejection,
but by a realistic acceptance of who we already are
and a desire to be the best possible version of that reality.[4]

MARCIA GERMAINE HUTCHINSON, *Love the Body You Have*

YOUR DIETING AND WEIGHT-LOSS IQ

Knowing the truth and the lies about diet and other weight-loss schemes can help you guide your daughter in making good choices. Yes, this is another area in which we must research and scrupulously determine the truth about diet and weight loss. (See recommended reading in the Resources section.)

When I began to experiment with destructive eating behaviors, I didn't think my choices were a big deal. But I was wrong. No one told me that the choices I was making with regard to food and my body could cause chemical changes in my brain, increasing my risk for depression, and could damage my liver, lungs, and heart. Debra Waterhouse warns, "Dieting is not a risk-free game of the incredible shrinking woman." She lists twenty-eight potential consequences of dieting, including hair loss, gallbladder problems, and sleep difficulties. She concludes, "Dieting is dangerous to all women, but our young daughters have the most extensive damage because they are dieting during their preadolescent and adolescent years—right when their cells are rapidly dividing, their first menstrual cycles are starting, and their bodies are maturing into women."[5] Spotting the lies and kindly sharing the truth with our daughters as early as possible can help them steer clear of destructive choices.

In the last chapter we talked about the importance of understanding that eating is not just about eating. Eating can be a form of expression that must be understood and responded to wisely. But eating and weight loss are also about health and nutrition. Balance is tricky, requiring that we be armed with sound nutritional and psychological information and that we start early in exposing lies and telling the truth, but that we encourage openness and individuality in our daughters at the same time.

Following are some of the lies about dieting and weight-loss schemes, as well as some ideas for winning your daughter to the truth.

THE LIES

1. Dieting is a good way to control weight.
After working with hundreds of women who have tried every diet imaginable, I am convinced that the only reasonable way to approach weight loss is by accepting our basic body structure and eating sensibly. I know it's boring and won't sell anything, but it's true. When your daughter wants to try Slim-Fast or some other weight-loss scheme, this is a good opportunity to tell her the truth: Dieting makes us fat. A girl who diets is *eight times* more likely to develop an eating disorder.[6] Nutritionists report that all dieters have a 95 percent probability of regaining any weight lost within two years.[7] When we diet and restrict ourselves, we eventually feel hungry or deprived. The pounds we initially lose are primarily water, and our system is thrown into disequilibrium. We respond by overeating and usually gaining back what we've lost, and more. Then we feel fatter and worse about ourselves and begin the whole process anew. Biologists and nutritionists can explain it in more scientific terms, but the bottom-line truth is that dieting tricks our metabolism so that we store fat more easily from fewer calories. (See the Resources section for books that explain this phenomenon.)

2. Dieting won't hurt me.
When we don't get well-balanced nutrition, we begin to feel tired, spaced out, even stupid. Dieting traps the brain in a cycle that has an impact on our emotions as well. When girls begin to go through puberty, their brain chemistry is in as much chaos as they are. Proper nutrients are essential to produce chemicals that fight mood swings as well as serious depression. Girls who starve themselves or repeatedly go on fad diets can be unknowingly sentencing themselves to a lifelong struggle with eating disorders or depression (see more about this in part 3). An adolescent might not understand the seriousness of this consequence. If you've struggled with depression or know someone who has, this would be a good time to talk to your daughter about how debilitating it can be.

3. Exercise is my punishment for being fat.

Girls need exercise and physical activity. But when it comes from self-contempt it can become a part of a destructive weight-loss scheme. Exercise that is not about a basic, joyful desire to move our bodies can be more harmful than healthful. Counselor Geneen Roth explains: "Somewhere between the ages of seven and thirteen, we lost the connection to our bodies. We lost the sense that what was inside us mattered, and began to treat our bodies as

JUST FOR THE TWO OF YOU

Consider together some of the truths about dieting listed below and ask your daughter to interact with you about them.

1. According to Dr. Mary Pipher, author of *Hunger Pains,* "Every day, 56% of the women in the United States are on diets. We have a 30-billion-dollar-a-year diet industry."[8] Make a list together of causes that you would donate the $30 billion to, if you could.

2. Go to the mall or park together and follow Geneen Roth's advice: "Stare at normal women's bodies (normal does not include models, actresses, and elite athletes)."[9] As you notice other girls and women, look at each other, and remind each other: "*You* are what a 'normal' woman [girl] looks like."

3. Ask your daughter if she's ever felt constantly judged and criticized by a teacher, coach, or even parent. How did it make her feel? When she tried to do better, was it a positive experience? Relate this to the body. What have our bodies done to us that make us want to punish them? Exercise that is motivated by shame, anger, or self-contempt will not be life-giving.

4. Ask your daughter what she would like to do for physical exercise. Dance? Mountain bike? Take walks? Swim? Geneen Roth concludes: "In the end, moving your body is not about flat stomachs or thin thighs; it is about being...a woman [or girl] who is lucky enough to have arms and legs that can surge with energy, be warmed by the sun,

objects that needed to be manipulated and sculpted so other people would love us. We started to diet. We started to binge. We stopped feeling the power and strength of our arms and legs and began to focus on cellulite instead."[10]

The mother at the beginning of this chapter might use the revelation of these lies to have a conversation with her daughter, Kelly:

- "When I was in my twenties I tried a grapefruit diet to change my body. It worked for a while, but eventually I gained all the weight

and slice through wind and water."[11] The earlier we celebrate this reality with our daughters, the better!

5. Discuss the fact that making healthy eating choices *feels good*. This is a wonderful opportunity to reinforce truths discussed in the last chapter: Hunger is good. Food is not the enemy. Satisfying your hunger with good food is the best way to energize yourself for the life you want to lead. You can be trusted with what you eat. Are you and your daughter walking hand in hand with these beliefs as your foundation?

6. If your daughter needs to lose weight in order to be optimally healthy, you can support her in reasonable strategies for weight loss. When Kristin began to ask me about dieting, we sat down and came up with our own dieting and weight-loss plans. We tried to have fun as well as be sensible. Some of our ideas include:
   - Don't do sit-ups after eating ice cream!
   - Don't eat out of only one food group.
   - See food as energy.
   - Do thirty minutes of physical activity every day.
   - Try a Tae-Bo or kick-boxing class.
   - Try Jazzercise. "Mom, you can do it." (Kristin's note to me)
   - Don't think self-hatred.
   - Don't ever take diet pills. Not only do diet pills mess with your metabolism, but recent studies suggest that they pose a serious risk of stroke or heart attack in young women.[12]
   - Don't talk about dieting. It's boring.
   - Keep gum in your purse.

back, and more. How about getting on the Internet to see how many kinds of diets we can find? How much do they cost? Do they sound reasonable? How long could we last on each particular diet? Who benefits most from selling these diets?"

- "Your friends at school think they're making a smart choice by drinking Slim-Fast because initially they are losing a few pounds. But they will eventually find out that their body is smarter than they are. Remember when we had contests to see who could hold their breath under water the longest? When we came up for air, we breathed harder and faster to replace the oxygen we'd deprived ourselves of. When you deprive your body of real food, it will crave and need even more to make up for what you've deprived it of."

- "When I tried dieting, I discovered that I was tired all the time, I couldn't think clearly, and I really didn't feel like doing a lot. It wasn't worth it. I love your passion and zest for life. I'd hate to see that go away because you're unhappy with your legs. If you could have the legs of your dreams, would it be worth it if you were always tired, depressed, and didn't feel like doing anything?"

- "I didn't exercise until I was in college, and then I learned that exercise helps me feel good about my body and gives me energy. Are there any physical activities you've wanted to try?"

Do you not know that your body is a temple of the Holy Spirit
who is in you?... Honor God with your body.

1 CORINTHIANS 6:19-20

YOUR EXPERIENCE

I recently spoke to a group of high school juniors and seniors at one of the Denver public schools. We talked about what they'd learned from their mothers about eating and body image and what they wished they'd learned. After the class was over, a beautiful young woman approached me. She bit her lip and said, "I think what you're saying about mothers and daughters talking is right. I take diet pills, but I would never tell my mother."

I asked her why. "My mom would freak out," the girl said. "She would tell me to get rid of them. And then I would get fat."

As she answered I thought about her reasons for disclosing her diet pill habit to me, a virtual stranger. I knew that she, like all of us, longs to be completely known. I also knew that although she looked quite grown up in her tight black pants and chic sweater, she still needed and wanted a mother—someone to guide her, stop her from harming herself, and help her to become the young woman she wants to be.

I thanked her for her "sacred disclosure," and then with my mother heart full of longing for this girl, I asked if she'd read the recent studies about the risk of diet pills. She hadn't. I asked her to please reconsider discussing the diet pills and her desire to be thin with her mother. I gave her my business card and promised, "If it goes badly, ask your mother to call me." I really didn't expect to hear from her again.

Just for You

Our experiences with eating and weight loss are our best education in helping our daughters with theirs. Consider your first awareness of body image and how you connected it to eating choices. Of course, you probably won't share every detail with your daughter, and you'll have to evaluate when she is ready to hear certain parts of your story.

1. What does your story reveal about your beliefs about body image and weight loss?

2. How have these beliefs hurt or helped you?

3. Go back and consider the lies and truths that have been discussed. In what ways have you lived in the truth? in a lie?

4. Did your mother disclose any experiences to you about her struggle with body image or her experimentation with different diets? If so, how did you respond? If she didn't, would you have liked her to?

5. What do you fear in telling your daughter about your own experience?

This morning at nine o'clock my telephone rang. I was expecting a call and answered the phone quickly but was surprised to hear a tentative, fearful voice. "You don't know me, but you spoke to my daughter's class a few weeks ago. She told me that you told her to tell me she's taking diet pills. I'm scared to death and don't know what to tell her."

I asked this mom what she was most afraid of and was stunned by her answer. "When I was in college, I used speed to control my weight. I got hooked on it, and I had to be hospitalized. I missed a whole semester of school. My daughter doesn't know, and I'm afraid to tell her."

What a joy to share with this mother that her story is not something to hide and fear! In his wonderful book *Telling the Truth*, theologian Frederick Buechner states: "Stories have such power for us.... They force us to consider."[13] I asked this mother to consider what her story tells about herself, her choices, and the lessons she's learned, and to write out what she could share with her daughter. She promised she would call me and let me know how their conversation went.

I understand that there is some controversy about disclosing our mistakes and frailties to our children. Some parenting experts suggest that we are to be role models and that children, even teenagers, are unformed and cannot process our mistakes and the lessons we have learned from them. I agree that with young children this may be true. But how young? Only you can judge your daughter's maturity, cognitive ability, and need for your story.

As our daughters enter preadolescence and their teen years, I firmly believe they will benefit from our stories with regard to body image, eating, and weight loss. You can be certain that your daughter is reading and watching other stories about body image and weight loss, that she and her friends are telling each other their own stories, and that she is wondering about your story. Your story is one of the best door openers to talking about the truth and lies with regard to body image, eating, and weight loss. Your daughter will want to be connected to you when you are honest about your own feelings, opinions, and experiences. When you know your story, are not afraid of it, and see the many wonderful lessons you have learned because of it, you will be ready to share it with your daughter along the way.

Since God has so generously let us in on what he is doing,
we're not about to throw up our hands and walk off the job
just because we run into occasional hard times.
We refuse to wear masks and play games.
We don't maneuver and manipulate behind the scenes.
And we don't twist God's Word to suit ourselves.
Rather, we keep everything we do and say out in the open,
the whole truth on display, so that those who want to
can see and judge for themselves in the presence of God.

2 CORINTHIANS 4:1-2, MSG

Authors and counselors Hugh and Gayle Prather explain, "Children are not a different life-form. They respond to fairness and unfairness, love and judgment, devotion and betrayal, gentleness and cruelty, appreciation and dismissal, openness and rigidity, in about the same way that adults respond. Most of our problems with our kids indicate our lack of *identification* with their needs, our failure to see that our kids' needs are our own and to treat them as our own."[14]

Theologian Brennan Manning offers an insightful model to evaluate why, when, and what we should disclose: "What is the purpose of self-disclosure? For anyone caught up in the oppression of thinking God works only through saints, it offers a word of encouragement. For those who have already blown it, it offers a word of liberation. For those trapped in cynicism, indifference, it offers a word of hope."[15]

Here are some conversational clues that your daughter might need a few lines of your story to validate her own, form a deeper connection with you, and facilitate her personal growth:

- "Mom, you don't understand. You've never worried about being fat."
- "I've already blown it, Mom. I've been taking diet pills for a year. It's too late to change."
- "I hate my body."

- "What difference does it make what I eat, or if I eat?"
- "I'll never feel good about myself."

The mother of the girl on diet pills just called back. It's 8:30 P.M. She and her daughter talked for two hours, she told me. They asked each other for forgiveness. They flushed the diet pills down the toilet. They asked for one counseling session with me to get further encouragement in putting their relationship back on track. And tomorrow they are going to find a health club or exercise class they can join together.

Self-contempt, discouragement, cynicism, indifference, and despair can be transformed into hope when we commit to walk hand in hand with our daughters, to harbor no more secrets, no more lies.

Part III

Conquering Roadblocks
to Relationship

While some people claim that when a daughter is rebellious her mother is to blame, this usually is not true. Blaming the daughter for the difficulties does nothing to resolve the situation either. There are many forces at play, and many circumstances contribute to the predicament. When a relationship is shaky or strained, there's bound to be something in both mother and daughter that desperately needs healing. As the mother and the adult, you have to make the overture toward this end.[1]

JUDY FORD AND AMANDA FORD, *Between Mother and Daughter*

Chapter 9

Anorexia

Once a rare and exotic disease, anorexia is now common.
It is estimated that the disease affects between one and six
of every two hundred women. Most victims are female
and many are between the ages of 12 and 25.
Tragically, anorexia is the leading cause of death among people
seeking psychiatric help.[1]

MARY PIPHER, *Hunger Pains*

norexia. The very word sounds scary. We have seen the horrifying pictures of emaciated girls with sunken eyes and protruding bones and cannot conceive of our daughters—the children we have devoted so much of our energy to feeding and nourishing—intentionally choosing to starve themselves.

A single chapter cannot thoroughly investigate all the biological and psychological dimensions of this complex disorder. The primary purpose of this chapter is to familiarize you with anorexia, alert you to warning signs in your daughter, and equip you to intervene in ways that might prevent this horrible struggle. A list of additional resources on anorexia is included in the Resources section.

Peggy Claude-Pierre, mother of two daughters who struggled with anorexia and the author of *The Secret Language of Eating Disorders,* pleads, "The key is early intervention. Eating disorders are insidious and difficult to treat once they become acute."[2] Nancy J. Kolodny, author of *When Food's a Foe,* agrees: "Eating disorders are tenacious and stay with a person for periods ranging on average from one to fifteen years."[3]

THE CONTINUUM OF ANOREXIA

Eating disorders exist along a continuum. The continuum for anorexia indicates the stages that may occur between the time a girl says she feels fat and when she ends up in the hospital slowly dying from starvation. By the time they're in the sixth grade, most girls will have wondered about their weight and expressed concern about their size or shape to their mothers. The preadolescent girl is on the brink of the time period when she will be most vulnerable to developing an eating disorder.

The most common time for the onset of an eating disorder is when girls' bodies and lives begin to change dramatically. Breasts as well as sexuality begin to bud, hips and an awareness of societal problems widen, and weight, along with pressures and responsibilities, begins to increase. We can help our daughters best at the *beginning* of the continuum with awareness and proactive intervention. At the end of the continuum, eating disorders will usually need to be addressed by doctors, psychiatrists, and sometimes hospitalization.

THE BEGINNING OF THE CONTINUUM

At the beginning of the continuum of anorexia, your daughter may skip a meal in order to lose a few pounds for an upcoming event. As your daughter experiments with eating and not eating, her choices may have a positive impact or only a minor negative impact on her overall well-being.

When Kristin was in gymnastics, she constantly worried about her weight. During the middle of the competitive season, she became sick with a persistent virus. She missed a week of gymnastics and lost a few pounds due to loss of appetite while she was sick. When she returned to the gym one of her coaches complimented her on losing weight. "You look great!" he announced. After practice Kristin came home and told me about her coach's approval and lamented, "I wish there was some way I could get rid of my appetite *all* the time."

I wanted to slug my daughter's coach and immediately lecture Kristin on the dangers of her thinking, but I waited until the next morning to talk with her. I told her that I know losing weight feels great, especially when people notice. But I told her I also know that the combined feelings of losing weight and being in control can become addictive, resulting in an eating disorder. She rolled her eyes a bit at what she knew was coming, but she was still young enough that she valued my opinions and listened to my warnings. We considered together the value of having an appetite, why God created us to eat and not simply absorb nutrients, the pleasure in good food, and the necessity of proper nutrition to perform well in her sport.

Kristin already knew of the high risk for eating disorders among gymnasts and was not surprised to hear me firmly reiterate, "When losing weight becomes more important than your love of the sport, you have to quit." I knew she would struggle with her size as long as she was in gymnastics, but I wanted her to know that I was watching and aware of the risk for eating disorders and that I would most assuredly intervene quickly. I cannot emphasize enough that this is the best time to intervene.

It all started when I hit my seventh-grade year.
I had always been considered "big-boned," "stocky"—
nice ways of saying "fat."
I started by dieting and working out.
I got so many comments from everyone when I started to lose weight
that I slowly became obsessed.
My whole life became centered around what I didn't eat
and how many times a day I worked out.

STACY, age 16

I have a friend whose thirteen-year-old daughter began to skip dinner occasionally. When her mother questioned her behavior, she explained that she wanted to lose weight for an upcoming school dance. The mother suggested they sign up with a personal trainer at their local recreation center for five visits and tone up together before the dance. My friend explained to her daughter that going to the personal trainer was contingent on her eating healthy meals. The daughter agreed and felt good about the results of the exercise. Her mother reinforced an important lesson: The only correct and effective approach to weight loss is healthy eating choices and good exercise.

Her story reminds me that early intervention means taking our daughters' concerns about weight and eating *seriously* right from the start and being willing to spend time and money to help them channel their concerns into healthy choices.

During adolescence our daughters will grow most gracefully into independence if they have confidence in our strength and stability. This includes the knowledge that we will not turn the other way when they make destructive choices but that they can count on us to intervene when their experiments become dangerous.

JUST FOR THE TWO OF YOU

At this stage on the continuum, your goal is to continue to reinforce the truth and lies about dieting and body image, using the exercises we have looked at previously. Some additional practical intervention might include the following:

1. Be very careful with compliments about weight loss or looking skinny. These remarks can promote destructive eating choices. If your daughter begins to skip meals, don't ignore the behavior. Ask what's behind her not eating and tell her the reason you want to know is that you want to support her in healthy ways. After she explains her desire (usually to lose a few pounds), help her come up with a healthy strategy.

2. Don't be afraid to warn about eating disorders. Now is the time to talk about anorexia, read together about this disorder, and watch movies about girls who have struggled (see the Resources section). The wisdom and warnings about eating should be a natural part of your dialogue with your daughter *before* eating disorders develop.

3. Even adolescent girls need to know that their mother is stronger than they are. Our knowledge and strength at this time on the continuum might prevent further progression into an eating disorder. Let your daughter know that she has control over her choices of food, but that when you observe she is not choosing food at all or eating very little, you will intervene.

4. Get rid of all scales and diet products.

The strength of my mother is incomprehensible to me.
She takes every challenge that we are ever faced with
and whips it into shape.

SARA, age 15

Intervention might be the loss of a sport (like gymnastics), or a decision that the two of you will go together to a nutritional consultant or therapist who knows about eating disorders, or that you will participate together in a seminar on eating disorders. Of course, your daughter may view your warnings as extreme and unnecessary. After all, she's just skipping a meal. But your warnings and early interventions may also be the safety net that keeps her from falling further into destructive eating behaviors.

THE MIDDLE OF THE CONTINUUM

Further along the continuum of anorexia is increased experimentation with dieting and exercise. A girl may eat only certain foods, she may eat only a small portion of each meal, or drink only water and diet drinks instead of eating. She may develop rituals in her eating like cutting food into tiny bites and only eating a portion. You will notice that she becomes increasingly anxious at meals. She may exercise with greater frequency and intensity. She will justify her behavior by saying things like "Everybody diets," "Being thin is healthy," "A lot of exercise is good for you," or "If diet pills or drinks were dangerous, they wouldn't be in the grocery store." Your daughter may begin to worry excessively about the calories and fat content of foods. She may constantly criticize herself and her appearance. What began as experimentation slowly becomes obsession.

People started to tell me I was getting too thin,
but to me that was a compliment.
Their remarks made me stronger to keep losing.

ELAINE, age 17

If your daughter is sliding into the middle of the continuum, she may be on the edge of an eating disorder. Ten percent of females between the ages of sixteen and twenty-five have subclinical anorexia, which means they exhibit some anorexic behavior.[4] Now is the time for intensified intervention.

As you help your daughter stay away from an eating disorder, you will have to learn to talk together about pain and negative feelings. Eating disorders are ways in which girls cope with things about themselves and their lives that are stressful or painful. One antidote to developing anorexia is for your daughter to learn to talk openly about her feelings. When she slides toward the middle of the continuum of anorexia, you will need to talk together about her life in order to prevent a further slide down the continuum.

The next two "Just for the Two of You" sections offer some ideas and questions that can open communication during this time and help your daughter directly connect her emotional life to her eating choices. You can help your daughter answer these questions by modeling to her your own connection with your internal world and answering the questions as well.

JUST FOR THE TWO OF YOU

1. Always begin any conversation with a desire to understand what is going on in your daughter's world. Explain to her that you know her eating choices (or her choice not to eat) and excessive exercise are rooted in reason. Help her articulate what she is hoping for, afraid of, or experiencing that justifies her eating and exercise. Help her consider different responses to her concerns.

2. Whenever your daughter puts herself down, fight her negative mind-set. Encourage, compliment, and remind her of what is true. My daughter goes through days when she hates the way that she looks. She never agrees with me when I tell her she looks great. But my job is to model for her how to fight the negative mind with loving, dogged persistence. One mother said to me, "When my daughter puts herself down, she's just looking for attention." My response: "Then give it to her."

3. Depression goes hand in hand with eating disorders. Experts debate whether depression causes the disorder or the nutritional imbalance

The End of the Continuum

When a girl reaches the end of the continuum of anorexia she may refuse food outright or eat in ritualized, robotic ways. Her lack of nutritional intake begins to show in a distinct sickly pallor, black circles under the eyes, cracked fingernails, dry skin, and insomnia, and she will have difficulty concentrating. If your daughter's eating behavior is on the end of the continuum, her personality has gradually changed. She's probably lost her sense of humor, become intolerant of herself and others, rigid in her values, and isolated from friends and other interests. At this end of the continuum, a girl struggling with anorexia must be regarded and treated as a critically ill patient.

At the end of the continuum you must take the responsibility for your daughter's recovery. Tell her that you love her and that you know she is exhausted and afraid. Reinforce that you believe in her and don't blame her for what she's done. Know that one of your daughter's first fears will be that you are going to make her fat. Assure her that you love her and that you won't let

causes depression. Talk to your daughter about the risk of depression and educate yourself and her on the debilitating consequences she is setting herself up for by depriving herself of necessary nutrients.

4. Take active steps to prevent depression. When day after day your daughter awakens moody and tired, craves carbohydrates, or doesn't eat at all, it might be a good idea to check with your doctor or healthcare provider about the possibility of depression. Often these symptoms arise from an imbalance of a powerful brain chemical, serotonin, that the body needs to function normally.

5. Understand and explain to your daughter that when nutrients are regularly missing in the diet, chemical changes in the brain alter perceptions. Not eating literally makes you crazy. Share with your daughter pictures and information about girls who are extremely thin and literally see themselves as fat when they look in the mirror (see Resources section).

her get fat. Explain that you are going to get through this *together.* Tell her that you will find a doctor and get a therapist for both of you (or the whole family).

I remember the day my mom told me we had to get help.
At that moment I hated her.
I told her to stay out of my life and just let me be.
I told her I didn't care if I died, as long as I died thin.
But she stuck by me, going to counseling with me
and keeping a loving eye on me.

RACHEL, age 17

GETTING TREATMENT

As you walk hand in hand with your daughter through the difficult and sometimes dangerous terrain of body image and eating disorders, you and your daughter may need to talk with a therapist. The best counseling will not replace your relationship with your daughter, but will enhance it by providing insight and guidance to strengthen your alliance. Listed on the following page are some tips for finding the best counselor and some suggestions when insurance or income is not available to cover the costs of counseling.

JUST FOR THE TWO OF YOU

1. Who or what in my life triggers the most painful or bad feelings?
2. Who or what in my life triggers the most pleasurable or good feelings?
3. What do others say about me that makes me feel good? bad?
4. Do certain people or events make me want to lose weight?
5. Is there a particular time of the month I feel the worst about myself?
6. How does not eating make me feel?
7. When am I the happiest? unhappiest?
8. When do I feel in control? out of control?
9. What is so scary about being out of control?

1. The best referrals usually come from those who have been through a similar struggle. If you don't know of anyone whose daughter has struggled with an eating disorder, contact youth pastors and/or school counselors and ask them if they can help you locate another parent who has sought counseling and help for her daughter.

2. Contact your insurance for a list of providers and information about how many sessions they will pay for and how much they will pay.

3. Choose a therapist whose work focuses on adolescents and eating disorders. Contact the National Eating Disorder Organization (918-481-4044) for a list of therapists and treatment centers in your area.

4. Interview at least three therapists (with your daughter) before choosing a counselor. It is important that your daughter feel like she is part of the process of choosing who will help her.

5. When you interview the counselor, explain that you want to be a part of your daughter's recovery and ask the therapist how he or she will incorporate you into the process.

6. If insurance is not available and money is tight, ask for a sliding scale. Many therapists will slide their fees to accommodate your income.

7. Ask your church about a counseling support fund. Often a church will pay half of the counseling fee, while you pay the other half.

8. If counseling is out of the question due to your financial situation, look for a support group in your community. Investigate and interview group leaders as carefully as you would a therapist.

    - Contact the National Mental Health Association Information Center (800-969-NMHA) for referrals to local support groups and/or community resources.
    - If your daughter's struggle is with compulsive overeating, contact Overeaters Anonymous (505-891-2664) for a group meeting near you.
    - Check with your local hospital about educational meetings and eating disorder support groups.
    - Investigate Internet resources:
      —http://edreferral.com includes information about eating disorders as well as further suggestions for finding a therapist
      —http://www.somethingfishy.org lists therapists, treatment facilities, dietitians, and support groups as well as provides online support.

If your daughter is near the very end of the continuum of anorexia, she may need hospitalization to restore some weight. It is almost impossible for a starving person to fight depression, develop self-esteem, and learn healthy ways of dealing with pain and stress. At no other time in her life will your daughter be hungrier for unconditional love. Even in the midst of these devastating circumstances, treat her with respect and kindness.

THE CAUSES OF ANOREXIA

Mother and daughter sat across from me in my counseling office. Their body language indicated that they were glad to be there together, that they liked each other, and that they were allies.

When Lauren and her mother, Susan, first came to see me for counseling

JUST FOR YOU

1. Evaluate the ways you are expressing your love for your daughter. Do you express love when she is "good"? When she eats? Do you react negatively when she doesn't eat? Your daughter's emotional health is as fragile as her physical health right now. Watch carefully that you don't send signals that suggest your love is conditional, reinforcing her belief that she doesn't deserve love or food.

2. You can walk hand in hand with your daughter during this time if you become allies together against the problem, which is anorexia, not your daughter. Your daughter is not your enemy. Put your arms around her, comfort her, fight her negative mind-set. Your daughter needs to know that you are stronger than her eating disorder. You might not feel this way, and so you will have to rest confidently in and run relentlessly to the truth that God is stronger. We will explore this more together in the final chapter.

3. Do not comment on body size or appearance.

4. Find another focus together besides the eating disorder. Take a class together in painting, poetry, creative writing, or cooking. Creative self-expression will be healing to both you and your daughter.

one year before, their moods had been drastically different. Susan had looked defeated, her shoulders slumped, as she nervously looked back and forth between her daughter and me. Lauren wouldn't even sit on the couch by her mom. She sat on the floor, legs crossed, arms folded, and stared out the window. Lauren was fifteen years old and seriously underweight. She hid her starving body beneath baggy overalls and an oversize sweatshirt. Neither Lauren nor her mom knew that they were about to begin an agonizing and amazing journey of healing *together.*

Today was their final counseling appointment with me. Lauren still wore baggy overalls and an oversize sweatshirt, but she no longer looked like a starving, sick child. She looked like a healthy adolescent girl. Susan ended our session with words that reveal, in large part, the reason for her daughter's healthy transformation: "We are so grateful for Lauren's anorexia. It shocked and scared us, but it also made us look at the truth about our family. It was a wake-up call. Lauren's struggle with anorexia saved us all."

Understanding anorexia is not simple. We don't need scientific research to confirm that females are complex and that our behaviors are just as complex. However, there are some commonalties in girls who struggle with anorexia that help pinpoint some of the roots of this potentially deadly disorder.

Girls who are most successful in fighting anorexia do so with the help of their families, and this means that treatment must include examining family dynamics. Please do not read this section and conclude that you are to blame for your daughter's struggle! You did not *cause* her condition, but you are responsible to help her. Part of that responsibility is looking at the components of your daughter's personality in the context of your family's personality style and relational dynamics. Is there is anything in the family dynamics that should change in order to help your daughter fight her eating disorder? Making your home a place of open communication and independent thinking as well as a safe place to make mistakes and test ideas is your responsibility as a parent.

I am hesitant to provide an opportunity for mothers to shoulder any more blame. You are not to blame. Prayerfully, draw the line between blame and responsibility as you read the rest of this section.

GIRLS WHO STRUGGLE WITH ANOREXIA
There are multitudinous reasons for girls getting trapped in anorexia. And certain personality traits or life experiences set girls up for this disorder.

- Girls who mature early and feel fat in comparison to their peers may begin dieting early. Especially when they are teased and ridiculed for their weight, girls may feel pressure to find their own solution and show everyone that they are not fat. They are faced with the dieting dilemma early and discover that they have to eat less and less to continue to lose weight. As we discussed in previous chapters, dieting slows the metabolism, requiring increasing deprivation to achieve weight loss. The findings of The Renfrew Center, an eating disorder clinic in Philadelphia, make sense. This highly acclaimed treatment center discovered that 88 percent of their patients, both anorexic and bulimic, had a history of prolonged dieting prior to the onset of their eating disorder.[5]
- Girls who have been physically abused often believe they don't deserve to eat or to be nourished.
- Girls who have been sexually abused may fear that their growing body will only invite more abuse. Thus, they determine to stay little girls.
- Girls whose parents are in the midst of a divorce or who live with parents who are depressed or abuse drugs or alcohol are prime candidates for an eating disorder. Instead of focusing on their real psychological needs (which they fear will not be met), they focus on food (and not eating) because it's something that they can control. Anorexic girls use a preoccupation with not eating or gaining weight to starve other feelings that are too painful. Anorexic behavior substitutes for dealing with tension, anxiety, conflict, or difficulties that girls feel they cannot express or resolve.
- Girls who tend be perfectionists often struggle with anorexia. Anorexia can be a result of striving to meet our cultural ideals or it can be an expression of finding control in an imperfect world. Many girls who struggle with anorexia count calories, create weight charts, make lists of good and bad food, and rate their eating behavior each day. These girls often have black-and-white thinking and see themselves as either good or bad. They may be extremely sensitive to any criticism and compensate by taking complete control of what they eat. They may weigh themselves every day and find great satisfaction in losing weight because they feel strong and in control.

- Girls with a misplaced sense of responsibility are vulnerable to anorexia. They may feel responsible for their parents' bad marriage or their brother's drug problem. Their antennae are alert to everyone around them, and they feel responsible for others' suffering. They begin to believe that they don't deserve anything pleasurable—which includes food. Their negative mind tells them that family difficulties are their fault or their responsibility to solve and that they don't deserve to eat until they have fixed the problems around them.
- Girls who participate in sports or activities that depend on thinness—gymnasts, dancers, models, and actresses—are candidates for anorexia.

FAMILIES OF ANOREXIC GIRLS

If you take a girl from one of the categories just mentioned and put her into one of the families described next, an eating disorder is highly probable.

- Anorexic girls usually come from families in which parents impose an identity upon their daughters. When parents have rigid ideas about who their daughter should be and are intolerant of her uniqueness, she may take control in the area of eating.
- Hilde Bruch, pioneer in the treatment of anorexic girls, explains that girls in rigid families that do not encourage and foster independence never develop a sense of self. When they approach adolescence, they are terrified to grow up and are afraid of the developmental hurdles. Starving is a way to stay small, asexual, and dependent.[6]
- At the other extreme are girls in families with parents who are distant or uninvolved. These girls often feel invisible and left to themselves to find their way in the world. Starving becomes a way to be in control and stay invisible—literally. Therapist Kathryn Zerbe, M.D., explains that whenever legitimate imperatives for nurturing are not met, "One outcome of this dilemma is a defensive strategy in which the individual gives up on having her needs met. In effect, she says to everyone in her life, 'I don't need anyone. I don't even need food.'"[7]
- Salvatore Minuchin, a respected family system theorist, believes that anorexic girls come from families that are intrusive, overprotective, and unable to deal with conflict. Girls learn to subordinate their needs

to those of the family. They are careful to never express negative feelings, and they take on a great responsibility for not embarrassing the
family. Once again, the only way to feel in control is by not eating.[8]

- Peggy Claude-Pierre, author of *The Secret Language of Eating Disorders,* believes that anorexia is rooted in negative thinking that
  can be fostered in a critical, demanding family. When love is conditional and only high achievement is rewarded, a girl can begin
  to believe she doesn't deserve to eat unless she performs well, and

Just for You

Listed below are some questions to help you examine the personality of
your family, as well as exercises to make changes, if necessary. If your
daughter has a personality that is vulnerable to anorexia and your family
personality is one that might foster this disorder, then you are responsible to address the family dynamics. As Lauren and Susan (the mother-
daughter team mentioned earlier) will testify, it is a process in which
everyone wins.

Complete each numbered statement with one of the seven lettered
responses at the end (all responses are not appropriate for some statements):

1. When my daughter chooses to wear something I don't like,
2. When my daughter expresses a dislike for a certain hobby or extracurricular activity and asks to drop it,
3. When my daughter spends her whole evening on the telephone and
   has to stay up late to finish her homework,
4. When my daughter makes a new friend whose language is distasteful
   to me,
5. When my daughter makes a B on her history test and has the choice
   to take the exam again to improve her grade,
6. When my daughter asks to eat only cereal or yogurt for breakfast and no
   longer wants the standard breakfast of eggs or pancakes I've been fixing,
7. When my daughter is late for curfew,
8. When my daughter wants to get her hair cut in a way I think won't be
   flattering for her,

her negative mind convinces her that she never performs well enough.

You can get a glimpse into your family dynamics by your answers in the exercise below. If you answer mostly *C* or *D,* your home is probably an environment where independence is being fostered and your daughter is developing her own sense of identity. However, if most of your responses are *A,* you might want to look at the message your lack of involvement in your daughter's life sends. If your responses are predominantly *B*s, your home may have

---

9. When my daughter wants to get a body part pierced,

10. When my daughter no longer wants to be involved in family devotions or other religious activities,

11. When my daughter goes to a party and tells me alcohol or drugs were there,

12. When my daughter's room is a mess,

13. When my daughter asks to take diet pills,

14. When my daughter asks to go to a movie that is somewhat objectionable to me,

15. When my daughter asks to stay home from school,

16. When my daughter skips dinner,

17. When my daughter is moody and depressed,

18. When my daughter says she hates herself and doesn't do anything right,

19. When my daughter wants to try something that I don't think she'll be very good at,

---

A. I let it go.

B. I make the decision for her.

C. I discuss it with her but give her the final choice.

D. I encourage her.

E. I let her know how disappointed I am.

F. I tell her she's being ridiculous.

G. I discipline her (loss of privileges, extra chores, etc.).

a climate of rigidity and intrusiveness that can be harmful to a girl who is vulnerable to an eating disorder. Likewise, if most of your responses are *E*, *F*, and *G*, your daughter may feel that your home is permeated with criticism and disapproval, especially if she has a sensitive personality.

If you answer *A, B, E, F,* or *G* to any of the statements, I encourage you to discuss that scenario with your daughter, ask her what she would like your answer to be, and ask her how your answer makes her feel. If most of your answers are *C*s and *D*s, I still encourage you to go over each of these statements with your daughter, asking her how *she* thinks you usually respond in such a situation and what she'd like your answer to be.

I was surprised when I did this last exercise with my daughter and discovered that she had experienced responses from me that were not consistent with my answers. Her perceptions informed me of some negative messages I was sending her, completely unknowingly. For example, when she is moody and depressed, my answer was that I would let it go. She said she perceived in my nonresponse that I was disappointed in her. She told me she would really like it if I said something like, "I know you're in a bad mood right now, and that's okay. Let me know if there's anything I can do."

Almost every month a new girl walks into my counseling office who has lost sight of everything else in life except controlling her weight. An amazing volleyball player is obsessed with her thighs, and she can't play volleyball anymore because she's lost too much weight. A gifted creative writer hates her hips so much that withholding food from herself seems like the only possible solution. The lack of nutrients she's getting as a result makes concentrating on writing impossible. A talented musician can only think of her fat calves and how she's not good enough in any way. The depression that comes from her resulting eating disorder has made her apathetic about music.

Meeting these casualties has made prevention my passion. Aware, watchful, diligent, determined, and proactive mothers can join hands with their daughters to prevent and overcome this deadly disorder. Together we can win a lifesaving and life-giving victory. Take it from sixteen-year-old Lauren, who has this to say about her mother, Susan: "Our relationship has saved me from anorexia. We have demonstrated pure commitment to each other. Our relationship is held together by honesty and complete trust. I am never going to find another who loves me as much as my mother."

Chapter 10

Bulimia

Bulimia is the epidemic of our time.
Eight to 20 percent of all high school girls are bulimic.
Psychologists are estimating the incidence rate for bulimia
among college-aged women
to be as high as one in every four or five.[1]

MARY PIPHER, *Hunger Pains*

If the word *anorexia* provokes fear within us, the word *bulimia* provokes an unsettled disgust. How, we wonder, could our beautiful, sweet-smelling, innocent little girl even consider sticking a finger down her throat to cause herself to vomit, or ingesting laxatives to produce chronic diarrhea?

The word *bulimia* literally means "ox hunger" and identifies girls who become caught in a vicious obsession. They are obsessed with not gaining weight, but at the same time obsessed with food. Once the behavior becomes entrenched, a girl who struggles with bulimia can't eat more than 400–500 calories without feeling guilty, but will binge on up to 12,000 calories only to purge herself by vomiting, using laxatives, or exercising excessively.

As in the previous chapter, we will not be able to conduct an exhaustive examination of bulimia in this book, but we will look at the continuum of bulimia with suggestions for intervention and prevention. We will also consider the causes of this disorder. Bulimic behavior is a difficult habit to break. The treatment for bulimia is often long-term and complicated, sometimes taking six months to two years before a girl even begins to find freedom from this form of disordered eating. Once again, *early intervention* is the best way to prevent bulimia and help our daughters get out of the life-draining quicksand of this disorder before it pulls them under completely.

THE CONTINUUM OF BULIMIA

Bulimia is usually more difficult to detect than anorexia. A girl who struggles with bulimia often maintains a healthy weight. She doesn't look sick and fragile like a girl who struggles with anorexia. The progression of this disorder can be slow. A girl may experiment with some form of purging and go months before she tries the behavior again. There are, however, early warning signs that moms can view as invitations to become proactively involved in their daughters' lives. In fact, the often slow progression of this disorder, especially in younger girls, should give us a lot of hope that we can intervene to prevent bulimia from taking over.

There are two important factors that are foundational in responding to our daughters wherever they might be on the continuum of bulimia. First, we must give them the message that we see what is happening and, second, that our love and respect for them is not diminished. The unseemly nature of this disorder is a perfect setup for denial. It takes courage to open our eyes to the possibility that our daughters might be dabbling in or practicing the behaviors of binging and purging. Girls who struggle with bulimia carry a tremendous amount of shame and guilt about their behaviors. The need to keep their eating and purging rituals secret is overwhelming.

By now I'd discovered that sugar could make me sleepy,
dull the edge of any feeling, take away any pain—at least for a while.
I took myself off to the candy machine, put my hand on the lever,
pulled it again and again. The sweets dropped like tiny bombs
into my hands, doing their own secret damage.
I wept alone, in the company of peanut bars and chocolate chip cookies.
In public, I kept on smiling, kept on studying,
kept on making the honor roll.[2]

MARGARET BULLITT-JONES, *Holy Hunger*

Eating disorder specialist Nancy J. Kolodny underscores the importance of actively looking for bulimic behaviors early when she reports: "Although bulimia is more common among older teenagers than younger ones, it is increasingly becoming a behavior 'tried on for size' by preteens and junior-high schoolers, especially those who have high-school or college-age siblings, relatives, friends, or acquaintances with whom they interact."[3]

The power of not only seeing but offering love and respect in response to bulimic behaviors is eloquently explained by a woman who struggled with bulimia for years: "All that I was giving myself was food, when what I really hungered for was embodied love. It wasn't doughnuts or brownies or cheese that I needed. It was companionship, the *compassionate attention* that could help me explore my feelings, give voice to my anger, release my tears" (emphasis mine).[4]

THE BEGINNING OF THE CONTINUUM

The seeds for bulimia are often planted in the decision to go on a diet. As we've discussed before, when a girl decides to skip a meal, fast for a day, or use diet pills, she inadvertently slows down her metabolism. When she goes off the diet, either because she can no longer stand the deprivation or because she's lost the desired weight, she will gain weight faster because of her slowed metabolism. This can be the beginning of yo-yo dieting, with which most American women are unfortunately familiar.

Any diet can be a first step in the direction of an eating disorder.[5]

MARY PIPHER, *Hunger Pains*

The beginning of bulimia is often a moment of desperation. After a failed diet and giving in to a forbidden food, a girl may gag herself to undo the damage. At first she finds purging difficult and disgusting and vows to never do it again. As her mother, you may never know of her early experimentation with purging. However, if you are paying close attention to her dieting behavior, you have an invitation to intervene to help prevent the seeds of this disorder from growing. This is a good time to evaluate yet again your own relationship with food and body image. A recent study of more than three thousand fifth graders through eighth graders by researchers at the Medical University of South Carolina in Charleston found that one of the most influential factors for girls who struggle with eating disorders is their mother's relationship with food and body image.[6]

Mothers often worry that talking about eating disorders might give their daughters the idea to engage in the behavior. It is true that eating disorders can be contagious and that peers often plant ideas for different behaviors in girls' minds. The suggestibility of adolescent girls requires that eating disorders be talked about most openly and thoroughly *between mother and daughter*, where all the facts are presented and mothers can outline for their daughters the certainty of their intervention if they observe any of these behaviors. Just as with anorexia, early on the continuum is the time to hang out the safety net of possible intervention.

Just for You

1. How comfortable do you feel with being vulnerable to others, including your daughter?
2. What have your past experiences been with personal disclosures?
3. How open was your own mother with you?
4. When you consider talking openly about your own eating and dieting choices, what is your greatest fear?
5. If your eating and dieting choices were displayed on a video screen for all to see, what would you feel?
6. Often, mothers begin to look honestly at their lives and make significant changes for the sake of their children. Is this true of you? If so, what kept you from feeling that these changes were justified for your own well-being?

Jessica's mom provides a good example of intervening early. When Jessica entered high school, she became conscious of her slightly larger size than some of the girls in her group. By midyear, her mother, Pam, observed that Jessica had been trying to diet, skipping meals, and making contemptuous comments about her body and size. Pam called me and said, "I have a feeling that Jessica may have gone into the bathroom and tried to throw up after dinner last night. I'm so afraid her concern about her weight is going to turn into an eating disorder. I just want to pick her up from school and take her away from all the pressures she is feeling right now."

I encouraged Pam to trust her intuition. Our intuition is a gift from God

Just for the Two of You

1. As you notice your daughter's attempts at dieting, vulnerably admit that you might have modeled this pattern to her. Registered dietitian Debra Waterhouse lists four behaviors that might send your daughter into an unhealthy relationship with her body and with food: (1) daily weighing with accompanying moaning and groaning; (2) mirror complaints as you look at your reflection; (3) bathing suit blues; and (4) body bashing. Waterhouse concludes: "A mother's own eating habits and weight concerns serve as modeling cues that a daughter internalizes as her own."[7]

2. When you see your daughter in the frustrating process of on-again, off-again dieting, now is the time to warn her about eating disorders. Explain that diets are not only ineffective, but they can open the door to destructive eating patterns. During adolescence it is likely that someone, usually a peer or older girl, will suggest to your daughter, "Throw up what you eat, and you won't have to worry about your weight." From age twelve, or even earlier, depending on your daughter's maturity and exposure to different eating behaviors, the truth about eating disorders should be talked about openly between the two of you.

3. In talking you will want to help your daughter understand the triggers for her behavior and support her in learning new behaviors. Following are a few questions that might help start the conversation. Model openness for your daughter by answering these questions yourself. As you are vulnerable about your own feelings, you will encourage your daughter to open up to you.
    *   Is being thin the most important thing to you?
    *   Do you think being thin makes your life better? How?
    *   What has been your experience with dieting?
    *   Is purging a form of weight control for you?
    *   What do you feel when the binge and purge is over?
    *   Is it hard for you to eat in front of others?
    *   Are you ever anxious that you won't get enough to eat?
    *   Do you feel different from everyone else? How?
    *   What are you most afraid of right now? most angry about?

that allows us to take our daughter's hand and lead or even pull her away from danger. Pam and I agreed that it's not possible to take our daughters out of this world and its unique pressures on adolescent girls, but I suggested that perhaps her inclination could guide her to action that was effective but a little less extreme.

Pam called me after that weekend to tell me what she'd done. She had picked up Jessica after school on Friday with their bags packed and announced she had planned a surprise getaway. Pam took her daughter to a mountain cabin that friends let them use for the weekend. The first night they went out to dinner and a movie in a nearby town. Saturday morning after breakfast Pam started a conversation: "I know that you've been trying so hard to fit in this year and that you've been worried about your weight. I've watched you try to lose a few pounds. I couldn't help but think of all the times that I've dieted and been frustrated. I don't know if you've ever felt desperate enough to try something like throwing up your food or using diet pills or laxatives. A lot of girls think that is the best way to lose weight. But once you start doing it, the obsession with eating and purging can take over your life."

Jessica was pretty quiet during this time, but her mom was well prepared. She'd brought a movie (see Resources section for suggestions) and asked Jessica to watch it with her. Once during the movie, Pam turned to Jessica and firmly said, "If I even thought you were binging and purging, I would get us both to a counselor who could help us."

After the movie, Jessica remained quiet. Her mom suggested, "Let's go into town and go shopping." They wandered through the shops, ate dinner, and had a lot of fun.

Sunday morning after breakfast Jessica said to her mom, "I have really wanted to lose weight. Will you help me?" Once again, Pam was well prepared. They agreed together to support each other in healthy food choices and to sign up for a Jazzercise class. They left their mountain retreat joined hand in hand against an encroaching eating disorder.

Jessica will no doubt continue to struggle with body image and wanting to lose weight. But the possibility of bulimia is now out in the open and she knows her mother will be looking for signs of trouble. Jessica also feels loved and supported because of the manner in which her mom had declared war on this eating disorder.

THE MIDDLE OF THE CONTINUUM

When a girl begins to experiment with binging, she may notice that initially she loses a few pounds. She will not know that the weight loss is generally only water weight that is temporarily decreased after purging. Unfortunately, for some girls the discomfort with vomiting or use of laxatives is outweighed by the benefit of losing weight. A girl in the middle stages of the continuum of bulimia may purge once a week, every other day, or only at lunch (where she is less likely to be detected by her mom.) Sometimes, girls in the middle stages only use laxatives.

During this stage, your daughter will continue to look normal. But you may begin to notice that she picks at her food and seldom sits around the table talking with the family after a meal, because binging takes place in private. When your daughter does eat with the family, pay close attention. Notice if she makes a trip to the bathroom immediately after a meal. Often a girl will turn on the shower or run water in the sink to cover up the sounds of her purging. You may notice that your once exuberant or lighthearted daughter is becoming more withdrawn and serious. Once bulimia gets its hooks into a girl, the obsession with eating and weight control slowly drains the joy and pleasure in life.

If your daughter is caught in the middle of the continuum of bulimia, it's very likely that she is suffering from depression. Based on recent research, experts believe that bulimia results when low serotonin levels (the brain chemical that results in a sense of well-being) trigger episodes of binge eating, especially of carbohydrates. The binges lead to a flurry of serotonin production within the brain, which reduces—at least temporarily—the feelings of stress and tension. The relief is short-lived, however, and is usually followed by feelings of guilt or low self-esteem, which trigger a desire to purge. These studies conclude that, "Low serotonin levels appear to be responsible for some of the personality traits commonly seen among people with bulimia—depression, impulsiveness, irritability, and emotional volatility."[8]

When getting a medical evaluation for your daughter during this stage, talk to your healthcare provider about treating depression. Depression can be treated in adolescents with antidepressants. There is also encouraging news that alternative healthcare providers are finding success in treating depression and eating disorders. Unfortunately, many conventional physicians are sometimes ignorant about the connection between eating disorders and depression. Bring your own research or find a physician who is knowledge-able about eating disorders.

Just for the Two of You

1. Now is the time to act upon the intervention you outlined in the early stages of this continuum. Intervention should include a medical consultation, an evaluation of the eating behaviors and climate of the entire family, and therapy for both you and your daughter with some-one who understands eating disorders.

2. Talk frankly about your daughter's anxiety. As you confront her behaviors she will be terrified that she is going to become grossly over-weight. Reinforce that you want to support her in liking her body. Remind her, with evidence (see Resources section), that purging does not result in permanent weight loss.

3. Binging and purging become central in the life of a girl who struggles with bulimia. The act of eating and purging becomes a way of dealing with tension. Explain to your daughter that you know she has a lot of stress in her life and that you want to help her find healthy ways to relieve that tension. Practice relaxation techniques or take a yoga class together. Learn about the benefits of a regular practice of deep breath-ing to reduce stress.

4. Contract together to eat three meals a day and three small snacks. Give your daughter a sense of control by allowing her to come up with a daily eating plan.

5. Throw away bathroom scales.

6. Support one another in not eating while you are watching television. The most vulnerable time for binging, according to the Academy of Pediatrics, is during television viewing.[9]

7. Agree with your daughter that you will each keep a journal on your eating. Your own vulnerability will help her trust you and confide in you. Pick out fun journals together. Record what you eat, what's going on during the time you're eating, and what you're feeling during these times. Look for patterns in your eating, and practice making a

distinction between eating when hungry and eating in response to other feelings. Make a list together of alternative responses to emotional tension.

8. Now is the time to encourage your daughter to take a class in some-thing she's been interested in, start a sport, or begin a hobby. Bulimics lose the ability to enjoy anything except binging. This is a crucial time to coach your daughter in having fun. Ask her, "If you could learn anything, do anything, be involved in any activity, what would it be?" And then do all you can to support her in this new endeavor. You may need to go with her initially or encourage her to bring a friend along.

THE END OF THE CONTINUUM

When your daughter reaches the end of the continuum of bulimia, she will begin to look ill. She will look drained from binging and purging. You will see a marked decrease in her energy. She may experience signs of dehydration, such as dry mouth, sunken eyeballs, dry, doughy skin that has lots its elasticity, extreme fatigue, dizziness and/or nausea, or little or no urine for eight to twelve hours. Many girls in this stage binge on such large quantities of food that it is impossible not to notice the ravenous progression of the disorder. You will notice that large amounts of food are disappearing and that money, which your daughter has used to buy additional food, may be missing. You may notice scars on the back of your daughter's finger from scraping it on her teeth when she induces vomiting. Her eyes will be bloodshot, and her face may look bloated. Her dentist may comment on eroding enamel or dental deterioration. Your daughter will gradually exclude friends and family and appear constantly agitated.

Every adolescent girl I have worked with in this stage has been caught in her bulimic behavior by friends and/or family. The bathroom reeks of vomit, and the toilet contains telltale signs of her behavior. You may find that she is hoarding food under her bed or in her closet. Her friends at school may report the behavior to their mothers or a school counselor, who then calls you.

At this stage of the disorder the behavior is so out of control that it is vir-tually impossible not to leave evidence. But I also believe that girls in this stage subconsciously *want* to get caught. Binging is no longer pleasurable. The binge-purge cycle has become the dominant force in your daughter's life. She feels guilty, depressed, and out of control. She also feels angry, nervous, disgusted with herself, afraid, and alone.

Although it is devastating to observe your daughter in this stage of the disorder, your insight, love, and respect will be what helps pull her to safety.

JUST FOR THE TWO OF YOU

1. At this stage medical intervention is essential. Your daughter may require hospitalization or in-patient treatment. Girls in this stage of bulimia often have electrolytes that are so out of balance they need intravenous treatment. Your daughter will also need treatment by a counselor who is well educated about this disorder. Assure your daughter that you will be with her every step of the way.

2. Lock all cupboards and your refrigerator. Explain to your daughter that this is not punishment but rather the opportunity for her to face her struggle and respond to it in a different manner. (We'll discuss this more fully as we look at the causes of bulimia.) She should not work in a place that serves or sells food during this time.

3. Eat together as often as possible. Encourage your daughter as she eats a healthy portion or eats a bad food. Let her talk about her anxiety. Support her through her courageous efforts to combat this formidable foe.

4. Never respond to your daughter's behaviors or feelings with shock or disgust.

THE CAUSES OF BULIMIA

Just as with anorexia, the causes of bulimia are complex. There are, however, some commonalties among the girls who struggle with bulimia and the families of those girls. Because I have experienced this eating disorder personally, I can speak with certainty that if your daughter is bulimic, she believes that she is gross, disgusting, and unlike anyone else. She believes that no one could know about her behavior and still love and respect her.

One of my favorite stories in the Bible is of Jesus and the woman at the well in John 4. Jesus met a woman who was at the town well during the noon hour. She was alone. It was customary for the townswomen to get water from the well together in the cool of the day. This woman's arrival at the well in the heat of the day, all by herself, suggests that she was an outcast from her peer group.

The humility of Jesus is evident as he asked this woman to give him a drink. She replied in surprise, " 'You are a Jew and I am a Samaritan woman. How can you ask me for a drink?' (For Jews do not associate with Samaritans.)" (John 4:9). Jesus immediately identified her loneliness, shame, and thirst for much more than a drink of water. He answered, "Everyone who drinks this water will be thirsty again, but whoever drinks the water I give him will never thirst. Indeed, the water I give him will become in him a spring of water welling up to eternal life" (John 4:13-14).

Jesus and the woman continued to talk as she expressed doubt that this "living water" that comes from a relationship with the Messiah could be for her because of her past shameful behavior. She confessed that she'd been married and rejected by five husbands and was now living with a sixth man (a scandalous act for that day). She expected to be rejected by the Messiah as well.

With a kindness and strength that must have been desperately absorbed by this thirsty woman, Jesus declared that her behavior did not in any way negate his offering to her. She dropped her empty water jug and ran to the town, shouting, without shame, "Come, see a man who told me everything I ever did. Could this be the Christ?" (John 4:29).

This wondrous story of redemption underscores a guiding truth for walking hand in hand with our daughters on the path of recovery from unsettling, shameful behavior. Did Jesus tell the Samaritan woman *everything* she'd ever done? It certainly is not recorded in the text. But in pinpointing her thirst, he told her the *reason* for everything she'd done. He knew she'd gone from man to man to soothe the pain of rejection and satisfy her thirst for lasting relationship.

Likewise, as we examine the roots of bulimia we can give a wondrous gift of redemption to our daughters as we help them understand the reasons for what they have done—reasons that are rooted in their unique personalities and experiences as well as the dynamics of the family. In helping them uncover the reasons for their eating disorder, we hand them back self-respect and give them hope for recovery and redemption.

GIRLS WHO STRUGGLE WITH BULIMIA

These girls are often people-pleasers. They don't want to disappoint others, and they try hard to meet the expectations of people they like and respect. Although they may overtly condemn a culture that ascribes value based on thinness and appearance, internally they want very much to live up to these ideals. Because these girls are so conscious of others' opinions, someone's casual remarks about their weight or appearance can trigger an eating disorder. A coach's demand, the cultural ideals of thinness, or a parent's preoccupation with weight, body size, and eating will have an impact on them.

Like girls who are vulnerable to anorexia, girls who mature early and feel bigger than other girls their age may be vulnerable to bulimia. Girls at risk also tend to have a hyperawareness of others that keeps them from focusing on their own internal world. They often sense when others are in pain or turmoil and feel responsible to help. Not knowing what to do with disappointment, sadness, or fear, they learn to numb these feelings with food. One woman explains, "Growing up, I had no clue about how to express my anger, or how to listen without panic to the anger of someone else."[10]

How much I wished this food would fill the hole in my heart.[11]

MARGARET BULLITT-JONES, *Holy Hunger*

An adolescent girl is not automatically equipped to resolve all the tensions she feels and soothe herself in wise ways. Food is an available, legal, predictable comforter. But because this girl wants to be liked, and that means meeting cultural ideals, she cannot allow herself to gain weight. She is vulnerable to the trap of bulimia.

Dr. Kathryn J. Zerbe writes powerfully about the predictability of bulimia when a girl with this personality type is left on her own to deal with the tensions of life: "The young bulimic-to-be searches (often in vain) for a protective, available, ready response from her mother. She looks for ways to self-soothe her inner state of restlessness, loneliness, and angst. When her mom doesn't fill the gap, the child will turn to food. Food symbolizes the mother by feeding the child, and has the power to soothe."[12]

FAMILIES OF BULIMIC GIRLS

The preceding quotation is a good segue into the family dynamics that foster an environment that might make a girl more vulnerable to bulimia. As we discussed in the previous chapter, understanding family dynamics is not about assigning blame; it is about accepting responsibility for what you can change to help your daughter overcome or prevent bulimia.

A comprehensive 1991 study best summarizes the differences in family dynamics in homes where girls struggle with anorexia compared with homes where girls struggle with bulimia. The study concludes, "In a sense the fundamental difference between the restricting [anorexic] and bulimic mode could be thought of as the [bulimic patient's] search for something to take in, compared to the [anorexic patient's] attempt to keep something out."[13]

For girls who are vulnerable, bulimia will be triggered in families where there is tension at mealtime, family dieting, parental discord, parents who are depressed or have substance abuse problems, or parents who are obese. An at-risk girl will most likely internalize all the emotions of her family, resulting in persistent anxiety. She will not be able to say, "I am anxious because my mom is depressed." That goes against her need to please others. Studies suggest that girls who struggle with bulimia often experience their mothers as unavailable psychologically, if not physically. The mother may be depressed or preoccupied with her own life. Many of the girls I see in treatment for bulimia talk about their loneliness and longing for something different from what their mothers offer.

I wish I knew a girl or woman like me.
Well, maybe not exactly like me,
but someone who "gets" what it's like to worry
about all the things I worry about.

AMY, age 14

Following are five questions that will help you define your daughter's vulnerabilities to bulimia, with suggestions for how you might help her understand the reason for her vulnerability. Each question also gives you an opportunity to examine your involvement in your daughter's life and to think through how you might be more present and supportive. As you think about your daughter's unique personality, you will probably come up with your own additional questions.

1. Do other people's moods affect your daughter?

Tell your daughter a story from early childhood about her sensitivity to others. As you explain that her empathy is a wonderful gift, you can also tell her that it has probably resulted in her feeling responsible for other people's happiness and that the feeling of responsibility produces an awful tension that she quite naturally has wanted to find some relief from.

My own daughter recently became distressed because her decision to go to the mall with a friend resulted in another friend expressing jealousy and hurt. Kristin concluded, "I just won't go at all. I can't stand for everybody to be mad at me." I assured her that her acceptance of her friend's invitation to the mall was not a bad thing and that she'd done nothing wrong. We talked about the insecurity and jealousy among girls her age and that she couldn't make them go away. She admitted that *everyone* wasn't mad at her and that she could invite her hurt friend to do something later. If that didn't satisfy the friend, then I suggested that her friend was choosing to be petty. I reassured Kristin that she is not responsible for others' bad behavior and that she can't take on the weight of trying to make everyone happy.

If you have not had the opportunity to ease the burden that your sensitive daughter carries around as she feels responsible for everyone's pain, let her know that you haven't helped her as you should and that you want to talk through those things with her from now on.

2. Is change hard for your daughter?

Once again you might think back to her early childhood. How did she do with a new baby-sitter or when you introduced new food? As you share these stories with your daughter, you can validate that adolescence is a time of incredible change and that she must be feeling a lot of internal pressure to handle all the changes well. If her life has been complicated by other changes, like a divorce in your family, illness among family members, or a sibling going off to college, then her turmoil has only been intensified. Explain that food and her rituals of binging and purging probably provide a sense of safety and predictability in the midst of her chaotic world. Ask if there are any changes going on that she's uncomfortable with, mad about, or grieving over.

If you've been unavailable during these changes and assumed that she was managing well, apologize for your oversight and talk about ways you can make things more stable in her life.

3. Does your daughter try hard to avoid making mistakes or forgetting things?

Take note of your daughter's striving to make good grades, practice her musical instrument or sport, and maintain a social life. Ask her if she feels pressure to do everything right so that no one gets mad at her. Ask how she feels when she does make a mistake. How do her friends or family members respond? Ask if her purging behavior has been an attempt to not feel unacceptable to others. Explain that living with the pressure of being perfect will make her feel and act crazy. Perhaps you can talk from your own experience.

Discuss cultural ideals and why it makes sense that your daughter would go to drastic lengths to keep from getting fat. As you reflect on your response to this facet of your daughter's personality, consider how diligent you have been in praising your daughter in unconditional ways. I was quite convicted when my daughter told me that she thought I was disappointed in her because she wasn't getting straight A's. When I asked how she had come to such a conclusion, she explained that I seemed to take it for granted that she did her homework on her own and kept up in school. She further complained that it seemed to her that because her work wasn't perfect, it wasn't worthy of comment from me.

4. Are friends (both girls and boys) important to your daughter?

Experts warn that the onset of an eating disorder can be triggered by rejection from a good friend during adolescence. The friendships of adolescents are complicated and almost always in flux. How aware are you of who is important to your daughter and how they are treating her? How much time does she spend daydreaming about a boyfriend? Is your tendency to dismiss this as teenage foolishness?

When I was in high school, a boy whom I had really liked told me that he had never liked me and never would and that I should get over it. When I sobbed about my breaking heart to my mom, she casually responded, "Oh, Sharon, you'll have lots of boyfriends, and there are lots of fish in the sea." She was right, of course, but her answer did nothing to soothe my very real pain.

When a girl is rejected by a friend—boy or girl—she needs help in making sense of it and finding comfort. If she doesn't, she will assume something about her provoked the rejection. And more often than not, girls assume that their appearance is the culprit. When her pain is dismissed or mocked, she will search for comfort elsewhere.

You can explain to your daughter that rejection is overwhelmingly confusing and that rejection might compel her to seek comfort in food, causing her to obsess about perceived faults in her physical appearance. Apologize if you've taken her social struggles with a grain of salt and not offered understanding and comfort. Ask if she is experiencing any troubling relationships currently.

5. Does your daughter have a hard time asking for help?

Every mother of an adolescent daughter has experienced a time when she has offered advice to her child only to be met with the contemptuous response, "Mom, I know. I can take care of this myself." But some girls consistently resist any help and support from others. Think back on your daughter's life— as she learned to ride a bike, complete homework assignments, or navigate the complexities of her first week of high school. Did she do these things alone, without any help or support? Girls who struggle with bulimia believe they can rely only on themselves. Bulimia is a way of saying, "I can eat whatever I want and control the outcome." It is a combination of behaviors that reinforce complete self-reliance. A girl who struggles with bulimia believes that no one can help her and still like her. So she is left to herself.

You can help your daughter understand that in her self-sufficiency she has become quite competent but has cut herself off from what she wants most—the compassionate attention of others. How have you contributed to her self-sufficiency? Have you been unavailable, or have you pushed her away when she expressed a desire for help? You might need to ask your daughter this question. When a girl is sensitive to rejection, *one* experience of being rebuffed when asking for help can foster a determination to never ask again.

Explain to your daughter that she is up against something she can't fight alone and that you *want* to be in the fight with her. You might have to prove this to her if this has not been the nature of your relationship. Even if she pushes you away, keep coming back.

Your daughter's struggle with bulimia can be the opportunity for you to develop a wonderful relationship with her, one in which there are mutually affirming bonds that continue growing. As you understand your daughter and her eating disorder and are transparent about your own life, you can have a relationship based on mutual respect and a deep understanding of each other's personal struggles. You can give your daughter permission to make mistakes as you acknowledge your own imperfections and offer her unconditional love and respect. The fierce presence of your mother heart for your daughter has the power to soothe and tame the wild hunger of her heart.

Chapter 11

Compulsive Overeating

I never felt like I fit in anywhere.
So I filled my loneliness with food—candy, to be specific.
When puberty set in, I started gaining weight by the week.
I went from a training bra to a 32D in one summer,
and cookies filled out the rest of me....
I felt like a giant, shapeless, androgynous balloon.[1]

TAMMY LYNN MICHAELS, star of the television show *Popular*

I was recently reminded of the sometimes cruel and unusual rites of passage in adolescence. My daughter's high school gym was filled with the sixty-five girls who'd tried out for cheerleader, Kristin and two of her closest friends among them. As friends and family looked on, the cheerleading coach announced that letters to each of the girls were on a table in the middle of the gym and that the girls could come and get their letter to learn the results. As girls ripped open their letters, some jumped up and down and shouted for joy, while others cried in disappointment or quietly slipped out of the gym.

Sixty-five girls. Each of them unique in her size, personality, and ability. Kristin didn't make the squad, nor did her two friends. But all of them faced the disappointment with grace and good sportsmanship.

Some of the girls who tried out for cheerleader are overweight. As I waited for Kristin to gather her things so we could leave, I stood by a group of students discussing the results of the tryouts. As the kids looked in the direction of one of the overweight "losers," one girl remarked, "I'm so glad the fat girl didn't make it. Her big butt would be an embarrassment to our entire school!"

This teenager's cruel remarks reflect a culture that does not have much tolerance for size differences. High school girls have told me that if a girl wears larger than a size ten, she will be considered fat. The average American woman wears a size twelve. That means that if most of us dared to walk down the hallways of high school today, we would be subject to disdain at best and taunts of "oink, oink" at worst. If a girl is truly overweight, the cruelty and rejection are often debilitating. The Children's Medical Center of Dallas reports that overweight children are not only prone to rejection by their peers, but to low self-esteem, depression, and health consequences.[2]

We are afraid of fat—for ourselves and our daughters—and for good reason. Statisticians report that overweight females are 40 percent less likely to go to college, 20 percent less likely to marry, apt to make less money per year, and even more likely to be found guilty by a jury![3] Even with all of the cruelty and prejudice that those who are overweight suffer, statistics startlingly suggest that one in four American children are overweight, and studies confirm that obese adolescents are at a high risk to be obese adults.[4]

As with the eating disorders of anorexia and bulimia, compulsive overeating and the obesity that often results have serious consequences that will not only impact your daughter's health but also her quality of life. Hand-in-hand mothering approaches the awkward and sensitive issues of overeating and obesity from the perspective that this is a *mother-daughter* problem.

Even if you have never struggled with your weight, your daughter's struggle must be approached with a "we're in this together" attitude. You can walk hand in hand with your daughter as you take responsibility for your part in encouraging, allowing, or overlooking her unhealthy eating and exercise habits. The fact that you don't have the same problem does not have to keep you from being in the same process. Let your daughter know that you join her in healthy eating choices and increased activity because you have a responsibility for her, you love her, and you're committed to being with her every step of the way. As you explain that you long for good health and self-esteem for your daughter, express even more passionately your longing for the changes that may be necessary to cement your relationship and draw you closer together.

This chapter will help you understand overeating and obesity and encourage you to work *with* your daughter to change eating patterns, engage in physical activity, and accept biological realities. If you set your daughter apart and single her out for treatment because of her weight problem, then you are only reinforcing the culture's cruel alienation. But if you become your daughter's ally in healthy patterns of living and self-acceptance, you will strengthen your relationship with your daughter and forge a solid foundation for her future.

UNDERSTANDING OVEREATING AND OBESITY

Recently, after I spoke to a group of middle school girls and their mothers about body image and eating disorders, a mother asked to talk to me.

"I wish my daughter was more concerned with body image," she confided. "She doesn't seem to care how she looks. She doesn't pay attention to what she eats, and I think she eats far more than she should, although I'm not exactly sure what she's eating."

I asked this concerned mother how she knew her daughter didn't care about body image and how she had determined that she was an overeater. Her answer reveals the confusion and paralysis that mothers often feel when their daughters struggle with a weight problem.

"I know she doesn't care about her body and she eats too much because she's overweight. She probably weighs thirty to forty-five pounds more than the other girls in her class. But she just won't talk about it with me. I've suggested diets and exercise classes, but she doesn't care!"

[Overweight girls] have experienced fat jokes, stares, and ridicule.
They have learned to feel anxious and defensive about their bodies.[5]

MARY PIPHER, *Hunger Pains*

This mother's assumption about her daughter's apathy, her fears about her daughter's weight, her uncertainty about her daughter's eating habits, and her frustration with her daughter's response or lack of response to her suggestions, are all too common between mothers and daughters who struggle with overeating and weight gain. Let's begin with a few facts about overeating and obesity that might begin to shed some light on this complex subject.

- The U.S. Surgeon General reports that the causes of obesity in children are genetic factors, lack of physical exercise, and unhealthy eating patterns.[6]
- According to Dr. Reginald Washington of the American Academy of Pediatricians, a girl is obese when she is 20 percent over her ideal weight.[7]
- Dr. Washington suggests that a child needs medical intervention if she is 40 percent over her ideal weight.[8]
- Don't rely only on a height and weight chart to determine your child's ideal weight. A physician will need to evaluate your child to determine a healthy weight by consulting your daughter's growth history as well as by measuring her body fat (a physician will use calipers to gently pinch the flesh on the trunk and the back of the upper arm). For example, if a girl's weight for her height is above the 95 percentile but her fat measurement is normal, then she will be considered to have a large frame but not too much fat.
- Disordered overeating is not the occasional indulgence in a calorie-laden food or a big meal. Compulsive overeating is eating with the feeling that you can't stop eating. A girl who struggles with compulsive overeating loses the ability to regulate herself with concerns about her appearance or her mother's or peers' concerns. She eats without thinking. She's often not aware of how much she's eating or even what she is eating.
- If your daughter is overweight, you can be certain that she knows better than anyone else that she has a weight problem, but she is afraid that acknowledging her problem will mean that she will be forced to stop eating the way she wants to.

Defining compulsive overeating and obesity only highlights the seriousness of this eating disorder. As we did with anorexia and bulimia, we will examine choices, preventive patterns of living, and intervention strategies. Since experts agree that the three predominant causes of obesity in children and adolescents are unhealthy eating habits, lack of physical activity, and genetic vulnerabilities, we will explore how you can walk hand in hand with your daughter in each of these areas.

Changing Eating Habits

Rather than examining the proportion and types of food you and your daughter eat, it will be most helpful to discover what kind of an eater you are. There are two kinds of eaters—those who eat according to external controls and those who eat in response to internal cues. The earlier and more consistently we can learn to eat when prompted by instinctive internal cues, the healthier our eating choices will be.

Girls and women who rely on internal cues eat when they are hungry and stop when they are satisfied. Those who rely on external controls rely on cues prompted by advertising, peers, dieting gurus, emotional tension, or even the

Just for the Two of You

1. When you and/or your daughter reach for a snack, ask:
    - Did something on television just remind me of food?
    - Am I bored?
    - Am I really thirsty instead of hungry?
    - Am I avoiding doing homework or laundry?
    - Am I stressed out about something?

    As I look back on my early parenting, I realize it's easier to give our children a snack than our time and attention. But helping your daughter to pay attention to her hunger and subsequent eating choices is a great gift. The more openly you discuss your own hunger and what mimics hunger for you, the more receptive she will be to reevaluate her own eating.

2. Make a list together of all of the possible emotions you could feel. When you and/or your daughter go in search of a snack when you're not really hungry, look at the list of emotions and identify what you're feeling. Talk about an alternative response to the emotion besides eating—like calling a friend, taking a walk, or having a good cry.

3. When you eat together, practice eating slowly, enjoying every bite. Ask one another: "Are you still hungry?" Learn to detect when you are full, and honor that internal cue.

smells from the food court in the mall. Of course, we're all influenced by the smells of food or pictures of advertisements to some extent. But when our eating choices are controlled entirely by external cues, we are set up for eating problems.

Other factors influence externally controlled eaters besides advertisements and food availability. Eating produces a natural sedation. Digestion activates the parasympathetic nerve system. This is the branch of the nervous systems that returns the body to normal after a stressful occurrence. When we discover that food has a sedative quality, stress may become an external cue that prompts eating. Eating can be used to medicate failure, loneliness, anxiety, or boredom. Using food to avoid or numb negative feelings can trap us in a vicious cycle. An overweight girl is more likely to be isolated and feel

4. Stock your cupboards with a variety of wholesome foods. Be sure to ask your daughter what she'd like you to have at home, and honor her requests.

5. Don't altogether forbid certain foods. Debra Waterhouse explains with startling clarity: "At every stage of development, restrictive feeding does not 'save' the daughter from an overweight fate, it ensures it."[9]

6. Make good nutrition a part of your approach to food by:
    • buying and preparing lean meats;
    • providing a variety of low-fat snacks;
    • becoming fast-food savvy. For example, a regular order of French fries has ten grams of fat, while a super size has twenty-six grams! All fast-food restaurants will provide nutritional information about their food if you ask. Become an expert so that you can help steer your daughter toward the best choices.

7. Watch television with your daughter and notice the advertisements for high-fat, sugary foods. How often do you see commercials for vegetables? When your daughter seeks a snack during television viewing, ask her if she's motivated by commercials. Talk about alternative, healthy snacks.

8. Boredom is a common external cue that sends children to the refrigerator. Make a list together of different responses to boredom than eating.

rejected. She needs comfort and may find it readily available in food. She grows more isolated and may become even more overweight.

As mothers we reinforce externally guided eating when we attempt to restrict, regulate, and control our daughters' eating. Of course, there is a tension here. When our daughters are young, we need to provide for them and guide them toward good nutrition. As they approach adolescence, however,

Just for You

1. Unsolicited advice will probably backfire. Before you begin a dialogue with your daughter about eating, consider how you will approach it. If you have participated in or allowed unhealthy eating behaviors, apologize to your daughter and talk about the changes you want to implement for the health of your family. Be specific. For example, you might say, "I recently learned that one of the main culprits in weight gain is soda. I didn't know this could be so harmful to us all. I'm going to stop buying soda on a regular basis so that we don't always have it in the house. I think it would make more sense for us to treat ourselves to a soda occasionally rather than regularly consume those empty calories." Ask if she has any concerns or objections to the change. If she opposes the change, negotiate a compromise (like one soda a day or every other day), with your goal being to avoid a power struggle while moving toward healthier choices.

2. Never suggest that your daughter eat just to be polite or to be a member of the clean-plate club. Your goal is to model healthy eating choices for your daughter and encourage her to pay attention to her own hunger and preferences so she can disregard the manipulation of others.

3. If you are significantly overweight, it is easier to deny your daughter's problem. For her sake, as well as your own, it's time to gently and firmly bring the truth into the light. You can tell your daughter that you have learned that being overweight can cause serious medical problems, like high blood pressure, diabetes, and heart disease. Courageously disclose your own struggles with self-esteem and other limitations you have experienced from being overweight. Explain that

we need to let go and cheer them on as they learn to guide themselves. Enforcing stricter eating rules, forbidding sugar or restricting fat intake, and trying to control your daughter's eating habits as she grows into adolescence will almost surely backfire, bringing about disordered eating or obesity.

Registered dietitian Debra Waterhouse cites countless studies that conclude that control is counterproductive. "A controlling parenting style hinders

you are going to change your eating patterns. Your modeling of a commitment to healthy eating patterns will be the best encouragement for your daughter.

4. Changes in diet are easier to take and maintain if they are made gradually. Try one or two changes a week:
    - Gradually eliminate all foods with empty calories (such as candy and soda, etc.) from your cupboards.
    - Gradually switch to low-fat foods.
    - Begin to limit fast foods.
    - Enjoy meals in the kitchen or dining room, with the television off.
    - Buy frozen fruit bars and sugarless pudding and Jell-O.
    - Keep pretzels and popcorn on hand for snacks.

5. Find a doctor who specializes in overweight children or adolescents. You will want a doctor who understands height and weight charts for children and adolescents and who factors in growth spurts. Interview the doctor to assess his or her compassion and understanding of overweight children. Before you make an appointment for your daughter, explain to the doctor your concerns for your daughter and enlist his or her help in encouraging your daughter to understand the seriousness of her weight problem and to make changes in her eating behaviors.

6. If you live in a city with a university-based medical center, look into their weight-control programs. The best programs provide a registered dietitian, an exercise consultant, a pediatrician, and a psychiatrist. Well-rounded programs provide a medical evaluation, involve the whole family, and focus on specific age groups.

the child's ability to develop internal self-control."[10] She further suggests that if *you* are a disordered eater, you are more likely to try to control your daughter's eating, and your daughter is more likely to become a disordered eater. Encouraging your daughter to be an instinctive eater (prompted by internal cues) will have lifelong rewards and can prevent your daughter from being trapped in compulsive overeating.

Early encouragement in eating according to internal cues is the key to preventing compulsive eating and the obesity that often results. If you suspect your daughter is vulnerable to overeating (maybe because you are aware of your own vulnerability) or is beginning to rely on food as a companion and comfort, now is the time to intervene.

A mother and daughter came to see me for counseling because the mom had discovered that her daughter was sneaking food into her bedroom. She was shocked to discover half-eaten apples and empty boxes of cereal under the bed. As we talked, we learned that the daughter (age eleven) liked the independence of feeding herself when she was hungry. Her well-meaning mother was in the habit of fixing all her daughter's snacks. The daughter also said that she felt more freedom to quit eating when she wasn't hungry if her mother wasn't watching over her eating.

Both mother and daughter were relieved to learn that this troubling behavior actually reflected some healthy attitudes toward food. But we all agreed that the sneaking of food needed to stop. The mom came up with a great solution when she suggested they buy a small refrigerator for her daughter to keep in her room. That way, she could keep her own healthy snacks on hand. I couldn't help but think, *What a cool mom!* And, *Maybe I should put a refrigerator in my bedroom!* I know the daughter left counseling thinking that her mom believed in her, which in turn bolstered her own self-confidence.

If your daughter is further along the continuum of overeating than an occasional overindulgence, the best goal is still to guide your daughter to becoming an instinctive eater. But, as noted, compulsive eating is accompanied by a lack of awareness about internal cues. Your daughter may resist your suggestions to change or refuse to talk about the problem at all. This chapter contains suggestions and ideas to foster self-awareness and to help you form an alliance with your daughter to change unhealthy eating patterns.

Keep in mind that if your daughter is not ready to change, then forcing her into a weight-management program will be a waste of time and may do more harm than good. Her failure in the program will further erode her self-esteem and increase her resistance to help in the future.

One wise mom I know responded to her reluctant daughter by telling her that she would not force her to enter the program, but that *she* was going to enter the program anyway. She also told her daughter that she would no longer be allowed to ignore the weight problem and that they would begin to talk to a counselor together and separately to try to understand her overeating and her reluctance to seek help. She promised her daughter that she could have the final say in the counselor they chose. They interviewed four counselors before her daughter found someone she liked and was willing to talk to.

The mom continued in the weight-loss program and occasionally shared with her daughter what she was learning and the changes she was implementing. Her daughter couldn't help but respect her mother's persistence, and she became increasingly curious about the program and its possible results. Through counseling she gradually began to talk about the pain of being overweight and her numbing of that pain through continued overeating. Gradually she became willing to make changes, and she eventually entered the weight-loss program.

At the suggestion of a friend, I went into therapy.
The more secrets I forced into the light of day,
the less I felt a need to shove food in my mouth.[11]

TAMMY LYNN MICHAELS, star of the television show *Popular*

INCREASING PHYSICAL ACTIVITY

A healthy body image isn't about changing your body. And it's not about changing your daughter's body either. *Body image is improved as we accept and take care of the body we already have.* To help our daughters boost their metabolism (which can certainly become sluggish from habitual overeating) and promote healthy weight loss, we have to model and encourage physical activity as part of healthy self-care.

The earlier you model physical activity as a part of your life, the more likely it will continue to be a part of your daughter's life as she gets older. A Boston University study reports that a mother's level of physical activity affects her children's approach to physical activity. If a mother exercises, her children are *twice* as likely to exercise![12]

If you have allowed and/or participated in a sedentary lifestyle, you will need to apologize to your daughter and explain your desire for healthy change. It's never too late to model a healthy lifestyle! You can encourage your daughter in the following ways:

- Model physical activity by your example. If you haven't been physically active, let your daughter see your commitment to making this change.
- Remind her that she doesn't have to exercise every day. Begin gradually by choosing an activity once a week. Work up to doing some type of exercise three to four times a week.

Just for the Two of You

1. Regulate television viewing. According to William H. Dietz, M.D., "Children use up more energy doing almost anything besides watching TV."[13] Researchers have discovered that television viewing reduces the metabolic rate in adolescent girls by 12-16 percent.[14] Agree to a rule that to earn an hour of television, you have to do some physical activity—take a walk, mow the lawn, go for a bike ride, wash the car.

2. Incorporate physical activity into your daily life. When you and your daughter are out together, park at the edge of the parking lot to give yourselves an opportunity for extra walking. Take the stairs instead of the elevator.

3. According to the U.S. Surgeon General, girls between the ages of six and eighteen experience a 36 percent decrease in activity.[15] Be aware of your daughter's changing interests and take the initiative to talk with her about new activities she might enjoy. Consider tennis lessons, trampolining, horseback riding, or in-line skating. Ask her what sounds like fun.

4. Agree that rewards will come in the form of activities, not food. Make a list together of possible treats—bowling, swimming, hiking, ice skating, etc.

- Let your daughter choose her own activity. One mother and daughter I know began to increase their activity by going on night walks. The daughter felt too awkward and embarrassed to do any other type of exercise. They bought flashlights and discovered their neighborhood in the dark.
- If your daughter refuses to increase her physical activity, insist that she begin to talk with a counselor to gain insight about her reluctance to make this healthy change.

ACCEPTING BIOLOGICAL REALITIES

We all know in our heads that human beings come in many shapes and sizes and that genes determine, in part, each person's size and shape. But accepting this truth in our hearts is not easy. Genetic vulnerability to weight gain is a reality for many. According to Mary Pipher, "A recent study by A. J. Stunkard involving more than five hundred adoptive children and both their biological and adoptive parents showed decisively that the genetic factor is all-important."[16]

If you and your daughter have faithfully worked at incorporating healthy eating habits and exercise into your lives and you still struggle with weight, how can you encourage your daughter? First, you have to deal with your own history of feeling like you don't belong in a superskinny society. When you hold on to the belief that you can or should change your basic body structure, you are passing these beliefs on to your daughter whether you articulate them or not. And these beliefs can lead to eating disorders. When we, as women, do not accept our own bodies, we create a climate for eating disorders to flourish in our daughters.

Understanding and accepting biology are essential in developing a healthy body image. But it's not easy. Admit it: You long for a magic pill or a program that will erase the struggle with weight—for yourself and especially for your daughter. That would be encouraging. But understanding our unique biology can encourage us to invite our daughters to a rich relationship with us as we form an alliance to make good eating choices, engage in enjoyable physical activity, and cultivate healthy self-acceptance—*together.*

JUST FOR YOU

1. Before you jump to the conclusion that your daughter is an overeater, examine if the root of this belief is only a *fear* that your daughter is fat. Where does this fear come from?

2. Do you struggle with your weight? Did you as a child? As you take another look at your own growth and development or chart the growth of women in your family, what is true about the bone structure, frame size, and shape of the women in your family?

3. Have others suggested that your daughter is fat? How did they reach this conclusion? What do they know about your daughter and family history?

4. If you and your daughter are part of a family that doesn't naturally fall into the acceptable measurements of our culture, *before* you look at overeating you will be encouraged by looking at a few basic biological realities.

   • Larger as well as smaller girls and women are metabolically and genetically different from one another, and no amount of starving or force-feeding is going to change that.[17] The advertisers for the dieting and exercise industries are committed to making us believe differently.

   • Going on a fad diet will make matters worse. Yo-yo dieting is largely responsible for the increase in obesity in our culture. Debra Waterhouse warns, "If you are overweight or have a long history of dieting and have a daughter who is overweight, if you encourage her to diet, you'll be jumpstarting the very condition you seek to prevent."[18]

   • If your family's biology predisposes you and your daughter to a larger size, then that does not mean your daughter is destined to struggle with overeating. Practically every study shows that a mother's *attitudes* about weight and food correlate with how the daughter forms her body image and structures her own eating behaviors.[19]

HONOR YOUR DAUGHTER REGARDLESS OF HER SIZE

If your daughter is overeating, she will not make changes in her eating habits out of shame or disapproval for her body. Positive change begins with self-acceptance and an attitude of genuine care.

This is a good time to ask yourself what you really want for your daughter. Do you want to promote health and well-being or weight loss and a certain look that is applauded by the culture? It is crucial that you be your daughter's advocate and ally by honoring her individuality—and her body.

One way in which you can honor your daughter while she is working to change eating patterns and increase physical activity is to fight "fatism." Look for the bias in the media and proactively challenge unkind remarks about size. This means that you are going to have to talk about the realities of being larger in our culture. Denial and silence will not help your daughter. Talk about the struggles in our biased culture as you and your daughter encounter them. Openness about the hard realities of being overweight will help your daughter relax and be more open with you as well, which may help her to be more open to the changes you suggest with regard to eating or physical activity. Your efforts to analyze the media and talk about its effect on self-esteem will have to be even more vigilant if your daughter struggles with weight.

I have a friend who took her children to Disneyland a few years ago. She noticed on the popular ride Pirates of the Caribbean that one of the points where everyone laughed hysterically was where the pirates were all chasing women, except for one overweight woman who was chasing the pirates. My friend cringed at the cruel portrayal of this brutish woman who, because of her size alone, was "scarier" than the pirates. She mentioned her concerns to her family and told them that she planned to write a letter highlighting the mockery and expressing that had it been turned on any other group, it would be considered prejudice.

Months after the trip, my friend's daughter wrote a paper in her seventh-grade English class about the person she admired most—her mother. She wrote about her mother's compassion and advocacy for others. Although the daughter is not overweight, she is bigger than most of the girls (and boys) in her class. She told her mother privately, "That letter you wrote to Disneyland let me know I could count on you to be there for me."

As important as your fight against fatism is, much more crucial are your

JUST FOR THE TWO OF YOU

1. When your daughter becomes discouraged and hard on herself for her body size, encourage her to ask herself these questions:
   - Would I ever judge a friend as I am judging myself?
   - Am I doing the best I can? If not, what can I change?

2. Write love notes to your daughter often, talking about your love for *her*. Complete sentences such as, "I love you because…" "I admire so many things about you, like…" "Being with you is wonderful because…"

3. If your daughter talks openly about being fat and how it affects her life, encourage her to do some "If I were thin" exercises to expose the myth that losing weight is the key to changing our lives for the better. For example, "If I were thin, I'd have better clothes." Ask your daughter how she can act on her desire *now*, as the size she is. Shopping might be in order! Buy attractive clothes. Size should never determine how fashionable and comfortable your daughter's clothes are. Feeling good about yourself while you are on the path toward weight loss is powerful motivation.

4. Throw away your scales. No one should be defined by the number on those unreliable tools. If your daughter is fighting obesity, let medical professionals keep the scales and chart her weight.

5. When you watch television, occasionally ask questions like: "Why aren't larger girls the stars?" "Who decides what size everyone should be on television?" "What other qualities do the girls/women have besides a perfect body size?"

6. Find a good massage therapist for your daughter (and yourself!). Girls who are overweight often feel untouchable. Massage not only fights depression but puts us back in touch with our bodies and combats the idea that we are too gross and fat to touch.

7. Share your struggles, discouragement, and successes as you participate together in changing your eating habits and trying new physical activities. Set goals and decide how you will reward yourselves when you reach the goal.

own words spoken to, about, and on behalf of your daughter. Once a mother's words are spoken, they are not easily forgotten. Juxtaposed against your efforts to incorporate healthy eating habits and exercise must be your advocacy for your daughter. Never stop noticing and enjoying her strengths, skills, accomplishments, and physical attributes.

Pioneering researcher on eating disorders Kathryn Zerbe, M.D., tells parents of children who struggle with eating and body image that "nothing is more crucial for individuals than to find a place where they feel valued for themselves as they are, regardless of what they weigh."[20] It is your job, as your daughter's mother, to hold in tension a need to make changes in diet and exercise *while* you honor her with compassion and support, regardless of her size.

The Rewards of Walking Hand In Hand

One mother-daughter duo I know came up with an "extreme dream." They jointly set a goal (with the help of their doctor and dietician) of each losing thirty-five pounds. They decided that when they reached this goal (which seemed pretty extreme at the beginning), that they would take a dream trip to Paris! Traveling overseas might not be in all our budgets, but this mother-daughter team matched their hard work with a big payoff! We don't have to minimize the hard work ahead, especially when it justifies a tantalizing reward.

I believe that one of the most important rewards of acknowledging our unique biology and facing head-on any propensity toward disordered eating will have both relational and spiritual rewards. Not only will we draw our daughters into deeper relationship with us, but we will also inevitably create a context for our daughters to seek out their Maker.

I have a dear friend who knew she was bigger than the other girls in her class in kindergarten. No one told her to lie about her weight, but when a science experiment in the second grade asked for her weight, she cut hers by twenty pounds. She vacillated between squeezing her body into horribly uncomfortable clothing to prove she could wear what everyone else was wearing, to attempting to hide in grossly oversize clothes. When she turned fifteen, her mother suggested she try smoking to curb her appetite and take off a few pounds! The shame, loneliness, and anger she has carried due to her larger size are far heavier than her actual weight.

Accepting her larger size and biological predisposition to easily gain weight did not automatically erase all her questions. But it did take her to the core question for anyone who struggles with being larger in a one-size-only society: *Why did God make me like this?* One of the gifts of our inevitable struggle in a culture that assaults body image on every side is that we can go to our Creator with our questions, hurts, and disappointments. Why did God allow such diversity in physical attributes, sizes, and shapes? Certainly he foresaw the prejudice and resulting hurt that would come against those who are not in the favored group.

The question "Why, God?" is one I am confronted with continually in my counseling practice. Why do some of us struggle with obesity, infertility, and health problems and others do not? I certainly am not wise enough to answer for each person, but I believe that God knows the environment in which we are individually most likely to seek a deeper relationship with him. And he allows or designs the unique contours of that environment, hoping that we will seek him as he is seeking us.

It is He who gives to all men life and breath and all things....
He created them to seek God, with the hope that they might grope
after Him in the shadows of their ignorance, and find Him.

ACTS 17:24-28, William Barclay's translation

If your daughter is larger than the cultural ideal, her size can become part of the context in which she seeks a relationship with God. Not surprisingly, it may also be the context in which she becomes angry with God and even rejects him for a time. Her struggle with God then becomes part of the unique landscape of *your* life in which you can look to your own relationship with God as you trust him with your daughter.

The bottom line is trust. Do you believe passionately (if falteringly) that God can be trusted—with your daughter and with you? The apostle Paul asked and answered this question: "But who are you, O man, to talk back to God? 'Shall what is formed say to him who formed it, "Why did you make me like this?"'... What if he did this to make the riches of his glory known to the objects of his mercy, whom he prepared in advance for glory?" (Romans 9:20-23).

A Holy Hunger

And so we know and rely on the love God has for us.

1 JOHN 4:16

It's Friday night and our daughter, Kristin, has big plans. She and a group of friends want to meet for dinner and then go to a movie. As she excitedly tells me everyone who is going to be there, I mentally calculate that her plans will put me in the car for about forty-five minutes.

It's Friday night and I'm tired. Even though the laundry room is over-flowing with dirty clothes, all I want to do is curl up with a good book and a pint of Ben & Jerry's Chunky Monkey ice cream and go to bed early. My husband and I flip a coin for driving responsibilities. I "win" the return drive. So much for getting to bed early. I might need a few cookies with that ice cream.

Kristin says good-bye to me with shoulders slumped. I don't even ask if there's a problem. *Mothers deserve a night off too,* I tell myself.

"I look awful," Kristin volunteers.

"You look wonderful," I try to respond confidently. I kiss her on the cheek and *run* to my bedroom. I'm not in the mood for the tricky task of encouraging a teenager.

When I pick up Kristin from the movie, her mood is not improved. I ask about the movie and try my best to keep the conversation light. I have spent the entire week talking to people about the depths of their emotions, and right now I just want to talk about Julia Roberts's new hairstyle.

"Mom, I feel so fat." Kristin ignores my interest in Julia. "How long will this last? Will I ever feel good about the way I look? I just feel so yucky!"

By this time we are pulling into our driveway. When we walk into the house, I hug Kristin and say, "I'm sure you'll feel better in the morning. Good night."

That was all the wisdom, advice, insight, and counsel I could summon right then. Besides, *I* felt fat after an evening spent with Chunky Monkey ice cream!

Real Moms, Real Lives

We have spent eleven chapters together looking at insights, ideas, and exercises for being proactive in our daughters' lives regarding eating and body image. It looks good on paper. But in reality, between parenting, spousing, and working, the cries of "Mom, I feel fat!" are sometimes drowned out by other demands. And there are moments when we just can't summon the words to encourage our daughters because we don't feel good about our own bodies. We find ourselves scanning the magazine covers at the checkout stand in the grocery store, wondering if perhaps it's time for a diet.

I have a picture in my office of a clownlike figure trying to juggle many objects of different sizes and colors. The artist has aptly inscribed beneath this painting, "I'm not so good at taking my own advice, but that doesn't mean I don't know what's right." As my own Friday night story of ice cream and minimal mothering suggests, I'm not writing this book because I have done it perfectly. I get tired, frustrated, and overwhelmed by the job requirements for being a mother. Hand-in-hand mothering is a task that reveals my weaknesses, frailties, and failures. But I am also learning that it's in the midst of mothering that I discover much about my strengths and about God's amazing love for me.

When I find myself hiding from my daughter or son, ignoring their struggles, and believing that I don't have anything to offer them, I know that I have to return to my point of reference in this whole parenting process: how God parents his children. His parenting is a model for me to emulate, but it is also an encouragement that I am not alone.

I've tried to prayerfully imagine who might be reading this book. I imagine there are moms with young daughters, and you are anticipating the fun you will have together as you walk hand in hand through the next few years. I imagine there are moms whose daughters are teenagers, and you're eager to read anything that will help you keep a good relationship. Perhaps you have struggled with an eating disorder yourself, and you want to understand your struggle as well as help your daughter avoid a similar one. And I imagine there are moms whose daughters are dabbling with or trapped by an eating disorder, and you are desperate for help and hope.

Wherever you are in your mothering, I know that you and your daughter will have unique experiences and responses as you interact with the material in this book. I know it doesn't come as a surprise to you when I say that this book doesn't have all the answers. And I'm glad. Because the encounters you and your daughter have with body image and eating struggles are wondrous opportunities to connect with God, the One who *does* have all the answers and is your living Source for mothering. When your daughter cries, "Mom, I feel fat!" the door opens for you to meet God, a God who takes *your* hand as you walk hand in hand with your child.

Coming Home

One of my favorite parenting stories is found in the Bible in the book of Luke. The story of the prodigal son and his eventual return to his home and his father has been the subject of many sermons and even entire books. It is a wondrous picture of God's love for his children, even when they wander far from home.

Have you ever noticed what drove the son away from his home and what drew him back? In both cases, it was his *appetite.* The son's hunger for adventure and independence lured him to seek satisfaction far away from his family. But his adventure was interrupted when famine hit the country where he was living and, again, he became hungry. The wayward son ended up working for a farmer who owned pigs. "He was so hungry he would have eaten the corncobs in the pig slop, but no one would give him any" (Luke 15:16, MSG). His hunger brought him to the pigpen, and then brought him to his senses. "He said, 'All those farmhands working for my father sit down to three meals a day, and here I am starving to death. I'm going back to my father'" (Luke 15:17-18, MSG).

After reading this book about eating, overeating, hunger, binging, and starving, perhaps you are, like I was, jolted by the relevance of this parable Jesus told. He seems to tell this story, in part, because he wants us to know that God understands hunger. He knows the places our hunger can take us—

sometimes to places of indulgence, shame, or deprivation. And just as the father in the story hopes for his son's return while he daily watches and waits for him, God hopes that our hunger will eventually lead us home.

Every time I read this story in Luke, I am amazed at its ending. The father gathers up his robes and runs with abandon to his son, joyously embracing him. The son expects to be dismissed, punished, or lectured, at the very least. But his father grabs his hand, holds it in front of his servants, and instructs them to put the family ring upon his son's finger. And then he culminates his welcome with an extravagant feast for his prodigal child.

Hunger—for physical food, to fit in and be liked, to look good, to mother daughters who like themselves and live confidently, to walk with our daughters through the mountains and ravines of eating disorders and body-image struggles—hunger can lead us home. And when we get there, standing face to face with our Father, what do we experience in his parenting of us? Your honest answer to that question will determine the course of your own parenting.

EXPERIENCING GOD

The apostle John wrote, "And so we know and rely on the love God has for us" (1 John 4:16). We read the word *know* and often attach it to our intellectual understanding of God's love. In the Bible, however, the knowledge referred to is *felt;* it comes from an *experience* of God.[1] In his compelling book *Ruthless Trust,* Brennan Manning quotes the Dutch theologian Edward Schillebeecks: "Christianity is not a message which has to be believed, but an experience of faith that becomes a message."[2]

Your own experience of God and his love is crucial because you will be able to translate only real-life *experience* to your daughter in your parenting, thereby inviting her to God as well. The amazing circle of the give-and-take of love is this: Our daughter's hunger brings her to us; our hunger to feed our daughter good things brings us to God; his hunger to love and feed us allows us to return to our daughter filled; and as we nourish her she receives a taste of God, which makes her hungrier for him.

In the midst of mothering a daughter through her struggles with eating and body image, there are an infinite number of opportunities for experiences with God. Just to get you started in looking for him and experiencing him in the ordinary moments of your daily life, let's examine three things that he longs for us to experience as we walk with him. Your recognition and experience of his welcoming grace, knowing mercy, and extravagant love will allow you to offer all three to your daughter in the days ahead.

WELCOMING GRACE

I imagine the son in Luke 15 making the long journey home, rehearsing over and over the speech he will make to his father. His first words to his father sound a bit prepared: "Father, I've sinned against God, I've sinned before you; I don't deserve to be called your son ever again" (verse 21, MSG).

The next sentence in the story is pivotal: "But the father wasn't listening" (verse 22, MSG).

In the split second of silence, the son might have thought it was too late, hopeless, impossible for him to return home. He'd starve! And then the father amazes his desperate son and everyone else with his instructions to honor his child and proceed with an extravagant celebration.

When have you received such a welcome? When you blow it and feel ashamed and hungry for reassurance, do you really believe that God is waiting, filled with hope, for you to come to him? Do you experience his welcoming embrace and hear him say, "We're going to feast! We're going to have a wonderful time!" (Luke 15:24, MSG)? When you *know* his welcoming grace, you will be able to welcome your daughter with grace.

One of my client's mothers taught me much about mothering with welcoming grace. Mary called me at half past eight on a Thursday night. Her daughter, Katie, had ingested a whole bottle of Excedrin and was at the hospital. Mary wondered if I could meet her in the emergency waiting room. I did.

Katie was sixteen years old and had been seeing me for help with her struggle with bulimia. She'd taken the Excedrin after a fight with her boyfriend. I prayed with Mary, and we waited to hear the news about Katie. After an hour, the doctor told us she would be fine. They had pumped her stomach, and she was out of danger from the overdose. But they had discovered that her potassium levels were dangerously low (a result of the bulimia), and she needed potassium administered intravenously.

We went in to see Katie for a few minutes. She apologized profusely. "I know I really screwed up this time. I'm so sorry. I wasn't thinking. I won't ever do it again." Her mom kissed her gently and said, "You just get your strength back."

Katie was especially distressed that she had left her purse and coat in the school bathroom after taking the pills. I offered to go look for her things so that Mary could stay with her daughter. The next morning I checked in at the school and searched high and low for the purse and coat with no luck. I called Mary to tell her the news and learned that Katie would be released from the hospital at five that afternoon.

I met Mary in the lobby of the hospital at five. She had just left Katie's room and said a nurse would bring Katie down in a wheelchair for discharge. When Katie saw us, she immediately looked downward in shame. Neither she nor I saw her mom pull a bag out from behind one of the couches in the lobby. As Katie stood to walk outside, her mom pulled a beautiful new coat from the bag and wrapped it around Katie. And then she pulled out a new purse and said, "I tried to fill it with all the things I know you like and thought you'd need."

Today Katie is a junior in college and is doing well. She's worked hard to overcome bulimia and its companion, depression, but I know she would tell you the work was possible because of that moment in the hospital, when she was welcomed back to life by her mother with such grace.

KNOWING MERCY

Recently I spent a weekend with a group of family and friends. I was startled by the appearance of one of my friend's teenage daughters. She had lost a noticeable amount of weight. As I watched her over the course of the weekend, I became more concerned about her eating behaviors. I approached her mother with some trepidation (I hesitate to comment on other people's children since I have my hands full with my own), but I could not ignore my concern. I asked my friend if she'd been monitoring her daughter's weight loss and eating choices, and she responded, "Oh, I know something is going on, but I just can't handle it right now. I don't even want to know if she's doing something."

I knew my friend was in the midst of a difficult time in her life and felt overwhelmed by her own struggles. I promised to pray for her and offered to help her find some information that might make her more confident in dealing with her daughter. I understood her fear and was reminded of what banishes our fear. When we experience the depth of God's mercy in the midst of our own messy lives, we can translate that into our human relationships.

In his masterful book about the account of the prodigal in Luke 15, Henri Nouwen describes Rembrandt's depiction of the condition of the son when he returned home:

> Rembrandt leaves little doubt about his condition. His head is shaven. No longer the long curly hair with which Rembrandt had painted himself as the proud, defiant prodigal son in the brothel.... The clothes Rembrandt gives him are underclothes, barely covering his emaciated body.... The yellow-brown, torn undergarment just covers his exhausted, worn-out body from which all strength is gone. The soles of his feet tell the story of a long and humiliating journey. The left foot, slipped out of its worn sandal, is scarred. The right food, only partially covered by a broken sandal, also speaks of suffering and misery.[3]

The son's condition only bolstered his belief that the only place for the likes of him at his father's home would be as a servant. To be seen in his misery and shame and at the same time welcomed as a celebrated son is the surprise ending of the story that no one, especially the prodigal, expects.

Similarly, we often do not believe that God can both know and handle all that goes on in our hearts and minds. Can he understand our hunger, our longings, our confusion, and even our doubt? Can he look at our mistakes, sins, and foolishness straight on and not turn away in dismay or disgust? When we conclude that he cannot, we hide the part of us that is in most need of his merciful touch. In order to mother mercifully, we must believe that God can know us *and* love us as we are.

Perhaps in the course of reading this book you have come face to face with some of the realities of your own heart. Maybe you've seen your own obsession with looking good. Perhaps you've recalled the days of your struggle with an eating disorder and shudder at the thought of anyone seeing you hunched over the toilet making yourself vomit. Or maybe you've seen clearly that your daughter is on the brink of an eating disorder. Have you experienced God's knowing mercy as you look at these things *with* him?

One of my clients called me this week with a story that illustrates the power of knowing mercy. She had been through a messy divorce and a year of trying to get on her feet and survive the transition. She'd watched her thirteen-year-old daughter gain over twenty-five pounds, while she tried to push away the notion that her daughter might be eating compulsively in order to numb her pain and anger about the divorce. My client told me, "I knew, but I didn't want to know, so I acted like I didn't know."

Her mother heart got the best of her one morning when she observed her daughter looking at herself in the mirror. Her daughter grimaced as she tugged at her tightly fitting skirt. This courageous mom walked over to her daughter, put her arms around her, and whispered, "I know." After a few moments, she continued, "I know you've been eating to try to soothe your pain and anger at your dad and me for our messy marriage and the divorce. I know you must be alarmed at the weight you've gained. I know you don't feel good about yourself. I know you need me to help you. And I know that right now nothing is more important than finding all the ways we can to help you with the pain and anger so you can feel good about yourself again."

Her daughter only murmured, "Okay." But her mother was not put off by the reticent response. She made a quick decision as she accessed her heart and discovered that her love for her daughter far surpassed her own fear, pain, and anger about her failed marriage. She told her daughter that they would not be going to work or school that day but were going on a mission to make over their eating and exercise habits. On their mission they discovered a health club for women only called Curves and signed up to begin an exercise program together. They went to Barnes and Noble and picked out a few books on healthy eating, including a cookbook. They ended their day at the mall with a free makeover at the makeup counter in a department store.

Before they went to bed that night, this hand-in-hand mom told her daughter, "I know you have a lot of questions and feelings inside that are really worth talking about. Let's make a date every Saturday to go for a walk or to eat tacos at midnight at Taco Bell while we talk." Her daughter, once again, replied, "Okay." When we have buried our feelings, it can take time to excavate them and to bring those feelings out into the open. This brave mom kissed her daughter and said, "I know I haven't been there for you and I'm sorry, but from now on, I will be."

Her daughter replied, "I know."

EXTRAVAGANT LOVE

Author and theologian Benard Lonergan writes, "Every authentic spiritual experience is an experience of unrestricted, unconditional being in love."[4] Certainly, the wayward son's older brother, and perhaps the community at large, thought that the father had become prodigal himself in his lavishing of love on his rebellious son. When have you experienced such extravagant love?

Find a picture of your daughter right now. Take a good look at what God has entrusted to you. The gift of your daughter was not contingent on your parenting skills, your background, or your success in life. In unrestricted, unconditional love, God gave you a daughter and made you a mother. No doubt you, like me, can rehearse all your shortcomings and failures in mothering. But I am coming to believe that the real sin is to miss God's love for me. Without experiencing that love, I lose touch with myself and frantically search in all the wrong places for what can only be found at home with my Father. The story of the prodigal reveals an extravagant love that always welcomes in grace and celebrates in mercy. And without experiencing that love, I cannot love my daughter extravagantly. And, oh, how I long to love her extravagantly!

When I met recently with a group of mothers and their adolescent daughters, I asked the girls to talk about how they had experienced their mothers' extravagant love. The girls talked of cookies made at midnight for the next day's school bake sale, comfort for a heart broken when a high school romance went sour, and forgiveness offered after a foolish choice or bad mistake. But the story I liked best was about Brussels sprouts.

Jenna told of going to her Aunt Delia's home for Easter dinner when she was nine years old. The meal was a main event for Aunt Delia, and she took it quite personally when others enjoyed (or didn't enjoy) her food. When

Jenna saw Brussels sprouts on the table for this Easter meal, she looked to her mother in panic. Her mom gave her a knowing look of empathy and quickly arranged the seats so that Jenna could sit next to her.

Jenna explained that she had tried Brussels sprouts before but could not eat them without gagging. The very sight of them almost made her sick. When the food was passed around the table, Jenna dutifully put one Brussels sprout on her plate. Aunt Delia chided, "Take more than that, honey. They are so good for you." Jenna said she was almost in tears as she put a spoonful of the dreadful things on her plate.

Both Jenna and her mom giggled as they told the rest of the story. Throughout the meal, whenever Aunt Delia's attention was elsewhere, Jenna's mom would quickly sneak a Brussels sprout from Jenna's plate and plop it into her own mouth. Their giggles turned to laughter when they told how the afternoon ended. As they left, Aunt Delia said, "You all will have to come back soon. I'll be sure to fix Brussels sprouts again, since Jenna liked them so much!"

Brussels sprouts, an empathetic mom, and a delightfully grateful daughter—I can't think of a more unlikely combination to illustrate extravagant love! The struggles our daughters likely will face with regard to body image and eating are unlikely invitations for us to experience God's grace, mercy, and love, and to share experiences with our daughters that will strengthen our relationship with each other for a lifetime.

HAND IN HAND

Hand-in-hand mothering begins with an understanding that we are all born hungry. Sadly, we live in a culture that "urges all of us to eat, shop, buy, acquire; for there in the material goods around us, in possession and commodities, prizes and grades, accomplishments and lovers, doughnuts and ice cream, [thinness and looking good], surely we'll find what we're looking for, our heart's desire."[5] Hand-in-hand mothering transcends the culture by creating a relationship with our daughters that is fueled by our holy hunger for a relationship with God. The amazing process of give-and-take in these vital relationships nourishes us with forgiveness, support, grace, guidance, mercy, and an unshakable commitment that satisfies the deepest desire of our heart—for perfect love. "No one has seen God, ever. But if we love one another, God dwells deeply within us, and his love becomes complete in us— perfect love!" (1 John 4:12, MSG).

Last night my daughter heard my part of a telephone conversation with a friend. She heard me moan to my friend, "I'm speaking at a ladies' retreat in three weeks, and I really wanted to lose a few pounds."

When I hung up the telephone, Kristin was waiting for me. She said, "Mom, all year long you have encouraged me to feel good about myself and to stop obsessing about feeling fat. I wanted to give back something to you, and so I wrote a poem for you for Mother's Day, but it sounds like you need it right now. I'm sorry it's not framed or wrapped."

She handed me a poem, handwritten and entitled "Mom." All of her *i*'s are dotted with hearts, and the poem is signed with a flourish *Kristin Hersh*. Her words remind me of the extravagant gift God has given me in my precious daughter, and of the amazing rewards in mothering—not because I do it perfectly, but because in loving, I discover love!

Mom

You are my hero, my love,
my friend.
You lift me up when I am down,
and help me back on my feet when I fall.
You show me unconditional love,
and teach me ongoing kindness.
You show me trust,
while still protecting me.
You encourage me, inspire me,
and motivate me.
You show me what it's like to be real.
I love you!
All of you!
Forever!

A Word for Daughters

When I was little, I wanted to fit into my mom's clothes. I would sneak into her room, put on one of her most beautiful dresses, and imagine actually fitting into it someday. When the day arrived that I was semiclose to fitting into one, it scared me a bit.

Most of the time it's hard for us to realize or admit just how important our mom's opinion is. We may try to deny it, but deep down in all of us girls, we long to be "just like her" and please her. Especially when it comes to outward appearance.

I used to be stick skinny. I ate basically anything I wanted, whenever I wanted. This was the reason for my nickname "toothpick" in school. As I got older, my body started to change, but my eating habits didn't. I had an undying love of sugar, and that was what I consumed most. Then all of a sudden, having just a Pop-Tart and a Frappuccino for breakfast affected me in ways it hadn't before. So all through my early teen years I was a bit chubby. And the only person in my life that ever said, "Maybe you should eat less sugar," or "How about exercising a bit more?" was my mom. She never said that I looked bad, needed to diet, or was fat—she just encouraged me that I could be healthier. We would come up with fun things to do together to help us stay in shape. We went on long walks, bought lots of fruit, and giggled together when we splurged on ice cream. I slowly began to realize that I needed to change my eating habits, but I didn't feel there was something wrong with me.

Whether your mom scrutinizes you or praises your every step, your opinion of yourself is largely based on what you assume she thinks of you. We live in an age where too-thin girls are on covers of magazines everywhere. Someone has to step up to the plate of being a godly example—to not be afraid of proclaiming wisdom and righteousness. Moms can help put in perspective what is truly important and magnify purity and inner beauty as something to be treasured.

Your mom's input in your life could be what you rely on as a steady foundation. It also can be part of a calling to be a woman of God and know a security you have never felt before as you see yourself through Christ's eyes. For "charm is deceptive, and beauty is fleeting; but a woman who fears the LORD is to be praised" (Proverbs 31:30). This is what we must focus on because this is all that matters in the end. And who better to set the example than the person we admire most? All of us need some encouragement from someone who loves us and will walk beside us always.

Relationships are hard, but you'll be thankful for sticking it out through the difficult moments with your mom. God has designed a divine connection between mother and daughter, one that is not of outward character but of heart and soul. That relationship may help both of you better understand what it means to be truly beautiful.

—NATALIE LARUE, recording artist and musician

RESOURCES

The resources listed below may not reinforce all of your personal beliefs and values. I have listed them as resources of information to help you walk hand in hand with your daughter, but you should screen and filter them before making them available to her.

FEMALE DEVELOPMENT

Bokram, Karen, Alexis Sinex, and Debbie Palen. *The Girls' Life Guide to Growing Up.* Hillsboro, Oreg.: Beyond Words Publishing, 2000.

Brio Magazine. Available from Focus on the Family, 1-800-A-FAMILY.

Harris, Robie H. *It's Perfectly Normal: A Book About Changing Bodies, Growing Up, Sex and Sexual Health.* Cambridge, Mass.: Candlewick, 1994.

Weston, Carol. *Girltalk: All the Stuff Your Sister Never Told You.* New York: HarperPerennial, 1997.

MOTHERING

Boyd, Charles F. *Different Children, Different Needs: The Art of Adjustable Parenting.* Sisters, Oreg.: Multnomah, 1994.

Cohen-Sandler, Roni, and Michelle Silver. *"I'm Not Mad, I Just Hate You!" A New Understanding of Mother-Daughter Conflict.* New York: Viking, 1999.

Madison, Lynda. *Keep Talking: A Mother-Daughter Guide to the Preteen Years.* Kansas City: Andrews and McMeel, 1997.

Pipher, Mary. *Reviving Ophelia: Saving the Selves of Adolescent Girls.* New York: Ballantine Books, 1994.

BODY IMAGE

Body Talk. 28-minute video on body acceptance. Order from Body Positive, 2417 Prospect St., #A, Berkeley, CA 94704. 510-841-9389.

Couchman, Judith. *The Woman Behind the Mirror: Finding Inward Satisfaction with Your Outward Appearance.* Nashville: Broadman & Holman, 1997.

Davis, Brangien. *What's Real, What's Ideal: Overcoming a Negative Body Image.* New York: Rosen Publishing, 1999.

Griffin, Marius. *Building Blocks for Children's Body Image.* From the Body Image Task Force, P. O. Box 360196, Melbourne, FL 32936.

Hutchinson, Marcia Germaine. *Transforming Body Image: Learning to Love the Body You Have.* New York: The Crossing Press, 1985.

Lee-Thorp, Karen, and Cynthia Hicks. *Why Beauty Matters.* Colorado Springs, Colo.: NavPress, 1997.

Luce, Katie. *The Pursuit of Beauty.* Green Forest, Ark.: New Leaf Press, 1998.

Radcliffe, Rebecca Ruggles. *Body Prayers: Finding Body Peace.* New York: EASE Publications, 1999.

Walker, Pamela. *Everything You Need to Know About Body Dysmorphic Disorder: Dealing with a Distorted Body Image.* New York: Rosen Publishing, 1999.

Dieting and Healthy Eating

Allen, Francine. *Eating Well in a Busy World Cookbook.* Berkeley, Calif.: Ten Speed Press, 1986.

Dietz, William H., ed., and Loraine Stern. *American Academy of Pediatrics Guide to Your Child's Nutrition: Feeding Children of All Ages.* New York: Villard, 1999.

Hirschmann, Jane R., and Lela Zaphiropoulous. *Preventing Childhood Eating Problems: A Practical Positive Approach to Raising Children Free of Food and Weight Conflict.* Santa Barbara, Calif.: Gürze Books, 1993.

Kano, Susan. *Making Peace with Food: Freeing Yourself from the Diet/Weight Obsession.* New York: Harper & Row, 1989.

Smith, Pamela M. *The Diet Trap: Your Seven-Week Plan to Lose Weight Without Losing Yourself.* Washington, D.C.: LifeLine Press, 2000.

Smith, Pamela M. *Food for Life: Breaking Free from the Food Trap.* Lake Mary, Fla.: Creation House, 1994.

Tribole, Evelyn. *Eating On the Run Cookbook.* Indianapolis: Human Kinetics Pub., 1991.

Warshaw, Hope S. *The American Diabetes Association Guide to Healthy Restaurant Eating,* Alexandria, Va.: American Diabetes Assoc., 1998.

Waterhouse, Debra. *Like Mother, Like Daughter: How Women Are Influenced by Their Mothers' Relationship with Food—and How to Break the Pattern.* New York: Hyperion, 1997.

Waterhouse, Debra. *Outsmarting the Female Fat Cell: The First Weight-Control Program Designed Specifically for Women.* New York: Hyperion, 1993.

DEPRESSION

Clarke, Julie M., and Anne Kirby-Payne. *Understanding Weight and Depression: A Teen Eating Disorder Prevention Book.* New York: Rosen Publishing, 2000.

Dowling, Colette. *You Mean I Don't Have to Feel This Way? New Help for Depression, Anxiety, and Addiction.* New York: Bantam Books, 1993.

Smith, Linda Wasmer. *Depression: What It Is, How to Beat It.* Berkely Heights, N.J.: Enslow Publishers, Inc., 2000.

EATING DISORDERS

Eating Disorders Awareness and Prevention, 603 Stewart Street, Suite 803, Seattle, WA 98101. 206-382-3587. http://www.edap.org

Kolodny, Nancy J. *When Food's a Foe: How You Can Confront and Conquer Your Eating Disorder.* Boston: Little, Brown, 1987.

Mirror-mirror. Information about eating disorders. http://www.mirror-mirror.org

Remuda Ranch, Center for Anorexia and Bulimia, P. O. Box 2481, Wickenburg, AZ 85358. 1-800-445-1900.

ANOREXIA

Bruch, Hilde. *The Golden Cage: The Enigma of Anorexia Nervosa.* New York: Vintage Books, 1979.

Gottlieb, Lori. *Stick Figure: A Diary of My Former Self.* New York: Berkley Books, 2001.

National Association of Anorexia Nervosa and Associated Disorders, Highland Hospital, Highland Park, IL 60035. 708-432-8000.

Ryan, Joan. *Little Girls in Pretty Boxes: The Making and Breaking of Elite Gymnasts and Figure Skaters.* New York Warner Books, 1996. (Information on obtaining the 1997 television movie based on the book can be found at http://www.lifetimetv.com.)

BULIMIA

Hall, Lindsey, and Leigh Cohn. *Bulimia: A Guide to Recovery: Understanding and Overcoming the Binge-Purge Syndrome.* Santa Barbara, Calif.: Gürze Books, 1986.

American Anorexia/Bulimia Association, 293 Central Park West, Suite 1R, New York, NY 10024.

Hornbacher, Marya. *Wasted: A Memoir of Anorexia and Bulimia.* New York: HarperCollins, 1998.

The following movies are shown periodically on television. You can find out when they might be shown at http://www.eonline.com/facts/movies.

Dying to Be Perfect: The Ellen Hart Pena Story, ABC television, 1996.

For the Love of Nancy, Lifetime television, 1994. Information at http://www.lifetimetv.com.

Kate's Secret, Lifetime television, 1986. Information at http://www.lifetimetv.com.

COMPULSIVE OVEREATING

Amplestuff. Catalog with larger sizes. P. O. Box 116, Bearsville, NY 12409. 914-679-3316. http://www.amplestuff.com.

National Center for Overcoming Overeating, P. O. Box 1257, Old Chelsea Station, New York, NY 10113-0920. 212-875-0442.

Pitman, Teresa, and Miriam Kaufman, M.D. *The Overweight Child: Promoting Fitness and Self-Esteem.* Toronto, Can.: Firefly Books, 2000.

Roth, Geneen. *Why Weight: A Guide to Ending Compulsive Eating.* New York: New American Library, 1989.

YOUTH CULTURE

Davis, Francis. *Living in the Image Culture: An Introductory Primer for Media Literacy Education.* Center for Media Literacy. 1-800-226-9494. http://www.medialit.org.

The Center for Parent Youth Understanding Newsletter, P. O. Box 414, Elizabethtown, PA 17022. 717-361-0031. http://www.cpyu.org.

Mueller, Walt. *Understanding Today's Youth Culture.* Wheaton, Ill.: Tyndale, 1994.

NOTES

INTRODUCTION: "FAT" IS NOT A FEELING

1. Judy Ford and Amanda Ford, *Between Mother and Daughter* (Berkeley, Calif.: Conari Press, 1999), 4.
2. Lori Gottlieb, "I Had an Eating Disorder and Didn't Even Know It!" *Cosmo-Girl,* April 2001, 149.
3. Jean Seligmann, "The Littlest Dieters," *Newsweek,* 27 July 1987, 48.

PART 1: UNDERSTANDING YOUR WORLDS

1. Gina Bria, *The Art of Family* (New York: Dell, 1998), 10.

CHAPTER 1: BEING A MOM

1. Sandra Susan Friedman, *When Girls Feel Fat* (Toronto, Can.: Firefly Books, 2000), 51.
2. Quoted by Hugh Prather and Gayle Prather, *Spiritual Parenting* (New York: Three Rivers Press, 1996), 25-6.
3. Margo Maine, *Father Hunger: Fathers, Daughters and Food* (Carlsbad, Calif.: Gürze Books, 1991), 3.
4. Janet Fitch, *White Oleander* (Boston: Little, Brown, 1999), 403.
5. Janet L. Surrey, "The Self-in-Relation: A Theory of Women's Development" in Judith Jordon et al., *Women's Growth in Connection: Writing from the Stone Center* (New York: Guilford Press, 1991), 51-64.
6. Adrienne Rich, *Of Woman Born: Motherhood As Experience and Institution* (New York: Norton, 1976), 28.

CHAPTER 2: YOUR MOTHERING STYLE

1. Rachel Billington, *The Great Umbilical: Mothers, Daughters, Mothers, the Unbreakable Bond* (London: Hutchinson, 1994), 6.
2. Foster Cline, M.D., and Jim Fay, *Parenting Teens with Love and Logic* (Colorado Springs, Colo.: Piñon Press, 1992), 34-5.
3. Quoted by Sarah Ban Breathnach in *Something More* (New York: Warner Books, 1998), 99.

4. Sara Shandler, *Ophelia Speaks: Adolescent Girls Write About Their Search for Self* (New York: HarperCollins, 1999), 68.

5. Gina Bria, *The Art of Family* (New York: Dell, 1998), 15-6.

6. Bria, *The Art of Family,* 10.

7. Linda Weber, *Mom You're Incredible!* (Colorado Springs, Colo.: Focus on the Family, 1994), 33.

CHAPTER 3: BEING A GIRL

1. Quoted by Rebecca Sinclair, "Surviving the Teenage Years," *Progressive Woman,* June 1992, 5.

2. Lisa Belkin, "Puberty Puzzle," *The Rocky Mountain News,* 4 February 2000, 14F.

3. Michael D. Lemonick, "Teens Before Their Time," *Time,* 30 October 2000, 66.

4. Lemonick, "Teens Before Their Time," 68.

5. Lemonick, "Teens Before Their Time," 68.

6. Annie G. Rogers, "Voice, Play, and a Practice of Ordinary Courage in Girls' and Women's Lives," *New Moon Parenting,* June/July 1993, 11-2.

7. Catherine Steiner Adair, Director of Education, Prevention, and Outreach at Harvard Eating Disorder Center, reported by Margery D. Rosen, "Is Your Child Headed for an Eating Disorder?" *Child,* August 2000, 63.

8. Quoted by Eugenia Allen, "What to Tell Your Daughter," *Time,* 30 October 2000, 70.

9. Quoted by Walt Mueller, "Feeling Like the Elephant Man," youthculture@2000, the newsletter of The Center for Parent-Youth Understanding, Summer 2000, 13.

10. Mueller, "Feeling Like the Elephant Man."

11. Geneen Roth, *When You Eat at the Refrigerator, Pull Up a Chair* (New York: Hyperion, 1998), 4.

12. Deborah Blum, *Sex on the Brain: The Biological Differences Between Men and Women* (New York: Viking, 1997), 53, 68.

13. Catherine Pines, as quoted by Janice Rosenberg, "True Friendships Rare Between Moms, Daughters," *Denver Post,* 2 October 2000, F3.

14. Quoted by Rosen, "Is Your Child Headed for an Eating Disorder?" 65.

15. Annie Dillard, *An American Childhood* (New York: Harper & Row, 1987), 11.

16. Emily Hancock, *The Girl Within* (New York: Fawcett Columbine, 1989), 6.

17. Rosen, "Is Your Child Headed for an Eating Disorder?" 65.

18. Stacey Colino, "Fear of Fat," *YM,* October 2000, 49.

19. Quoted by Gail E. Hudson in "I Want Mommy!" *Child,* August 2000, 66.

Chapter 4: Your Daughter's Culture

1. Quentin J. Schultze, *Dancing in the Dark* (Grand Rapids: Eerdmans, 1991), 87.

2. "A Body to Die For," *People,* 30 October 2000, 109.

3. Mary Pipher, *Reviving Ophelia* (New York: Ballantine Books, 1994), 22.

4. Dean Borgman, *When Kumbaya Is Not Enough: A Practical Theology for Youth Ministry* (Peabody, Mass.: Hendrickson Publishers, 1997), 87.

5. Walt Mueller, "Feeling like the Elephant Man," youthculture@2000, the newsletter of The Center for Parent-Youth Understanding, Summer 2000, 13.

6. Borgman, *When Kumbaya Is Not Enough,* 87.

7. Tom Piotrowski, "Mediaware: Read Your TV," youthculture@2000, the newsletter of The Center for Parent-Youth Understanding, Summer 2000, 13.

8. Borgman, *When Kumbaya Is Not Enough,* 75.

9. Ernest Kurtz and Katherine Ketcham, *The Spirituality of Imperfection* (New York: Bantam Books, 1994), 9.

10. Shari Levine, "Real Girls, Real Strategies," *Mary-Kate and Ashley Magazine,* April-May 2001, 105.

11. Margie Boule, "Brave 16-year-old Reveals Skewed Thinking and Body Image of Anorexia," *The Oregonian,* August 2000, C7.

12. Karen Lee Fontaine, "The Conspiracy of Culture: Women's Issues in Body Size," *Nursing Clinics of North America* 26, no. 3 (September 1991): 673.

13. Quoted by John Charles Ryle, *Christian Leaders of the Eighteenth Century* (Carlisle, Pa.: Banner of Truth Trust, 1978), 297.

14. Borgman, *When Kumbaya Is Not Enough,* 113-4.

15. Borgman, *When Kumbaya Is Not Enough,* 118-9.

16. Quoted by Douglas Foster, "If the Symptoms Are Rapid Increases in Teen Deaths from Murder, Suicide, and Car Crashes, Alcohol and Drugs…the Disease is Adolescence," *Rolling Stone,* 9 December 1993, 55.

Part 2: Building a Bridge Between Your Worlds

1. Flavia Weedn and Lisa Weedn, *Across the Porch from God* (San Rafael, Calif.: Cedco Publishing., 1999), 89, 91.

CHAPTER 5: "MOM, YOU JUST DON'T UNDERSTAND!"

1. Roni Cohen-Sandler and Michelle Silver, *"I'm Not Mad, I Just Hate You!"* (New York: Penguin Books, 1999), 21.

2. E. Z. Tronick and A. Gianinon, "Interactive Mismatch and Repair: Challenges to the Coping Infant," *Zero to Three: Bulletin for the National Center for Clinical Infant Programs,* February 1986, 1-6.

3. Judi Craig, *You're Grounded Till You're Thirty!* (New York: Hearst Books, 1996), 22.

4. Cohen-Sandler and Silver, *"I'm Not Mad, I Just Hate You!"* 6.

5. Cohen-Sandler and Silver, *"I'm Not Mad, I Just Hate You!"* 117.

6. Hilda Bruch, *Conversations with Anorexics* (New York: Basic Books, 1988); Craig L. Johnson, *Psychodynamic Treatment of Anorexia Nervosa and Bulimia* (New York: Guilford, 1991); and Maria Selvini-Palazzoli, *Self-Starvation* (New York: Jason Aronson, 1978).

7. Kathryn Zerbe, M.D., *The Body Betrayed* (Carlsbad, Calif.: Gürze, 1995), 52.

8. Joyce L. Vedral, *My Teenager Is Driving Me Crazy!* (New York: Ballantine Books, 1997), 89.

9. Harriet Lerner, *The Dance of Anger* (New York: HarperCollins, 1997), 8.

10. Hugh Prather, *The Little Books of Letting Go* (Berkeley, Calif.: Conari Press, 2000), 17.

CHAPTER 6: "MOM, I HATE MY THIGHS!"

1. Marcia Germaine Hutchinson, *Love the Body You Have* (Freedom, Calif.: The Crossing Press, 1985), 16.

2. Paul Schilder, *The Image and Appearance of the Human Body: Studies in the Constructive Energies of the Psyche* (New York: International Universities Press, 1950), 201.

3. Debra Waterhouse, *Like Mother, Like Daughter* (New York: Hyperion, 1997), 109.

4. A. M. Gustafson-Larson et al., "Weight-Related Behaviors and Concerns of Fourth-grade Children," *Journal of the American Dietetic Association* 92 (1992): 818.

5. Reported by Margery D. Rosen in "Is Your Child Headed for an Eating Disorder?" *Child,* August 2000, 62.

6. Lynn Jaffee and Rebecca Manzer, "Girls' Perspectives, Physical Activity and Self Esteem," *Melpomene Journal* 11, no. 3 (1992): 19.

7. Harriet Lerner, *The Mother Dance: How Children Change Your Life* (New York: HarperCollins, 1999), 177.

8. Schilder, *The Image and Appearance of the Human Body,* 210.

9. Deborah Blum, *Sex on the Brain: The Biological Differences Between Men and Women* (New York: Viking, 1997), 43.

10 Kathryn J. Zerbe, M.D., *The Body Betrayed* (Carlsbad, Calif.: Gürze Books, 1993), 155.

11. Zerbe, *The Body Betrayed,* 46.

12. Zerbe, *The Body Betrayed,* 168.

13. Jeanne Elium and Don Elium, *Raising a Daughter* (Berkeley, Calif.: Celestial Arts, 1994), 159.

14. Elium and Elium, *Raising a Daughter,* 160-1.

15. Mary Pipher, *Reviving Ophelia* (New York: Ballantine Books, 1994), 57.

16. Naomi Wolf, *The Beauty Myth* (New York: Morrow, 1991), 11, 185.

17. Barbara Moe. *Coping with Eating Disorders* (New York: Rosen Publishing, 1991), 31.

Chapter 7: "Mom, I Can't Eat *That*"

1. Mary Pipher, *Hunger Pains* (Holbrook, Mass.: Adams Publishing, 1995), 20.

2. Margaret Bullitt-Jones, *Holy Hunger* (New York: Alfred A. Knopf, 1999), 11, 25.

3. Peggy Claude-Pierre, *The Secret Language of Eating Disorders* (New York: Random House, 1997), 4-5.

4. Margery D. Rosen, "Is Your Child Headed for an Eating Disorder?" *Child Magazine,* August 2000, 65.

5. Rosen, "Is Your Child Headed for an Eating Disorder?" 63. Dr. Susan Sherkow is a psychiatrist in New York who directs a therapeutic and preventive nursery for mothers and children with eating disorders.

6. "What's Your Food Attitude?" *YM,* October 2000, 39.

7. Geneen Roth, *When You Eat at the Refrigerator, Pull Up a Chair* (New York: Hyperion, 1998), 21.

8. Geneen Roth, *When Food Is Love: Exploring the Relationship Between Eating and Intimacy* (New York: Plume, 1993), 103.

9. Kathryn J. Zerbe, M.D., *The Body Betrayed* (Carlsbad, Calif.: Gürze Books, 1993), 72.

CHAPTER 8: "MOM, WHY CAN'T I USE SLIM-FAST?"

1. Debra Waterhouse, *Like Mother, Like Daughter* (New York: Hyperion, 1997), 15.
2. Nancy J. Kolodny, *When Food's a Foe* (Boston: Little, Brown, 1987), 18.
3. Gesele Lajoie, Alyson McLellan, and Cindi Seddon, *Take Action Against Bullying* (Coquitlam, British Columbia, Can.: Bully B'Ware Productions, 1997), videocassette.
4. Marcia Germaine Hutchinson, *Love the Body You Have* (Freedom, Calif.: The Crossing Press, 1985), 16.
5. Waterhouse, *Like Mother, Like Daughter,* 43-4.
6. E. Koff et al., "Perceptions of Weight and Attitudes Toward Eating in Early Adolescent Girls," *Journal of Adolescent Health* 12 (1991): 307.
7. Waterhouse, *Like Mother, Like Daughter,* 58.
8. Mary Pipher, *Hunger Pains* (Holbrook, Mass.: Adams Publishing, 1995), 12.
9. Geneen Roth, *When You Eat at the Refrigerator, Pull Up a Chair* (New York: Hyperion, 1998), 99.
10. Roth, *When You Eat at the Refrigerator,* 167.
11. Roth, *When You Eat at the Refrigerator,* 162.
12. Lauren Neergaard, "Figuring Out Ephedra: Since Recent Deaths, the FDA Is Studying Dangers of Ephedra," Associated Press, 17 April 2000, and Jeff Gerth and Sheryl Gay Stolberg, "Another Part of the Battle," *New York Times,* 13 December 2000.
13. Frederick Buechner, *Telling the Truth* (New York: HarperCollins, 1966), 59.
14. Hugh Prather and Gayle Prather, *Spiritual Parenting* (New York: Three Rivers Press, 1996), 280.
15. Brennan Manning, *Abba's Child* (Colorado Springs, Colo.: NavPress, 1994), 133.

PART 3: CONQUERING ROADBLOCKS TO RELATIONSHIP

1. Judy Ford and Amanda Ford, *Between Mother and Daughter* (Berkeley, Calif.: Conari Press, 1999), 55.

CHAPTER 9: ANOREXIA

1. Mary Pipher, *Hunger Pains* (Holbrook, Mass.: Adams Publishing, 1995), 72.

2. Peggy Claude-Pierre, *The Secret Language of Eating Disorders* (New York: Random House, 1997), 185.

3. Nancy J. Kolodny, *When Food Is Foe,* rev. ed. (Boston: Little, Brown, 1998), 40.

4. Philip Mehler, "Eating Disorders: 2," *Hospital Practice* (15 February 1996): 109.

5. R. R. Radcliffe, "What a New Study Reveals About Eating Disorders," *Shape Magazine,* October 1987, 78.

6. Hilde Bruch, *The Golden Cage* (New York: Vintage, 1979), 76.

7. Kathryn J. Zerbe, M.D., *The Body Betrayed* (Carlsbad, Calif.: Gürze Books, 199), 324-5.

8. Pipher, *Hunger Pains,* 77.

CHAPTER 10: BULIMIA

1. Mary Pipher, *Hunger Pains* (Holbrook, Mass.: Adams Publishing, 1995), 53.

2. Margaret Bullitt-Jones, *Holy Hunger* (New York: Knopf, 1999), 24-5.

3. Nancy J. Kolodny, *When Food's a Foe* (New York: Little, Brown, 1998), 59.

4. Bullitt-Jones, *Holy Hunger,* 65.

5. Pipher, *Hunger Pains,* 55.

6. Margery Rosen, "Is Your Child Headed for an Eating Disorder?" *Child,* August 2000, 61-2.

7. Debra Waterhouse, *Like Mother, Like Daughter* (New York: Hyperion, 1997), 32-4.

8. T. E. Weltzin et al., "Acute Tryptophan Depletion and Increased Food Intake and Irritability in Bulimia Nervosa," *American Journal of Psychiatry* 152 (1995): 1668-71.

9. William H. Dietz, M.D., ed., and Loraine Stern (American Academy of Pediatrics), *The Official, Complete Home Reference Guide to Your Child's Nutrition* (New York: Villard, 1999), 55.

10. Bullitt-Jones, *Holy Hunger,* 53.

11. Bullitt-Jones, *Holy Hunger,* 20.

12. Kathryn J. Zerbe, M.D., *The Body Betrayed* (Carlsbad, Calif.: Gürze Books, 1993), 64.

13. Craig L. Johnson, ed., *Psychodynamic Treatment of Anorexia Nervosa and Bulimia* (New York: Guilford, 1991), 171.

CHAPTER 11: COMPULSIVE OVEREATING

1. Tammy Lynn Michaels, "A Weighty Issue," *Teen Vogue,* spring 2001, 120.

2. Charles M. Ginsburg, M.D., "Weight Control," *Pediatric Primer,* March 2001, 1-2.

3. Debra Waterhouse, *Like Mother, Like Daughter* (New York: Hyperion, 1997), 40.

4. *Helping Your Overweight Child* (Bethesda, Md.: Weight-Control Information Network, 2000), 1.

5. Mary Pipher, *Hunger Pains* (Holbrook, Mass.: Adams Publishing, 1995), 92.

6. "Getting Children off the Couch and onto the Field," *American Psychological Association,* 1996. http://helping.apa.org/family/kidsport.html.

7. Zondra Hughes, "What to Do If Your Child Is Too Fat," *Ebony,* July 2000, 1.

8. Hughes, "What to Do If Your Child Is Too Fat."

9. Waterhouse, *Like Mother, Like Daughter,* 27.

10. Waterhouse, *Like Mother, Like Daughter,* 26.

11. Michaels, "A Weighty Issue," 120.

12. J. Martin, "Fitness Fun for the Whole Family," *American Health* (July-August 1995): 70.

13. William H. Dietz, M.D., *Guide to Your Child's Nutrition* (New York: Villard, 1999), 127.

14. "More on the Pitfalls of Television Watching," *Tufts University Diet and Nutrition Letter,* vol. 10, 1992, 6.

15. "Getting Children off the Couch and onto the Field," *American Psychological Association,* 1996. http://helping.apa.org/family/kidsport.html.

16. Pipher, *Hunger Pains,* 95.

17. G. A. Rose and R. T. Williams, "Metabolic Studies and Large and Small Eaters," *British Journal of Nutrition* 15 (1961): 1.

18. Waterhouse, *Like Mother, Like Daughter,* 15.

19. D. C. Moore, "Body Image and Eating Behavior in Adolescent Girls," *American Journal of Diseases of Children* 142 (1988): 1114.

20. Kathryn Zerbe, *The Body Betrayed* (Carlsbad, Calif.: Gürze Books, 1951), 312.

Conclusion: A Holy Hunger

1. John L. McKenzie, *Dictionary of the Bible* (New York: Macmillan, 1965), 269.

2. Brennan Manning, *Ruthless Trust* (San Francisco: HarperCollins, 2000), 88.

3. Henri J. Nouwen, *The Return of the Prodigal* (New York: Doubleday, 1994), 46.

4. Bernard Lonergan, *Insight* (London: Dartman, Longman and Todd, 1957), 38.

5. Margaret Bullitt-Jones, *Holy Hunger* (New York: Knopf, 1998), 243.

ABOUT THE AUTHOR

Sharon A. Hersh is a licensed professional counselor who coaches mothers and daughters to use the challenges in their relationships to strengthen their bonds. She is the author of *Bravehearts: Unlocking the Courage to Love with Abandon* and the director of Women's Recovery and Renewal, a ministry of counseling, retreat, and support services for women. She and her husband, Dave, speak for FamilyLife, a worldwide ministry of Campus Crusade for Christ. They live in Lone Tree, Colorado, with their two children, Kristin and Graham.